MORE THAN JUST HEALING

Penny Perigan, MSW

More Than Just Healing
© 2017 by Penny Perigan
Cover photo © by

Published by Penny Perigan

ISBN 978-0-996-45697-5

CONTENTS

ABOUT THE BOOK

I began writing *More Than Just Healing* when Brian was first diagnosed in 1977. I thought that if I wrote things down it would help me better understand the medical community. But after several weeks my collection of terms turned into a daily journal. When God gave my writings a name, I understood that the purpose of the writings was to keep me focused on Him. Each day through tears, I poured my heart out to the Lord, and He faithfully filled me up with His love.

Forty-two written pages along with hundreds of documents, pamphlets, and case notes sat untouched in a very large file cabinet until 2005 when I decided to organize the paperwork and tell Brian's story. My family and I revisited that very painful time in our lives for several months, and then I returned the documents to the file cabinet.

Two years ago, after a bout with cancer, my own experiences reminded me how Brian had handled his own battle with cancer. It was truly an extraordinary time in our lives. I began re-writing the story, but this time I was determined to include every painful detail. My daughter, an English major and the editor-in-chief for a travel magazine, worked through each chapter with me. We shared many tears, but at the end of our journey the lessons still rang true.

I know your loss is difficult, but I want to encourage you to go forward. Don't give up or lose hope. God's love surrounds you. He is there; He is with you right now; His compassions never fail.

In His Love,
Penny

ACKNOWLEDGMENTS

I gratefully extend my appreciation for the people who helped me bring this book to print. I want to thank my husband, Kevin, for being my main support and praying me through the tears and nightmares.

I also want to thank my daughter, Crystal, who took time away from her busy schedule to work with me on this project. She always came with helpful solutions and words of encouragement. She was the first person I called when I had a problem or a question.

I want to give a very special thank-you to our dear friend Bob Stebbins, who traveled with us throughout this journey. He and his wife, Bonnie, spent many hours praying for us and were instrumental in giving Brian the "Best Christmas Ever." Bob was the first person I asked to read the book. As a former school teacher, he faithfully read every page and gave me feedback and even made corrections. I know how difficult it was for him to re-live this time in our lives.

Last, I want to thank Susan Osborn with Christian Communicators for connecting me with Gwen Ellis at Seaside Creative Services. Gwen critiqued the book and helped me navigate through this world of writing.

I could not have seen this project through to completion without each one of you. Thank you so much for your continued love and support!

PICTURE HIM RUNNING

Our son, Brian, was born on April 27, 1974. To this day it is still very disturbing to me that his cancer went undetected for three long years. There had been multiple well-baby checkups, scheduled vaccines, and, during that second year, weekly appointments for chronic ear infections, and still no one noticed the large tumor that spread throughout his entire abdomen. By the time it was discovered, it was already too late.

Brian endured an enormous amount of pain in his short life, and yet he continued to live life fully. His sweet, joyful spirit remained until the day he took his last breath. Just four weeks before he died, during periods of incapacitating pain, he wrote this:

> God Is Good
> God is good, He is not bad.
> Jesus is good, and we are glad.
> Angels we know are above our heads
> While God is watching over us, as we lay down our head.
> Everybody knows God will come down soon
> And later we will be right over the moon.

God was still good, even when his suffering was great. Brian still believed that he was surrounded by angels even though his lot in life had been seeded in a field of darkness. And even when death stood in front of him, he eagerly waited for heaven to open its doors. That was Brian.

Brian was born on a Saturday morning. Labor was induced, but he fought long and hard to stay where he was, warm and safe. We named him Brian Anthony, after my dad because I had always been daddy's little girl and could not think of a better way to honor my father. Brian was our second child. Unlike his sister, his skin was olive and he had deep dark brown eyes and brown hair that lightened to blond in the summer sun. He weighed seven pounds and nine ounces at birth and with all of his fingers and toes; he appeared to be a healthy baby boy.

Brian's *first* surgical procedure happened on April 29, two days after he was born. Like most baby boys, he was circumcised before he left the hospital. It's such a common practice here in the United States that I almost failed to recognize the significance of the first cutting away of flesh. Today more than sixty-five percent of all male babies are circumcised at birth.

Although we were fairly new Christians, we did not have him circumcised because of a deep religious belief, nor was it based on any cultural rationale. In fact, I cannot even remember giving the procedure much thought at all. My husband, Kevin, and I were distracted and neither one of us remember signing consent forms. After all, I was recovering from a difficult labor and Kevin was celebrating the birth of his son.

Meanwhile, my new baby boy was in the nursery, alone, he too having just endured a difficult labor. Out of the womb, having just lost the warmth and protection of it, he was forced to endure a twenty-minute procedure that would bring several hours of intense pain and take ten days to completely heal. For the parents the recovery process seemed so simple and natural, but for Brian, he learned a very hard lesson about life; he would have to endure pain alone. Others may try to help and support you, but pain is really a personal thing. When you are faced with it you only have one of two choices. You get to choose whether to rise above it or fall under its oppression. It will either make you bitter or sweet; and then that choice determines your outcome. Becoming the victor over your circumstances does not come easy. There will always be battles, but if you choose to become the victim there will be no reward.

Days after the circumcision we took Brian to church and participated in a ceremony that initially dedicated our son to the Lord. Maybe if I had paid more attention to why God wanted male babies circumcised or if I had grasped the depth of the meaning of a baby dedication, I would have been more prepared for what was to come; but my mind simply skipped over any depth of meaning that these rituals held. I had dutifully done what was required of me as a new parent. Brian's physical and spiritual needs had been met. I never realized at the time that so much more was required.

Brian was brave from the beginning, he never cried or fussed. When we brought him home he adjusted. He slept through the night and tolerated his feedings. If he had pain, no one knew about it.

Brian welcomed life's other difficulties in much the same way. After his cancer diagnosis and the beginning of intensive treatments and hospital stays, he accepted his intricate lifestyle as nothing other than normal. He never used his illness as a crutch. He forbade me to even mention it to strangers. He never wanted sympathy for what he could not do. He only wanted praise for all he had accomplished. His ability to overcome his suffering sharpened his focus and gave him great wisdom. While he was fully aware of what was happening to him, he was able to appreciate the things that were truly important to him. He enjoyed the simple beauty of clouds in the sky, birds singing in the trees, and people who were kind. Most of all he had a supernatural confidence that Jesus was always with him. Brian's awareness of the presence of Jesus gave him such a joyful spirit, purity of mind, and clarity of thought that it caused me to pause and wonder if he had tapped into the "abundant life," the life that Jesus had promised us. He believed he had it all. He believed that everything he needed was provided.

He also believed that if he couldn't handle something, I was not to worry because Jesus would be there with him. The illness, the procedures, and the pain could not stop him from completing his purpose here on earth. He would continue to move forward no matter what it cost him.

I longed to walk with him on his journey, but that was not possible. God had a different road for me to travel. Through the years I struggled with just letting God be God. I fought with him for the power to control my own life which only carved out paths that led me away from him and not to him.

I knew better than to question God. As gut-wrenching as the diagnosis was, I feared God and never asked, "Why me?" or dared to blame him for the illness. I didn't take issue with the fact that my son was sick. I understood that being a Christian did not exempt us from coming under attack; after all, bad things happen in a fallen world. But I believed God would lead us to victory. The way I saw it, the cancer might come but it would not stay.

But still, when my son was first diagnosed, my initial response had been far from accepting. I held on tightly to a promise that he would be healed. I don't know why I thought I could choose my own destiny and then claim it in the name of Jesus. That is not how it works. Only God, our creator, can set our feet on the right path. When Jesus faced the hardest decision of his life, he prayed, "Not my will, but yours." He turned to his Father and acknowledged that God's purpose for his life was worth any sacrifice. Yet at the time of Brian's illness, even knowing that Jesus himself, facing crucifixion, had prayed that God's will be done, even with all my study of the Word of God and all the teaching we received at church, a complete surrender to God's will was a much harder lesson to learn than you might think.

After battling the disease for five years, Brian died from cancer at just eight years of age. I never believed that God would take my child's life. But as his condition got worse, I could only hold on to the hope that God would not give Brian more than he could handle. I was certain that God would not allow a child to endure years and years of relentless pain—not when we were committed to him, when we depended on him, and when we were trying to do everything right—and yet he did allow it.

As I worked through Brian's suffering, I was pulled into God's presence and was eventually able to accept the gifts that were mine for the taking. The keys to the kingdom have always been within our grasp, but we have a part to play. We must come to the throne to accept them.

Right after his death, I tried to remember whether we had any signs of what was to come. When Brian came into the world, I was unaware of any signs indicating that he had a terminal disease. But just as I had been unaware of the pain that comes from cutting away the flesh in circumcision, I had not realized that by dedicating my child to God I had made a covenant with him to bring Brian into a relationship with him. I didn't know that Brian's chronic ear pain indicated a more serious problem.

In the years ahead I would learn to read the physical signs and identify medical issues, but I would also learn to follow the spiritual signs that reminded me over and over again to turn to God. So many times I heard his voice and turned to the light and then lost focus. We all lose our way and fall down; but when we turn to him, God is faithful and he picks us up again. We might lose heart, but his love for us remains unchanged.

With each surgery, the cutting away of Brian's flesh would teach me new lessons of faith that only worked to solidify my walk with God. There would be ten surgeries and ten lessons that taught me how to deal with human suffering and deepened my relationship with him. Each lesson cut deep into my heart, allowing a circumcision that is not performed by man, but by the hand of God. It is only when we allow God's hand to touch our heart that we are able to produce eternal rewards.

God who created us and knows our successes, as well as our failures, ascribes each of us with a weight of glory. In life we are often judged by our performances. We miss the mark when we don't get an A in school, a promotion at work, or fail to make a relationship work. But God does not use a human standard to measure our worth. Instead, he looks at our heart and identifies the parts in it that look like him.

The reflection of himself that he sees in us is called "the glory." It is the very essence of God. It is made up of his presence and his character. As God begins to transform our lives into the image of Jesus, we feel his glory as an awareness of something that is greater than ourselves. Sometimes his presence is described as a heaviness that has fallen on us. In the Hebrew language glory is *kabod* (glory).[1] It describes the physical aspect of the word as a weight/burden; glorious.

There were some important lessons to learn about the circumcision of the heart. To help me remember I assigned a letter to each lesson, forming the ten-letter acrostic C-I-R-C-U-M-C-I-S-E.

Lesson 1: <u>C</u>ommit Yourself to the Lord

Without ever realizing what I was doing, by following in a tradition of both circumcision and dedication, I was asking God to set my child apart and to make him his own. When I surrendered him to the Lord at church that day, I had actually given my newborn son, my most precious gift, to God. I hadn't realized how such a commitment would impact my own life. When I finally began to understand what God had asked me to do, my whole world had been turned upside down; he had my full attention and I was ready to learn the first lesson. I committed myself to him.

And at the end of our journey, fully awakened by his presence, I would fall on my knees and praise God knowing that his purpose outweighed my pain. As I walked through the fire in each affliction, every distraction dissipated and nothing else remained except what was made from the substance of God—the weight of his glory. For the believer, his glory is pure gold.

> For momentary, light affliction is producing for us an eternal weight of glory far beyond all comparison (2 Corinthians 4:17 NASB).

1

1977

We had just moved from West Covina into our new home in Walnut, California, and I was preparing for Brian's third birthday. We had decided to keep it simple—just a small party at McDonald's, Brian's favorite place to eat. Brian had been in good spirits that day. Only once did I think that anything might be wrong with him—and that was when it came time to leave for the restaurant, I couldn't find him. Not being able to find Brian was unusual because he was usually right by my side. He should have been underfoot eagerly waiting for all of us to climb into the car. When I called for him a couple of times and he didn't answer, I started to worry. I searched the house, checking and double-checking every room.

And then I found him, appearing not to be at all hurt or sick, but perfectly fine. Lying on the floor of his sister's room, one leg crossed and waving in the air, he was looking rather carefree as he pretended to be reading an upside down book.

I laughed because he was only playing at nonchalance. In reality he was so excited to get the party underway that he couldn't stop squirming. Giving a halfhearted reprimand, I tried to make him sit still so I could trim his hair before we left. Cut in a Beatle style with long, thick bangs that failed to hide his big dark eyes, Brian's hair grew so fast—I was always trimming it. "McDonald's! McDonald's!" he screamed happily all the way to the restaurant. As soon as we got the birthday presents on the table, Brian and a few of his friends started to hover attentively around them, trying to guess at what was inside.

We sat and waited for a few minutes for the rest of the guests to arrive. McDonald's was a place we visited frequently. It was one of the few restaurants we could afford. I was a stay-at-home mom, but kept busy helping at the school and at church. Kevin worked for the phone company, following in his dad's footsteps. With the new house, most of our money was going to pay for the mortgage payments and the rest of the money went for household bills. Money was always tight, but we managed.

Brian was usually shy, but when our McDonald's Party Host brought out hats and party favors he could barely contain himself. By the end of the day, though, he had become unusually quiet. I thought maybe he had gotten so excited that he tired himself out. I tucked him into bed and he was out by the time his head hit the pillow.

Two weeks later Brian started running a fever. When it reached 101, I called his pediatrician. Brian had chronic ear problems from the time he was two years old, and that day our pediatrician was dismissive of the problem, telling me this was likely another ear infection and that bed rest and a baby aspirin would help. But I went ahead and made an appointment for the next day.

On Friday morning, what I'd expected to be a routine trip to the doctor's office followed by a simple prescription for an antibiotic turned into something entirely different. The doctor checked Brian and did not notice anything in his ears. When he completed the physical he said he thought that he felt something irregular in his abdomen. The doctor thought Brian was having an appendicitis attack. He said, "Keep an eye on him and call me if he starts vomiting, and we'll get him over to the hospital for some more tests."

Appendicitis? Our three-year-old might have to have surgery? Of course, looking back, appendicitis doesn't sound nearly so momentous. But that day, the doctor's words were sobering. I had expected to be sent home with medication. The idea that our three-year-old might have to have surgery—for any reason—caught me very much off guard.

That night Brian was still awake at 11:30 PM and I was getting anxious because he was feeling nauseated. I called the pediatrician and he told me Brian would probably be fine overnight, but we should bring him into his office the first thing in the morning. Thankfully, Brian went right to sleep after the call. But I sat near his bed keeping a watchful eye over him throughout the night. I had never noticed that his stomach was swollen, or that his breathing was labored. I thought the gasps for air were the result of discomfort and that his round little body looked perfectly normal for a child that age.

The next morning, Brian woke up in pain. His stomach hurt and his temperature had risen to 103 degrees. At 8:00 AM Saturday morning, just after the babysitter arrived to take care of our daughter, Kevin and I took Brian to the pediatrician's office.

By noon, on May 14, Brian had been admitted to Presbyterian Intercommunity Hospital in Whittier, California, where a series of tests began: blood work, two chest x-rays, x-rays of the abdomen, and two tests done on his kidneys. I thought the kidney tests must be precautionary steps before they proceeded with the appendectomy. It never occurred to me that something else might be wrong.

At 3:00 PM we were sure they would be doing the surgery and that we wouldn't be returning home any time soon, so we called to ask the grandparents to pick up our daughter. Then I called several of our Christian friends to pray for us. The idea that our son was having surgery at such a young age was very unsettling, but we believed the hospital would be able to take care of the problem.

We sat for hours in the hospital just waiting for someone to come into Brian's room and tell us what was going on, but no one came. Even with the hours ticking away, I thought that the possibility of one of our children becoming seriously ill seemed remote—even impossible. I couldn't see anything that would single us out, nothing that would leave us especially vulnerable to some unforeseen crisis. All those tragic events . . . they always happen to other people . . . don't they?

We were good people. After all, I had always been there to help and support others in a time of crisis. I felt sure that I had always done the right thing when people needed me. I was the friend and neighbor who, upon hearing bad news, ran to be by the side of that "other" human being. I made a phone call and left a casserole on the doorstep.

I had a grateful heart. I thanked God for my family and children. I held my children a little tighter and recognized how lucky I was to have two beautiful, healthy children when I heard about a two-year-old who had drowned in the family pool, or a neighbor's child who had accidentally been killed by the family car, or a newborn who had died suddenly from SIDS. My heart went out to those families. But we hadn't done anything that could possibly warrant us losing our child.

Looking back, I see that my attitude was not only naïve, but my acts of compassion toward others were unrefined. Showing up and saying a few kind words and even performing a few thoughtful deeds for people who had just lost a child doesn't even begin to touch the gravity of the situation. It wasn't until it happened to me, until it was my child that I began to understand. Everything you had, everyone you loved, and everything you believed in could just disappear in one catastrophic moment, and that moment left you forever changed. You would never be the same, would never return to a "normal" life again. Casseroles could not fix it; you needed someone to jump into the pit with you, to love and support you until you learned how to climb out and face the world again.

Kevin and I had recommitted our lives to Christ before Brian was born, first attending a Southern Baptist Church and then moving our membership to a non-denominational church near our new home.

When we first made the decision to fully commit our lives to Jesus, the most difficult challenge we had faced was that being "born again" did not sit well with our Catholic families or our non-believing friends. I still remember the look on my dad's face when he asked me about the "marijuana" sticker on my car. He thought the cult I was in was ruining my life. He said, "I understand that you got saved and you are going to a new church, but can you at least get rid of that sticker?" I laughed, "You mean the Maranatha sticker? It means 'the Lord has come.'"[2] We obviously had not even figured out how to send the right message to the people we loved.

In the beginning we had such a hunger to learn and to grow that we showed up every time the church doors opened. We attended seminars with Bill Gothard, worked at Billy Graham Crusades, completed the Bible Study Series by Bill Bright, studied Francis Schaeffer and C.S. Lewis. God was laying a foundation for us—but we were still so new. When Brian became ill, we came with simple faith. It was all we had. And we believed that if you had a problem, you gave it to the Lord and he fixed it.

We were still waiting at the hospital when the clock struck the dinner hour. It still never occurred to me that Brian's doctors might have found anything wrong other than the appendicitis. I dismissed the delay, thinking the hospital must be searching for a surgeon available on the weekend. More hours passed, the hospital room Brian was in seemed to turn cold and dark, and we were still waiting for answers. Having been up with Brian the previous night, sleep deprived and exhausted from waiting, I finally broke down and cried uncontrollably. Why did Brian have to wait so long to get the help he needed?

Finally, at 7:30 PM, almost eleven hours after we had left the house that morning, our pediatrician and a surgeon contracted with Children's Hospital came into the room to tell us that Brian had a large abdominal mass on his right side. It was most likely a type of kidney cancer. They called it Wilms' Tumor. In the morning they would be sending us to Children's Hospital for surgery to remove it.

I had never heard of Wilms' Tumor until that day. I knew nothing about cancer. I was dismissive of the diagnosis thinking that no one in either of our immediate families had cancer. Then I remembered my aunt had been fighting breast cancer for ten years and I had a cousin who died in his 40s from a brain tumor. I wondered if it was hereditary. Had I given this to Brian?

The pamphlet that I was handed in the hospital was titled, "What you need to know about Wilms' Tumor." It read:

Wilms' Tumor is almost always a case of kidney cancer. It occurs in children from infancy to age 15. In Wilms' Tumor the cell division is abnormal. Masses of tissue called malignant tumors threaten one's life. When new growth spreads to nearby organs or other parts of the body by way of the blood stream or lymphatic system they are called metastases. Nearly 10% of patients have tumors in both kidneys. Treatment is a combination of surgery, radiation therapy and chemotherapy. Overall more than 8 out of 10 youngsters with Wilms' Tumor can expect to achieve the long term disease-free status that, for this cancer, is the equivalent of a cure.[3]

The pamphlet ended somewhat optimistically telling us that more than eight out of ten children could expect the "equivalent of a cure," but Kevin and I were both in shock. "It is most likely cancer?" Neither of us said a word in response to the diagnosis. Before the doctors left the room, I found my voice, "Is this as serious as it sounds?" Both men turned to assure me that in fact Brian's condition was very serious. When the doctors left the room, a nurse brought Brian some Jell-O. He had not eaten all day, but he didn't want anything. He was so worn out, he just wanted to sleep. When she closed the privacy curtain around us, it only added to the intense isolation we were already beginning to feel.

We did not know what to do next. We sat for several hours in silence watching Brian sleep. We were numb. I finally got up and again called friends and family and asked them to pray for us because now we thought Brian had cancer. With every call, the grave reality settled in a little deeper. I kept thinking that it was strange how that one word—cancer—could bring on such intense emotion. But then Brian was going to die, wasn't he?

Kevin finally went home to get some sleep and I stayed in the hospital bed next to Brian. I prayed that God would completely heal the cancer; that it would be gone in the name of Jesus. I had brought my Bible with me that morning. I could not have gone through an appendectomy without the Lord, and I certainly would not be able to endure a diagnosis of cancer without having his Word in my hand. I searched the scriptures for comfort but God led me in another direction.

> Search me, O God, and know my heart; test me and know my anxious thoughts. See if there is any offensive way in me, and lead me in the everlasting way (Psalm 139:23–24 NIV).

I wondered if this was a test to see how strong our faith was. I was committed to Jesus; I was willing to do whatever it took. That night I wanted nothing more than to pray for Brian's healing, but before that could happen, God needed for me to examine my own heart. I had sin in my life. We are all sinners saved by grace. Sinning is what we do best when we take control over our life, break speeding laws, spend more money than we can afford, and get angry at our friends and neighbors.

I stopped and took a hard look at whether my desires and motives to come to the Lord were pure. How could God ever begin to fill me with his power and the knowledge of his ways if I was already so full of my own stuff? I had to be willing to empty myself, be set apart, and become a sanctified vessel.

Brian's circumcision had been an outward sign that we were committed to God. He required more. He wanted a heart that was circumcised. A heart set apart for him through repentance and inward changes. So often we have a "come to Jesus moment," and promise to attend church more often and read the Bible. He wants more from us than just a change in our pattern of behavior. I began to confess my sins and turn away from all the distractions in my life. I wanted to be right with God. I bowed at his feet and began again with him with a deeper understanding of his call on my life. I prayed a sinner's prayer:

Lord, I come humbly before you in the name of Jesus. Thank you for sending your son, to die on the cross, for me. Thank you that his blood washed away my sins and that I am forgiven. God give me a pure heart and your strength today as I lay my child down before you. My emotions are filled with sorrow, but I am in pursuit of your will for my life and my son's life. Father, I place Brian into your hands for healing. I know that I can be strong because you are with me. Teach me to live a life that will bring glory and honor to you. Amen.

2

CHILDREN'S HOSPITAL

Sunday morning, we were sent to Children's Hospital in Los Angeles for the surgery. We checked in at noon but waited for hours to be admitted. It was a busy weekend and there were very few staff members to handle all the new admits. I went to the front desk several times hoping to get Brian into a room. He still had fever and was irritable. I thought he might feel better in a quieter place, but the receptionist finally told us that there weren't any rooms available; they did not have enough beds for all the people waiting to be admitted that day.

The wait continued and became grueling as more and more people infiltrated the waiting area. We had not eaten all day, and we had not slept for three days, but just looking into the faces all around us, I knew our situation was not unique. Finally, sometime after 5 PM, the receptionist said they could put Brian into the nursery with three babies.

We went into the office and signed all of the hospital's forms. We had signed similar paperwork at the hospital in Whittier; the only difference was the emphasis concerning the financial arrangement. We were told that by signing the form we would agree to pay all charges that were not covered by our medical insurance plan. I assured the woman on the other side of the desk that we were fully covered by our medical plan; after all Kevin had been working with the same company for more than eight years. She just smiled at me. I smiled back. Medical coverage was the least of our problems.

I was so grateful that we had a room. I could not wait to get settled in and get Brian into a bed where he could sleep, but Brian did not feel the same way about being in a room for babies. He did not understand why he had to be placed in a crib. He stood up in it, sobbing, "I am not a baby." He felt punished. His sobs hit a nerve. We all felt punished. How easy it would have been for me to cry out to God in protest, "Why are you doing this to Brian? He hasn't done anything wrong!" However, I was not angry. I did not believe God was cruel, inflicting this cancer on a three-year-old as punishment. I only feared the uncertainty of our situation. Would God really take Brian's life? No, that didn't sound right. But even if he did take him to heaven, that would be a good thing, wouldn't it?

From a very young age I had believed in Heaven. It was a perfect place without pain or sorrow. My grandmother had quoted her favorite scripture to me so many times that I had it memorized.

In my Father's house are many rooms; if it were not so,
I would have told you. I am going there to prepare a place
for you (John 14:2 NIV).

She believed those words with all her heart and so did I. I learned from her that we serve a loving God who had prepared a place for us. Heaven was a beautiful place with streets of gold, but getting there was the difficult part. Would Brian be ripped from my arms and die in surgery? I wondered. I cried out deep within my soul, "Please, Lord, give me strength to get through this."

Later that evening a real bed became available and we were moved out of the crib room into a room with three other older children. Finally, Brian was able to settle down and get some rest before his surgery. I thanked God for answering our prayers.

At first we waited patiently for a doctor to come in and talk to us about the surgery. Then we finally came to realize we were not a high priority. We were just one of many families with a very sick child. Nothing was going to happen this late in the day. During the night shift, doctors made their rounds but we were ignored, since we were newly admitted. The team of doctors stopped at each bed in our room and openly discussed each child's case. The first little boy was a seven-year-old diagnosed with Wilms' Tumor, just like Brian. He had done well after the surgery, but now his parents were discussing his progress with radiation therapy. The little boy seemed to be in a lot of discomfort with the treatment. I remember thinking he looked so frail and his skin color was so ash grey.

The next child was five. He came in with seizures and had been diagnosed with a brain tumor. The last child was just eighteen months old. She was recovering from heart surgery. These children were all very sick and the parents looked so tired. Only one family sobbed openly when they were given the worst possible news: "We don't think your child is going to make it."

With Brian sound asleep at the hospital, we finally left and drove home, hoping to get a few hours of sleep ourselves. The next day, Monday, Kevin and I arrived early anticipating that this would be the day Brian had surgery. But instead, Children's Hospital re-did all the tests that had been done at our local hospital. A CAT (computerized axial tomography) scan, a nephro-tomography, and an ultrasound were done. We were told these tests would determine whether or not the suspected mass was a cyst or tumor. I wasn't sure what they were talking about but assumed the cancer diagnosis was still in place. I was hopeful that maybe God had already healed Brian and all the tests would come back negative and the nightmare would be over.

We learned very quickly that mornings were the busiest time at the hospital. During rounds, a large number of staff went in and out of the rooms, reviewing the charts of each patient. Then they would circulate through the hospital individually. One by one each staff member proceeded to ask the same questions as the previous member.

- Do you understand what Wilms' Tumor is?
- Do you know what the treatment will be?
- Has anyone explained the side effects of chemotherapy?
- Tell me how you got here.

I would tell our story from the beginning, starting with the fever and the fact that we thought Brian had an ear infection. When I finished, another member of the team would enter the room and we would start again. I repeated our story over and over again until late into the evening. After several rounds, the questions became annoying. I was growing impatient. When would they help Brian?

It wasn't long before staff labeled me as being "an accurate historian." I assume the title was a compliment, but I only wanted this terrible cancer out of my son. No one that we talked to seemed to be in much of a hurry to make that happen. At the end of the day the only thing we had learned was that Brian would be receiving a blood transfusion before his surgery.

In time I realized Children's Hospital was a teaching hospital. This was the reason that the same questions were being asked by each member of the medical team assigned to Brian. Our team was made up of one member from each of the following medical providers:

- **Resident at postgraduate level two** has completed internship and one or two years of specialized pediatric training.

- **Fellow/physician associate** has completed internship and residency programs and is receiving additional specialized training. They are certified and state licensed to practice medicine under direct supervision for two years.

- **Attending Physician**—a full-time professional staff member who holds a teaching position at the University of Southern California School of Medicine.

The hospital had over 650 pediatric specialists and 65 residents and interns when we were there. Receiving treatment at a teaching hospital had its advantages. This hospital in particular was on the cutting edge of treating pediatric cancer. It provided opportunities for the staff to engage in discussion with each other, to take part in innovative research on site, and to tap into resources all over the world. On the other hand, as we witnessed during our first hospital stay, inexperienced staff members often took hours to perform simple tasks and made many mistakes.

That night Brian was still sick with fever and very uncomfortable. I don't think any of the staff even considered the amount of pain he was in because he had not been given any medication since he had been admitted. We were still expecting that there would be a surgery soon. But while we waited, I didn't know what else I could do for my son. Only a day had passed, but it felt like it had been weeks.

I began talking to the other parents in the room. By now, we all knew each other's stories by heart. The first child with Wilms' Tumor would be going home soon but would continue with the radiation therapy as an outpatient for an entire month. The second child with the brain tumor was not expected to live, but surgery had been scheduled—despite the fact that the survival rate was low. The bouncy, bubbly adorable little girl who had a heart defect had made a remarkable recovery from her surgery and was waiting to be discharged in a few hours. It was helpful to talk to other parents and to hear their stories. They helped me understand the process. Kevin and I knew nothing about how the medical community worked.

That night, I placed the timing of the surgery in God's hands, where it belonged. All day long I had fought with God over who was going to control Brian's life. I wanted a complete healing so we could leave the hospital; but that didn't seem to be happening. Then I decided that it was ridiculous that we had to wait so long; but that got me nowhere. I knew that God ultimately was able to take care of us. I just had to let go and let him take the reins.

Lesson 2: *Nothing Is Impossible with God*

Later that evening, after I had resigned myself to the idea that God was able to handle the situation without my help, a nurse came in to give Brian a blood transfusion. I wondered, is it really that easy? I just give my concerns over to you and you take care of them?

The nurse explained that the extra blood would prepare Brian for the loss of blood he would experience during the surgery the next day. I paused. "He'll be having surgery tomorrow? No one told us." But I was thankful. We wouldn't have to wait any longer. I felt such relief.

I wasn't particularly in favor of the blood transfusion because there had been so much in the news about people receiving "bad" blood, but I was too tired to put up a fight. I had to remind myself that when I asked God to take care of everything that concerned Brian, my part was to trust that he would.

When Brian finally fell asleep that night, we said a prayer for him and then drove home for a short nap, a shower, and some clean clothes. Before we left, the nursing staff told us to be back by 8:30 AM if we wanted to see Brian before his surgery.

Kevin rested and I searched for the story of Abraham and Isaac. I was struggling. I had prayed for healing and Brian was not healed. Although I did not question our faith, many of our Christian friends were already doing just that. Some people told me we were not seeing a healing because our faith was weak; others admonished us that we needed to get right with God. Still others had asked us what terrible thing we had done to bring this on our child. None of that had been helpful, only confusing and hurtful. Even if our faith had wavered, didn't God's Word promise that when we are weak, he is strong, that when we are without faith, he is faithful (2 Corinthians 12:10; 2 Timothy 2:13)?

I trusted that God would help us through each step of the journey. I could not put my faith in anyone but him. As I read the story of Abraham and Isaac, I felt like I was reading it for the first time. I felt the sadness, the heavy heart Abraham must have had as he took out the knife.

Then God said, "Take your son, your only son, Isaac, whom you love, and go to the region of Moriah. Sacrifice him there as a burnt offering on one of the mountains I will tell you about.". . . Then he reached out his hand and took the knife to slay his son. But the angel of the Lord called to him from heaven, "Abraham, Abraham!" "Here I am," he replied. "Do not lay a hand on the boy." "Do not do anything to him. Now I know that you fear God, because you have not withheld from me your son, your only son" (Genesis 22:2, 10–12 NIV).

I sincerely wanted to surrender my child to God, to trust his will. Deep in my heart, I hoped God would rescue the child I had not withheld. Had I missed the central message of Abraham's story? I saw what I wanted to see—that when Abraham had demonstrated his devotion to God, Isaac was spared. But Abraham hadn't known that God would spare Isaac. And still his allegiance to God and his trust in God's provision took precedence even above the life of his own child. I prayed, "Lord, I do give my son completely to you." Then I whispered, "No matter what the outcome."

I felt I had managed to surrender the outcome of surgery in that moment. But real surrender, permanent surrender, would come later and be much harder. It would not be just for that one-time but an ongoing process. I would have to learn to surrender to God at every step, and it would completely break my heart . . . just as Abraham's heart must have broken when he made up his mind to sacrifice Isaac.

3

SURGERY

When we arrived at the hospital early Tuesday morning, Brian had already been taken up to the top floor for surgery. Nursing staff had told us that we needed to be back at the hospital by 8:30 AM to see him prior to the surgery, it was only 7 AM! We had driven in early so we would have plenty of time to explain to him what was going on, but I never got that chance. I was angry and I let the hospital staff know it. "How could you take away our last few precious moments with our son?" I pleaded. Then I sobbed, "I just wanted to hold him one last time."

Brian had never been through anything like this before. I had not yet talked to him about the surgery because I did not want to frighten him. I had planned on telling him that morning just before they sedated him. I wanted to be there to comfort him and pray for him.

The nurse told me that a 7:30 AM slot had opened up unexpectedly and that's why they had taken him. I asked, "Was he upset?" But the look on her face told me she was done. She told me to just calm down and go to the waiting room. The other parents in the room told us Brian had been crying. He must have felt so afraid, and I felt so sad. How does this happen at a hospital that caters to children's needs?

We walked down the hall to the elevator and went up to the waiting room. It was Tuesday, May 17th, 7:30 AM, and Brian was undergoing his *second* procedure. Again, at the hands of a skillful surgeon, there would be a cutting away of skin, only this time an entire organ would be removed. We did not know if Brian would live through the surgery. If he did live, we didn't know for how long. The doctors couldn't tell us if he would live for six weeks or six months. Until the surgeon could go in and take a look at the tumor we had no idea how involved it had become with Brian's vital organs.

Kevin and I sat in silence, squished in between other parents who were waiting to hear about their children. All of us in the room were experiencing our own personal hell, paralyzed with fear that we would never see our children alive again. We all stared at the closed narrow door that led to the operating room, hoping to see our surgeon come back through that door with a delivery of good news. And yet everyone feared the worst—that we would be told that our child had not made it.

As I emotionally de-escalated, I realized I should be grateful that Brian was able to go in early. What if he had to wait for hours because they had gotten backed-up? The hospital was so busy. I settled in and opened my Bible to Ephesians. I needed to turn my heart and mind back to God.

> For our struggle is not against flesh and blood, but against the rulers, against the powers, against the world forces of this darkness, against the spiritual forces of wickedness in the heavenly places. Therefore, take up the full armor of God, that you may be able to resist in the evil day, and having done everything to stand firm (Ephesians 6:12–13 NASB).

In Ephesians 6, the apostle Paul writes to the church in Ephesus, urging his fellow soldiers to be strengthened by the might of Jesus to fight the good fight. As I read Paul's letter, I began to see that my situation could also be called a battle. But in my initial shock, I thought I was simply fighting against the illness that had attacked my child. I came to realize the nature of the battle that God's people are called to fight. I understood it was not about an emotional battle or even a physical battle; I was about to enter into spiritual warfare where good and evil battle for souls. I was beginning to learn how unfamiliar this new territory was to me. I would need to stay strong, believe God would take care of Brian, and not let this situation break me. But I still thought that when the battle was won the cancer would be gone and my child would live.

As we sat and waited, I ruminated about what God was doing in our lives. Brian didn't get a miracle; he still had to go through the surgery. I knew God was not limited in resources and that he also used doctors and medicine to accomplish healings, and to me, none of those things diminished his power. Still in the back of my mind I was acutely aware that God might perform the ultimate healing and take Brian to a place where there was no pain or suffering—heaven.

While I wondered what God was going to do, time continued to pass. The surgery was supposed to only take two hours. I turned to my Bible and in childlike faith I asked the Lord, "Will Brian go to heaven today?" My eyes fell on this scripture:

The Lord will sustain him on his sickbed and restore him from his bed of illness (Psalm 41:3 NIV).

This time the words ministered to me. They gave me such peace. I no longer felt fearful. Just as I turned to Kevin to tell him everything would be okay, our surgeon walked into the waiting room.

It was just before noon when he told us that Brian had come through the surgery in good condition. The radial nephrectomy had taken well over three hours. They had removed the right kidney without complications. It did not appear that the cancer had been involved with any other nearby organs. Brian would be out of the recovery room in two hours and then moved down into ICU on the second floor, where we would be able to see him. Days later, the medical report near Brian's bed described what the surgeon had done:

Three-year-old with abdominal mass: Wilms' Tumor stage 1 on right side. Large portions of the tissue surrounding the kidney and neighboring lymph nodes were removed. The tumor weighed 480 grams [*just over a pound, four times the weight of a normal kidney*]. It was 14 x 12 x 8 cms. in diameter [*5.5 x 4.7 x 3 inches; a normal kidney is 2 inches x 1 inch*]. The large yellow mass was removed and the left kidney was normal.[4]

I was grateful the surgery had been a success. But I didn't know what this "success" meant in terms of Brian's future health, and the surgeon didn't say. The medical pamphlets referred to a "success" as someone who lived three to five years after they were diagnosed. That didn't sound like much of a success to me. What the surgeon did say was that because of the size of the tumor, they thought that Brian must have been born with cancer.

Was it true that he had never been healthy? Had he always been a sick child? We had brought our son to the hospital at the first sign of trouble, and the tumor was already so advanced that the doctors had to remove his entire right kidney.

How could we have missed all the signs? And how did two other doctors who examined him regularly overlook such a large tumor? How did his grandmother, who was a nurse, and his mother, who bathed him and fed him and nurtured him daily, miss something that was so intrusive?

When we first saw Brian after the surgery, his skin tone was that grey color we had seen in the other children; that color of death. His lips were deep purple. He didn't look like the same child. I suddenly realized how much this experience would change him. All I wanted to do was hold him and tell him everything would be okay, but there were nurses all around his bed and I couldn't even get near him. Tears began to well up in my eyes.

Neither Kevin nor I had ever seen anyone in ICU before; it was devastating. He had tubes coming out everywhere. He had a catheter, oxygen, drainage tubes, and heart monitors. The oxygen mask covered almost his entire face. He was heavily sedated and yet when we walked into the room, he was very aware of our presence. Every time I moved away from the bed he moaned. He didn't want us to leave.

We stayed late into the evening, but there was little we could do for him. With the nursing staff working with him constantly, we felt like we were in the way. I felt guilty when we finally did leave just a few minutes after midnight. I was physically and emotionally drained. I tried to relieve my guilt over leaving by telling myself that Brian was doing okay, that most of the children in ICU looked much worse than he did. Years later, I would learn that in fact ICU was the best place to leave your child alone in the hospital because it provides such a high level of care.

In the morning I arrived early to find Brian awake. I tried to explain all the tubes and machines that were hooked up to him, but he just wanted to know when they would all be removed. He kept trying to form a word that sounded like "off." I sat next to him and patted his arm telling him that soon they would take everything off.

Brian's cheeks no longer looked sullen; his coloring was coming back and he was breathing easier. When the doctor came in during morning rounds, he told us Brian was doing well and he thought the cancer was Stage 1, which was really good news because that meant that it was treatable and had not spread to any other organs. He also told us that Brian's heart was strong and that now we were just waiting for the sole surviving kidney to start functioning on its own before he could be moved out of ICU.

By the afternoon, all the tubes were gone except for his catheter and the nurses started preparing Brian for the move into a regular room. Brian moaned and grabbed at my hand and held it tightly. In less than 24 hours from the time of his surgery, the kidney began working and Brian was out of ICU and on his way down to the second floor where he would stay for the next five days. I was thankful he was doing so well. Nothing was impossible with God; he saved my son's life.

Nursing staff moved Brian into a room shared with two other little boys, but it would take Brian several days before he was aware that there were others in the room with us. He was still heavily sedated but because he was less restricted by tubes and machines every move triggered the painful effects of having such a large incision. During fitful periods of being unconscious followed by consciousness he would cry out to me, "I hurt, Mommy." They tried to manage his pain with Thorazine, but after several dosages he had already figured out that he did not like the effects of that drug and moaned each time the nurses came into his room to give him another dose. "No!" he cried out, "it makes me feel dizzy."

Throughout the hospital stay, Brian had blood draws at all hours of the day and night even though we were told that he had lost a minimum amount of blood during the surgery. The staff had explained that after such a major surgery, these kinds of precautionary measures were routinely taken should he encounter a problem and need yet another blood transfusion.

That evening, the night nurse came in and uncovered his incision. I gasped; I had only seen the bandages and not the actual incision. It was so long and raw looking. The incision came down under his right arm and crossed his entire belly and ended near his left hip. The poking around must have hurt because my three-year-old asked me for another pain pill. When Brian fell asleep late that night, I went home overwhelmed by the amount of aftercare he was going to need when he got out of the hospital. Feeling both physically and emotionally exhausted, I laid down on the sofa and fell right to sleep.

In the morning, I left the house just before 6:30 and still hit all the morning rush hour traffic. I was trying to arrive at the hospital before Brian woke up because it was his first morning in the new room. I was surprised when I walked into the room to see he already had a visitor at 8 AM. The hospital's school teacher, Patti, was tall, pretty, about fifteen years older than I. She loved her job and Brian liked her right away. She sat near Brian's bed, reading him a book. Brian was still in pretty bad shape and could barely open his eyes, but she continued to read to him anyway. He had never looked so content with a stranger by his side. They formed a tight bond that day. In fact, Patti made a point of coming to check on Brian every time he returned to the hospital over the next five years.

After she left, the morning got very busy. We had three little boys in our room; all needed a lot of care. The oldest boy in Brian's room was nine years old. He had no hair on the top of his head, just patches around the sides, and his emaciated body gave him the appearance of being a little old man. When you gazed into his eyes you could tell he had suffered much pain. He had been battling cancer for five years, more than half of his life span. He knew everything about the hospital and about his cancer. He could explain any procedure or surgery with such great detail that you would have thought that you were speaking with a physician. His cancer had spread from his hip to his knees and then to his brain. He had such a long history with chemotherapy that just mentioning it by name made him wretch. He would yell at the nurses, "Don't talk about it or you will make me sick!"

That night the doctors had come into the room to tell his parents that their son's journey was almost over. They discharged him that same evening and sent him home to die. The parents looked stoic, there were no tears as they packed up their belongings and left the hospital. I wondered how they could be so strong, but then it hit me they probably had no tears left. It had been a long journey of sadness for them. I wanted to comfort their son. He was so bright and so brave. It must have been frightening to have to face death at nine. I hoped the doctors were wrong.

The other child was an out-of-control six-year-old. The child had been hit by a car and was in the hospital for observation, but he did not seem to be injured. In fact, he was very active. He screamed, jumped on the bed, and ran around the hospital room. He threw food, pulled out IVs, and flipped the television stations. His constant demands kept his parents hopping from the gift shop downstairs to the cafeteria. Every time a doctor entered the room, all of the parents in that wing of the hospital prayed they had come to discharge this little boy back home, but it wasn't meant to be.

At first Brian cried and whimpered when the tantrums were loud or lasted too long, but by the time the little boy was ready for discharge on that third day, Brian had become thoroughly entertained by his extreme behaviors.

Early Friday morning the two boys had been discharged and Brian and I celebrated that the room was all ours. It was so quiet and calm, that we snuggled in and watched cartoons. Those few precious hours gave us time to relax and catch our breath. By noon the entire floor was mourning the return of the nine-year-old who had just been sent home. His cancer was spreading so quickly that his parents could not manage his pain. His parents told me that his last x-ray revealed the cancer had spread to his sinuses. His breathing was slow and labored. His parents were inconsolable, and so was everyone who knew them. In just twenty-four hours his suffering would be over.

The smell of death, the sterile walls of the hospital, and all the sick children started to take a toll on me. I prayed and read my Bible every day, but there were moments when I just wanted to bolt out the door and take Brian with me. I opened my Bible to read more about this battle I was facing.

> Stand firm therefore, having girded your loins with truth, and having put on the breastplate of righteousness, and having shod your feet with the preparation of the gospel of peace (Ephesians 6:14–15 NASB).

There must have been a reason for Paul to repeatedly remind the Ephesians that they needed to stand firm. Whatever they were facing, they must have wanted to flee as much as I did. But I had chosen to follow Christ, and the spiritual armor he had given me was designed for soldiers as they marched forward into battle. As one Bible commentary put it, "There is no armor specified for the back, but only for the front of the body, implying that we must never turn our back to the foe; our only safety is in resisting ceaselessly."[5]

I needed to resist the urge to run. I was uncomfortable, but it was temporary; besides, running away would not make this all go away. I needed to rethink my situation. The Lord had been our strength and the worst of the battle was over. I was well protected by righteousness and held tightly together by the band of truth—the gospel of Jesus Christ. I would just have to trust God a little longer. He had taken care of Brian so far, hadn't he? Brian was healing so quickly. I just had to be patient until we got to go home.

During rounds the next morning, after all the annoying questions, an intern came over to Brian's bedside and told me the cancer had spread to the liver. Then he started talking to me about chemotherapy. I was stunned. "So the cancer has spread?" I asked. Then I argued, "But the surgeon told us that the cancer was Stage 1." I started feeling anxious again. I wondered if I had misunderstood. The long explanation we had gotten from the surgeon told us Brian's cancer had not spread. It was the best possible outcome given the size of his tumor.

A few minutes later our surgeon came into the room; he wanted to clarify the intern's statements. He said, "There was a small defect in the liver where the tumor had laid up against it, but the tumor itself was contained. Brian will be going home soon. But he will have to come back to the hospital to follow up with chemotherapy and radiation treatment." I took a deep breath; so we were still looking at a Stage 1 cancer, the type of cancer that has a good prognosis. But I did not understand the rush to start chemotherapy; surely Brian would have several weeks at home to heal.

The thought of going home made me feel so much better, like I was getting a handle on things again. I was ready to take back the control over my life. I could not wait for the discharge paperwork. Even though we would be spending another night at the hospital, I started packing up some of Brian's things. I would be driving Brian home. Kevin had gone back to work on Friday and was trying to pick up a few extra hours by working on the weekend. Crystal was still staying with my parents so I could stay at the hospital.

For parents who spent the night in the hospital, the most important thing they could do during the day was to secure a second blue chair. It was a difficult task because the hospital was always so crowded and often family members would notice that you had two chairs and would need to borrow one during a visit. It was essential to stick around until their visit was over so you could retrieve the chair. Having two chairs almost guaranteed two to three hours of sleep during the night. But during most of the night I just walked the halls; it was hard to sleep with so many people coming in and out of the room. I was looking forward to the day when I could go home and sleep in a real bed.

I thought of all the things I had neglected over the past week, including my daughter. She needed to be back home so she could return to school. I wanted to start putting the pieces of our family life back together; our crisis was over.

Late Monday morning, Brian's pediatrician had stopped by to see how Brian was doing. He had always been kind. I know he felt bad about not finding the tumor sooner. He was happy to see that Brian looked so good. I told him we had just been waiting for Brian to get strong enough to go home, and this morning they had given us the good news, that he was ready to go!

But hours later on May 23, we were still waiting to be discharged. Brian and I had just started a new book that the schoolteacher had dropped off when the social worker came into the room and directed me to follow her down the hall. I told her I was waiting for discharge papers and that I did not want to miss seeing Brian's doctor, but she insisted that I leave with her. Brian started to cry; he did not understand why I had to leave—without him. I couldn't understand why the one person at the hospital whom I had come to know as a friend was suddenly making such demands. My instincts told me to stay with my child, but instead I followed her into the elevator. We went to the third floor of the outpatient clinic.

When the elevator stopped I stepped into the pediatric cancer clinic. Then she gave me a tour of the place where Brian would be receiving treatment after his discharge. She told me that over 400 children were being treated at the cancer clinic. She said that because of the large number of kids that were treated daily that I should expect to be at the clinic all day and not make any other plans.

She explained the steps: "First check-in at the lab and pick up a blood slip. Expect to wait two to three hours before a lab tech is available to draw the blood. The results will be ready in time for your afternoon clinic."

"The lab results are important because the chemotherapy kills all of the blood cells, not just the cells that have cancer. So whether or not your child will receive treatment is dependent on the number of cells that survived from the last round of treatment. You will probably be able to determine if Brian is ready for his next round of treatment by the level of activity he exhibits. If he has been very tired, experiences shortness of breath, or has nosebleeds, his white blood count is probably too low and you will be sent home to watch for signs of fever, sore throat, or a cough. A normal range for the white cell count runs from 4,000 to 11,000, and anything below this number puts your child at risk."

"When you are finished at the lab, go directly to the outpatient clinic and check in there. You will wait two to five hours to see a doctor. There is a cafeteria on the ground floor of the hospital if you get hungry. Breakfast is from 3 AM to 10:45 AM, lunch from 11:15 AM to 3 PM and dinner is from 4 PM to 8 PM The waiting room is usually filled with patients so you need to arrive early if you want to find a place to sit down. There are toys in the waiting room . . ."

There was so much new information and I wasn't sure how to process it. I found myself gathering handouts that were strategically placed throughout the clinic. I remember telling myself that day that I must write everything down, because there were so many terms that I did not understand. I never realized those daily entries would someday turn into Brian's story.

The social worker continued. She barely paused to catch her breath. "When your name is called you will be placed in a small room. The doctor will review the outcome of Brian's tests, and based on the results, he will either approve or delay the chemotherapy treatment for that day. If chemotherapy is to be given, it will take two to four hours depending on the number of drugs and the amount of time that it takes to administer them."

Then she proceeded to tell me about Brian's specific treatment plan. "He will receive chemotherapy every four to six weeks. He most likely will be treated with any number of the following drugs: Vincristine, Cytoxan, and Adriamycin D.[6] The side effects of these drugs will cause hair loss, constipation or diarrhea, nausea, vomiting, loss of appetite, mouth sores, muscle weakness, sterility, and liver dysfunction."

As we continued to walk the halls, I realized I had become disoriented. I wasn't sure how we had gotten to the basement but the social worker was inviting me into her office to see if I had any questions. I sat quietly, giving myself a moment to let all her words sink in. I was alarmed at the fact that my child would lose his hair but I guessed that was to be expected. I had gotten used to all those little bald heads in the hospital. The loss of hair was trivial compared to how sick the drugs would make him. But now the social worker was telling me my child would also be sterile, that he could never have children. I would be taking that right away from him when I signed the consent papers. But then it crossed my mind that my only alternative was to just let him die. It was a lot to take in.

I was feeling trapped; this was my new life whether I liked it or not. For the next year, this was what it was going to be like. I knew that the social worker was only doing her job, sharing information I would need to have in the future, but I was having trouble accepting it. Now she was sitting in front of me asking me how I felt. With each question I was building a bigger wall inside, even as tears were flowing from my eyes. I was still quiet, mourning the loss of what our family used to be. Overwhelmed, I shut down. I didn't know how to express all that I felt. All I really wanted to know was, when do we get to go home?

4

CHEMOTHERAPY

When I returned to Brian's room, several staff members stood blocking the doorway. I saw a person with a needle standing at Brian's bed, and I could hear Brian crying. Apparently they had come in to start the chemotherapy treatment—but why were they doing that without my consent? I couldn't remember if I had signed anything that allowed the treatment to start. I could see Brian's arms were covered in blood from multiple needle sticks—had they not been able to find a good vein? I started counting the bloody sites on his arm; there were more than five.

I felt betrayed. Had the hospital tricked me by sending the social worker in to get me out of the room? The timing was certainly suspicious. I was so tired that paranoia was setting in. No one had mentioned to me that treatment would start in the hospital. The surgeon had emphasized that there would need to be time to heal after such a major surgery. I understood that to mean that Brian would need several weeks of bed rest at home. Based on the limited knowledge that I had about this potentially life threatening treatment I feared that starting the chemotherapy before Brian was healed could possibly kill him. This had to be a mistake; they were giving the drug too soon.

I stepped in closer to the bed so Brian could see me. The person administering the drug looked so young. Brian looked scared. He was frozen in place. The chemotherapy was given in a flash, and then the student left. I had kept silent, afraid I would only make the situation worse. But once it was over I rushed to Brian's side. Brian had been alone with them for more than forty-five minutes.

I held him close, thinking about all he had experienced while he was in the hospital.

At just three, he had already learned:

- children die from cancer
- what intense pain felt like
- when to ask for a pain pill
- and that not all people are kind

These were all hard lessons to grasp. I told him I was so sorry.

Minutes later, a nurse came in and took the time to give me a thorough explanation about the drugs Brian had just received and the side effects I should be aware of. She said Brian had received injections of Vincristine and Adriamycin. The dosage was lowered to reduce the side effects of nausea and vomiting so that the surgical wounds could heal.

When she left, I began telling Brian why he needed the chemotherapy. I told him stories about how the medicine attacked all the bad cancer and killed it. After he calmed down and fell asleep, I picked up my Bible. It was becoming my life manual, because it provided instructions for each step of my journey. I read Paul's next explanation about the battle.

> In addition to all, taking up the shield of faith, with which you will be able to extinguish the flaming missiles of the evil one. And take the helmet of salvation, and the sword of the Spirit, which is the word of God. With all prayer and petition pray at all times in the Spirit, and with this in view, be on the alert with all perseverance and petition for all the saints (Ephesians 6:16–18 NASB).

Paul's declaration said I would be able to extinguish the flaming missiles, but missiles seemed to shoot by on all sides with no end in sight. I had the sword, God's Word, in my hand, so what was I supposed to do? Pray for others? Really?

I wasn't in a position to question because I was so new to this new journey God had me on. I had just realized that being obedient meant that I had to walk with him daily. Walking in obedience allowed me the privilege of hearing his voice. I was amazed by the fact that he seemed to lead me to the Bible verses that I needed at that moment.

God's Word was telling me that I needed to pray for others. I began thinking about all the people I knew who were struggling—who were ill and did not know the Lord. By the time I finished my list, I counted seventy-nine people that I would pray for daily. I decided that this exercise would take me out of my own circumstances and help me to heal. By setting my own concerns aside, I could see that God was looking at a much bigger picture.

Hours passed, and then finally a nurse came in and medicated Brian with Thorazine. She said they would be taking him downstairs for a liver scan in a few minutes. Brian started to have some anxiety about leaving me, but I quickly reminded him that he had done this before and I would be in the room waiting for him when he got done.

When they came, he didn't fight or cry, instead he just looked defeated, like his mother. He was gone for a whole hour, but when he returned he had a shy little smile on his face. We were going home.

The forty-five-minute car ride was difficult for him. I could tell he was in so much pain. I couldn't imagine how it felt to be tossed about by the speed bumps, sharp turns, and rough roads with so many sutures in his little body. When we got home, Brian wanted to walk into the house by himself. He moved slowly but his gait was steady. I asked him to come out in the back yard so I could take a couple of pictures. We didn't have very many pictures of the kids—typically the camera only came out on special occasions, so Brian wasn't used to having his picture taken. He was still dressed in his hospital pajamas, and he looked so pale. He had no expression. He hurt, so I quickly got him back inside and into bed.

At that moment I thought it would be my last chance to capture a picture of my son. Somewhere deep in my heart, I knew that the cancer would kill him and I might not even have a recent picture to remember him by. I sat by Brian's bed, wondering what he was feeling. It must have seemed like he had been away from home for a very long time, but it had only been nine days. He lay very still and waited for sleep to come. Without the IV drips of Demerol, I could see that the days ahead of us would be very difficult.

Brian was sound asleep when I left his room sobbing. I knew now that every moment I had left with him was precious. I was overcome with the thoughts of losing him. The child I had seen through the lens of the camera had no future. He wasn't even the same child anymore. I feared he would never go to school, have friends, drive a car, get married, or have children. I worried that I would never know his dreams or hopes, that I might no longer get to see him laugh or play in the mud. His innocence was gone and he already knew too much about physical and emotional pain. I would never be able to look at him the same way, or treat him the same. From now on every time I did something for him I would feel like I was doing it for the last time. I felt a grief so raw that I wasn't sure I would even be able to go on without him.

I washed his clothes and put away the toys he had played with before he went to the hospital. Then I started to fix dinner. It was hard to believe that the last time I made dinner no one knew Brian was ill. Yet life had been precious then too; why hadn't I realized that? That's all I could think about until Kevin finally came home with Crystal and the three of us had dinner. Brian slept.

We had only been home for two days before we had to return to the hospital. Something horrible was happening to Brian's arm. It was swollen and had turned bright red. The flesh looked raw and was oozing fluids. It seemed to happen overnight. I was very concerned. The lab tech tried to explain to me that the first treatment of chemotherapy had infiltrated into his right arm.

The chemotherapy was so toxic that the person administering the drug must push it directly into a vein that had not been punctured or damaged in anyway. If the drug leaked out into the surrounding delicate tissue the result was a chemical burn. Brian had only complained that he did not feel well. He had not let me know that it was his arm that hurt. The core of the burn looked small, and yet it was already restricting any use of that arm.

We spent the entire day at the outpatient clinic. The lab had taken blood for the CBC (complete blood count) to determine if his bone marrow was working normally and to check the platelet count. It only took an hour to get the blood work done in the lab that morning, but when we got to the clinic, it was already full. We were lucky that a stranger was willing to give up her seat so we could sit down. We sat waiting in the clinic for hours. Brian slept and I read pamphlets about blood slips. When I finished reading them I slipped the handouts into my purse so I could add them to my collections of what was becoming, "Brian's medical file."

I had already heard that the goal of the cancer treatment was to interfere with the growth of the cancer cells and destroy them; what I didn't realize, even though the social worker had tried to explain it to me, was how all cells were affected. I learned how blood cells were produced by the bone marrow, and that single cells coming from the bone marrow were called stem cells. The pamphlet I was reading gave specific information about three types of cells and the things that could go wrong when those cell counts became too low.

It's the stem cells that turn into one of three major types of blood cells: red cell, white cell, or platelets. These three types of blood cells must become mature to carry out their jobs properly.

- **Red cells:** red blood cells contain hemoglobin and carry oxygen from the lungs to the cells. If the hemoglobin drops below 10, the patient is considered anemic. Warning signs: tired, dizzy, short of breath.

- **Platelets:** platelets are tiny particles that help the blood to clot. If the count falls below 50,000, spontaneous bleeding can result. A count below 5,000 is life threatening. Warning signs: nosebleeds, easy bruising, brown or red colored urine.

- **White cells:** white blood cells prevent and fight infections. A low count is below 4,000. Warning signs: fever over 100, sore throat/cough, shaking, chills.[7]

Despite Brian's bright red arm, the doctor ordered that a low dosage of Vincristine be given that day. The doctor tried to lower my high level of anxiety that Brian's life was in danger just like the nurse had done in the hospital, by telling me that decreasing the dosage lessens the risks. He ended the appointment by scheduling a consult with the burn center, ASAP!

As we walked into the burn center on June 1, Brian protected his arm by holding it close to his body. He had been refusing to use the arm or straighten it for an entire week now. The doctor took one look at his arm and said that the chemical burn could cause permanent damage without physical therapy. Brian cried out when the physical therapist came in and tried to extend the arm to take a measurement. The doctor continued to explain the nature of the burn. He said that by the time we could see the burn, it had already eaten through all the soft tissue as it burned from the core, the inside of the arm, and radiated into the outer layers of the skin. That meant that veins and muscles and in some circumstances even the bone were all damaged by the toxic drug. The doctor also pointed out the grave concern he had about the amount of damage that had been done to the joint. Without physical therapy the elbow could become frozen in place. He also warned that we should not have any expectation that the arm would ever be normal because even if the arm healed there would be interference with its normal functioning because of the scar tissue that remained.

Brian would have to have therapy at the hospital for the next thirty days, and in addition to the trips to the hospital I would need to work with Brian several times a day at home to help accelerate the progress. As we left I was handed a prescription for pain medicine and was told that Brian would need to take one pill four times a day.

The daily trips to the hospital were tough in the summer-like temperatures and downtown traffic. Each morning for the first few weeks, I had to wait until it was time to drop Crystal off for school, before we could leave. By the time I got to the highway it was already filled with early morning commuters. I worried all day long that we would be delayed and I wouldn't make it back to the school in time to pick up Crystal.

Once we were home, I was busy with Brian's stretching exercises, then making dinner, cleaning the house, and putting the kids to bed. It was our normal routine now, but it was both physically and emotionally draining. Each night, regardless of how exhausted I felt, I remembered to pray for the people on my list; it was what I was expected to do, if I wanted to be obedient to God's Word.

Crystal's classes ended on the ninth, but chemotherapy started back up on the tenth. The first day back at the cancer clinic, both of the children were scheduled to see the psychiatrist for an assessment. It was one of many support services provided by the hospital.

We arrived early for the blood work and checked in at the clinic, alerting staff that we would be at Physical Therapy for an hour. After lunch at the cafeteria, Brian went through a thirty-minute psycho-social assessment exam, and when it was over I chatted briefly with the psychiatrist. The results were good, Brian was adjusting. The psychiatrist thought Brian was a little withdrawn and certainly less trusting. I wasn't too worried because Brian had always been a little shy and hesitant when he approached something new; it was just part of his personality. I was pleased that I could see his old personality returning now that the incision had become less painful. He really hadn't lost himself in this process after all.

Crystal's test took a full hour because she was older. I had to leave her with the psychiatrist while I waited with Brian to see his cancer doctor.

The whole day had become a juggling act. When the hour was up staff watched Brian while I talked to the psychiatrist about Crystal's results. I had been so worried that she would feel left out because she was the "other" child, the one that wasn't sick, but the psychiatrist did not believe that at this early stage in the process either child had any issues resulting from the hospitalization. He did think that the way Crystal processed information might indicate that her IQ scores would be high. I could only hope that somehow having a higher IQ would make it easier for her to pass on to the next grade despite all of her absences. We returned to the clinic just in time for Brian's physical. Brian was cleared to receive another low dosage of Vincristine.

By the end of the week, Brian no longer needed any pain medication. Both the burn and the incision were healing nicely. His arm had only a few minor mobility issues, but the staff at the burn center was certain that he would regain full use of his arm by the time he had completed the full thirty days of physical therapy. We had so much to be thankful for; Brian's recovery had been a miracle. God had truly blessed us!

5

A NEW KIND
OF LIFE

Once the physical therapy ended, I tried to make the most of our time at home. I had a hard time adjusting because everything that we had done in our former life had changed with one exception: the kids still wanted spaghetti for dinner, but that was the only thing I could count on to stay the same during the remainder of this journey.

Our home life had turned upside down because of the constant intrusions stemming from Brian's medical condition. There were many scheduled appointments that were followed by a host of impromptu visits to doctors, clinics, and hospitals. Among those were calls to repeat a test, consults on test results, and paperwork that needed to be signed. There were several emergency visits when Brian got sick, required a blood transfusion, or when a lifesaving vaccine had to be given. Many appointments were rescheduled because staff was unavailable, a machine broke down, or the medication had not come in yet. I was always on alert because a call from the hospital could come at any hour of the day.

Because of the mayhem I abandoned all the house rules. There was no need for any discipline or chores or schedules. We all just robotically moved from one day to the next, hoping that the next call would not require yet another trip downtown.

While I tried to do things that would make our home a happier place, it was difficult because Brian never felt well. Trying to make up for our dreadful circumstances, Kevin and I bought the kids a new toy every time we visited a store, kept Sesame Street playing on the television all day long, and we celebrated almost anything with ice cream.

I felt conflicted most of the time. On one hand I encouraged Brian to go outside and play with the neighbors, while on the other hand I felt a sigh of relief when he said he did not feel up to it. Playing with others carried so many risks. I had to constantly supervise Brian's activity because a simple cut could cause uncontrollable bleeding. If a new child showed up at our house, I had to run interference with the parents, asking about vaccines and recent exposures to contagious diseases. I had been told that a simple cold could put him into the hospital and that chicken pox or measles could kill him. As much as I wanted our family to fit into a normal life style, the extreme side effects of Brian's treatment prohibited it.

In July, we took a five-day vacation to Northern California that would change everything. On the way to Kevin's uncle's house, I was embarrassed when we had to call to get the van towed because the brakes were going out, then horrified when it was broken into and all of the contents stolen. Yet in another way everything seemed trivial in the light that we had almost lost our child to cancer. I reminded myself that broken and stolen things were replaceable.

We spent three days on thirteen acres in El Dorado County. The town of Placerville was an old mining town discovered during the gold rush in 1848. Kevin's uncle lived on the top of a crest with a breathtaking 360-degree view of the mountains and valley. The air was so crisp and clean. Even in the heat of summer, unlike in Los Angeles, you could see for miles. Standing on the pinnacle of the majestic view, Kevin's uncle dared me to yell out so I could hear my echo in the canyon. Without hesitation, with a force that even shocked my children, I screamed. A little embarrassed that I had not simply yelled out "Hello," I could not help what came out of me. I was releasing all pain that had been pent up inside and it felt so good.

The view was beautiful. I breathed in the serenity of this place and exhaled all the challenges that waited for us when we returned to Los Angeles. Kevin and I both loved the idea of living in the country but never thought it would really happen.

While we were in Placerville we fully embraced life on the farm. During the day, the kids explored the outdoors and fed the goats, ducks, and the donkey. At night the adults barbequed and sat in the backyard and caught up on all the family gossip.

Brian still had all of his hair and no longer looked or acted like a sick child. He enjoyed the attention he was getting from his older cousins. He seemed so happy, running through the meadows laughing and playing. We seemed to forget that he was a very sick child.

Kevin's uncle sold insurance, and when we told him our van had been broken into, he encouraged us to file a claim for our lost articles. He helped us with the paperwork and just like that, the things that were lost would be restored. We would receive a check in the mail in a few weeks.

I remember wishing that my old life could be restored that easily, but I knew it could never be just like it was. It was the same with the things we had lost. The new clothes I had so carefully picked out for the children and bought on sale would not be the same as the clothes bought to replace them. The new Bible would not have all my favorite verses underlined, but I would learn to adjust. If God would just make us whole again, then we could have a new life that was similar to the old one. I bargained with God, adding in the provision that in this new life we would actually become a better version of ourselves because of all we had been through.

The last day in the foothills, we took the kids to the county fair. Brian's big brown eyes lit up when he saw all the 4-H animals and all the children grooming their prize pets. We ate hot dogs and cotton candy. We rode on a few of the children's rides and then won a couple of stuffed animals and a goldfish playing carnival games. We had a great time but the kids were starting to get tired, so we headed back to the farm. The next day we had planned on leaving for home, when Brian woke up sick. I panicked; he had a fever. We had exposed him to so many elements by taking him to the fair. What was I thinking?

We drove to the local hospital and waited in the emergency room for hours. We finally got placed in a small room and then we waited there for a very long time. When the doctor came in he told us we were not a priority and that we should not be in the emergency room. I told him Brian was on chemotherapy and was having trouble breathing. I also mentioned that Brian's doctor had told us that if there was a high fever, he should be admitted to the emergency room for an assessment.

The doctor never looked at me, he just told us to go home because Brian had the flu. We went back to Kevin's uncle's house to pack up our things and drove straight to the emergency room at Children's Hospital, 450 miles away. Brian's white cell count had dropped and that evening he was given a blood transfusion. We were thankful there was no need to keep him overnight and the hospital allowed us to return home that evening. The vacation was over.

On Friday, July 22, Brian went in for his physical and some testing. His first full dosages of treatment would begin on Monday. The appointment did not go as I had expected. This time, Brian's doctor had good news for us. He said he felt very encouraged by Brian's test results and it looked like Brian's treatment would be coming to an end in March. I was shocked; Brian wasn't going to die? The cancer hadn't showed up on any of the other organs, including Brian's good kidney. The chemotherapy was still going to be rough, but it was just a precautionary measure to ensure that any stray cancer cells would be destroyed. I felt so hopeful.

My entire outlook changed that day. I no longer complained about the forty-three-mile drive or all the downtown traffic. I let my guard down and began to feel comfortable at the hospital. I didn't get lost anymore in those long hallways. I felt confident; I knew my way around. I didn't have trouble finding a place to park; I knew where the overflow parking was located and could even park at a meter if I needed to. I knew the staff by name, understood the medical jargon and the purpose of the procedures. I no longer feared that Brian would die. I felt great relief because everything was working out as it should. For the next eight months the hospital would became a welcomed support system for our family, replacing our community and friends.

On Monday morning, the clinic was even more crowded than usual, but I no longer saw the long lines and lack of chairs at clinic as a problem. We settled into a spot on the floor. When other appointments took priority and we had to wait even longer, we ate ice cream and visited the school's classrooms. I knew that we were the lucky ones. God had blessed us with such a gift that I felt compelled to connect more with the other parents and help those who were new to this journey.

Outside of the hospital, cancer kids were isolated from the general public, but at the clinic when the children shared food and toys there was a false sense of safety because we all shared a common bond. I began to enjoy sharing tips with the other parents about how to manage long days with sick kids. We talked about packing lunches and bringing pillows and blankets from home. Having lost all of my initial feelings of resistance, I found the process flowed so much easier.

Almost every visit to the hospital afforded Brian the opportunity to go to school with his teacher, Patti, in the hospital classroom. Sometimes, I would sneak Brian out of clinic so he could visit for just a minute or two. The classroom was always buzzing with lots of children working with teachers' aides, but because Brian was only three, he was able to bypass all the rules and run straight to Patti, his teacher. She patiently turned his attention to the lesson of the day and continued teaching.

Brian's favorite part of school was the homework assignments. Patti always gave Brian something to do and warned him not to come back until it was finished. He thought it was a game and never wanted to disappoint her. It was great training for a three-year-old.

Back at the clinic we killed time by drawing pictures of the bad cancer cells and Brian would pretend to be the chemotherapy and cross them all out with a big black marker. Other times we would draw goofy looking animals.

The infusion center was our last stop and always the hardest part of the daily routine. The nurses were kind and we never had problems with burns or multiple sticks there. But it still broke my heart to see so many children forced to receive the mixture of toxic drugs designed to fight cancer. Each child was wrapped in a warm blanket to help curb the uncontrollable shaking from the infusions. All children had access to a small blue bowl to throw up in.

At the end of the week Brian looked like all the other children. He was extremely ill. The increase in medication clearly redefined what treatment was all about. Brian couldn't move without throwing up. He had to sleep with a pail near his bed. He was weak and lost massive amounts of weight. I worried about him becoming dehydrated . . . and I worried about how I was going to pull off Crystal's birthday party.

I had already been warned that seven to fourteen days after the treatment was the "nadir"—the lowest point. There would be a massive decrease in the white blood cells followed by a vulnerability to infections. I would have to be on the lookout for shortness of breath, fever, and nosebleeds. I watched for mood swings and any signs of depression. There would be little that I could do to comfort him during that time. All we could do was to just wait until the blood count recovered.

And then, when the count was normal and he began to feel like himself, we would start the whole process again. There would be no reprieve; it was the second cruelest consequence of going through chemotherapy treatment. We would not learn the worst consequence of all until the following year.

Crystal's ice cream social was held on Sunday afternoon. I sat Brian down that morning and asked him if he felt like he could attend the party. It was the first time I let him be part of any decision making process. I was happy to hear him say he wanted to go have some ice cream. It told me there was still a part of him left that did not want to miss out on what was going on around him.

We drove to Farrell's Ice Cream Parlor in the Whittwood Mall while Kevin worked. My mother and aunt had agreed to help host the party while I held Brian on my lap. Once the presents were placed on the table, Brian popped out of my arms and flew across to the table top to see what kind of presents his big sister was getting. I was glad I hadn't let the cancer rob us of the opportunity to celebrate Crystal's sixth birthday.

Several weeks later, just before the next round of treatment, we squeezed in a trip to Disneyland with a neighbor from West Covina. Her little girl went to kindergarten with Crystal and her son was Brian's age. It was a nice day at the park; we took pictures of the kids with Mickey, Pooh, and Dopey. Crystal was in love with Mickey and ran to greet him while Brian watched from a safe distance. We strolled down Main Street, waited in line to ride the train and It's a Small World. At the end of the day we stopped at the Castle and bought Mickey Mouse ears for everyone and then came home.

Brian had two offsite appointments in August. The first was with his pediatrician in Whittier and the second was a follow-up appointment with his surgeon in West Covina. At the first visit, our pediatrician was eager to see how Brian was doing, but I realized immediately that keeping the appointment had been a mistake. Brian was already seeing so many doctors that he didn't need any extra needle sticks or probing exams. After that appointment, trips to the pediatrician focused primarily on Crystal's needs.

The appointment with Brian's surgeon was less intrusive. He only wanted to take a look at the incision. When I asked a few questions about the surgery, he allowed me to review the file and look at the pictures that had been taken during the procedure.

"The enlarged kidney, yellow in color, filled the entire chest cavity." I had read that in the report, but actually seeing it was something entirely different. It still made me angry that a mass that size could be overlooked. I asked for a copy of the description of the tumor.

Chemotherapy continued on August 19 even though Brian's physical appearance had changed dramatically. Just days before, he had been wearing his Superman cape and flying around the family room, but now his hair was gone, he was too thin, and his bright brown eyes were dull. He had changed. He became so self-conscious about the way he looked that he refused to go outside. He didn't like people staring at him or asking me questions about his illness. He didn't want to look different. The baseball cap we bought for him was scratchy and made sores on his head so he would not wear it. We finally found a soft cap but he would only wear it to the clinic. At home, he was withdrawn. Even when some of the neighborhood moms bought hats for their children too, it didn't help. I felt sad that he felt like an outcast in his own neighborhood.

Brian wasn't the only one who felt "different." As a family, we were all affected by the changes we had to make. Kevin had to work long hours and on the weekends to keep up with all the medical bills. Crystal missed school days and couldn't have friends come to the house. My spiritual life was being stretched, my faith tested, relationships with my friends and neighbors were changing, and our financial stability was slowly slipping away.

My life stopped the moment Brian was diagnosed with cancer. And yet after three months, having heard the best possible prognosis, we were still having trouble adjusting. While I was developing a deeper relationship with the God I had worshipped for so many years, every semblance of my old life had fallen away. In the beginning when friends wanted to go to lunch or shopping, I didn't feel right about leaving my sick child so I could have a break. After all, Brian never got a day off. I felt a tremendous burden to make the right decisions for my child while I took care of the entire family. The physical and emotional demands kept me turning to God's Word for answers and searching medical journals for new cancer treatments.

My family called me a "radical" Christian. They were alarmed that I had, in their eyes, turned my back on the Catholic church—even though some of them had not been to church for years. I tried to tell them that even though I was not Catholic, I was still worshipping the same Jesus we had all grown up with. I wondered if they might be open to further discussion about their own faith and mine after they discovered that I had prayed with one of my cousins and I had simply encouraged her to find a church where she felt comfortable.

But I felt I had pulled back from many friendships. It took months before I realized I wasn't the only one who had changed and withdrawn, that many people we knew were also behaving differently toward us. The daily hospital visits, Brian's restrictions, and the cancer diagnosis created distance between us and our church and friends. No one dropped by anymore and most of our calls were from the hospital. I understood that some people avoided us because our situation made them feel uncomfortable. At twenty-seven years of age, I had never been around anyone who had cancer either. I wondered if people thought we were contagious. When friends or neighbors accidentally ran into me at the grocery store, they usually just told me that I looked terrible and never asked about Brian.

Sometimes, people we knew well spoke words to us that were hurtful without ever realizing it. They seemed to look at Brian's illness as a puzzle in which they held the missing piece. I knew which piece they held when they asked the question: "Does cancer run in your family?" Bingo! It's genetic . . . we don't have that gene. Or maybe they would ask, "Have you become a vegetarian?" I knew it; you've been eating red meat! Even one of my cousin's had scolded me, "Your kids slept in flame retardant pajamas, didn't they?" But no, my children never slept in them.

I wondered why it was so important to force a wedge between us. The truth was that they were just like me; we grew up in the same communities, went to the same schools, and were married within months of each other and our kids were all the same age. Like Brian, I didn't want to be pointed at and shamed. As far as I could tell, cancer didn't play by any set of rules; it struck three out of four families, putting us all at risk. It could happen to anyone.

I remember someone once telling me that "some Christians are so spiritually minded that they are no earthly good." Many would argue that this saying is overused and does not really apply, but it was how I felt about a few outspoken members of our church. They believed in a health and wealth gospel. Their strict doctrine promised material wealth and a life free from disease just by making a positive confession. I knew that just speaking a word doesn't make it come to pass. They often quoted from Isaiah 53:5, "By his stripes we are healed," which I had come to understand meant that believers were made spiritually whole by Christ's atonement on the cross. But to them it meant that believers should by faith consider themselves already healed of all physical disease, even in the face of contrary evidence. The teaching seemed like a blatant denial of reality when a broken leg in a cast, a cold or fever, diabetes, or any medical condition was healed, regardless of whether symptoms continued or medical treatment was needed. For them, illnesses were just distractions which they refused to acknowledge.

They had the same line of thinking when it came to money. They claimed that strong faith, what they called "million-dollar faith," would make you a millionaire. Just as you should consider yourself healed even if you were ill, you should also consider yourself wealthy even if you could not pay your rent.

Though we had different beliefs, the truth was I had not cared much about how others at church worked out their salvation until a group of church members approached me to say they had decided that Brian's cancer was a religious problem caused by sin, specifically, my sin. They said if I only believed and had faith like theirs, Brian would be healed. They were not the only ones who said such things directly to us. Throughout Brian's illness, many hoped to rescue us by simply pointing out our personal failures, but on one occasion we suffered an especially vicious attack.

We went to a Bible study one Wednesday evening to hear a speaker. After his lecture, the speaker overheard me talking to someone about Brian and stepped in to inform me that Brian was sick because God was teaching me a lesson. It was humiliating. I wanted to avoid making a scene and turned quickly to leave. Kevin and I were tired but otherwise in a good place. Brian was on the road to recovery and we felt God had answered our prayers. I knew I served a loving God who did not punish children for the sins of their parents, but this man insisted we were the impediment to Brian's healing and that it had nothing to do with God's will. All of the people at the meeting encircled us and were staring at us now. I turned to face my accuser but I never got a chance to reply; I didn't have to. The other members of our fellowship group, defenders of the faith, outnumbered our attacker and spoke up in our defense, winning the battle for us that night. Grateful for the support, we knew it had been God that silenced our enemy. But there would be many more painful encounters.

The attacks were hurtful because I did not disagree. God does bless us and wants us to live an abundant life; but I believe his emphasis is on our spiritual life. After all physical health and material wealth are temporal; they come and go but our relationship with him is eternal. We believed in the power of God to heal. But God heals according to his will for our lives. And when healing comes, it's a miracle that cannot be denied; there would be no need to fake it, no need to make claims that were not true. Like them I sought God's favor and wanted nothing more in my life, but I was put off by partial truths which only seemed to foster a self-righteous attitude. Why did they think that because their child did not have cancer and mine did they were spiritually superior?

Fortunately, we never heard this philosophy from the pulpit, but the beauty of belonging to a non-denominational church was the diversity that people bring because they come from many different backgrounds. Before Brian had gotten sick I had felt like my life had been enriched when others shared their beliefs. Now that I had become so vulnerable it was harder to process the words that seemed to be directed at my family.

Each Sunday, I made every effort to be in church during that first year even though I feared being confronted again in a public forum. I needed the fellowship and I needed to hear a message that could carry me through to the next week. Usually at church, we were surrounded by our closest friends during the services. They were our prayer warriors who fasted and prayed on Brian's behalf. Many church members sent words of encouragement, homemade gifts, and shared with us about personal battles with cancer. But there were many awkward moments that made me shy away from crowds. Often couples would share how blessed they were that their children did not have cancer or how happy they were that it was us and not them who had to go through it. I knew they were well meaning and had no idea what it was like to actually watch your child suffer from the disease. All I could do was smile and pat their hands.

I spent many nights reading inspirational books, but none were as comforting to me and spoke to suffering like the story in the Bible about Job.

- **Job** was a righteous man. He served God, had great wealth, many friends, and he was well respected. God gives Satan power to test Job, but he stipulates that Job's life is to be spared. So Job does not lose his life. But he does lose his children, his material possessions, and his health. His friends, Eliphaz, Bildad, and Zophar show up and the first thing they do is sit with Job for seven days in silence. But it isn't long before they start blaming him for his circumstances.

- **Eliphaz** asks, "Where were the upright destroyed?" Then he tells Job, "Blessed is the one God corrects," implying that Job is being disciplined because he has been evil (Job 4:7; 5:17 NASB).

- **Bildad** tells Job to "seek God" or he will die because "the light of the wicked goes out" (Job 8:5; 18:5 NASB).

- **Zophar** tells Job to "direct his heart right," suggesting, like Bildad, that Job is guilty of wickedness, that his suffering is "a wicked man's portion" (Job 11:13; 20:29 NASB).

Lesson 3: _Resolute Trust_

Job's friends essentially told him he had sinned and that God was punishing him, that he would die from his wickedness and finally that he must be getting what he deserved. None of these accusations were true. Not only had Job done nothing to deserve his calamity but throughout the trial he stood firm and put all of his trust in God. He never abandoned God even at his weakest point. When it was over, God restored Job's fortunes and increased all he had by twofold. All three of Job's friends were ordered by God to seek forgiveness from Job and to present a sacrifice before God.

Although I would never suffer like Job, his experience felt similar to mine. There was much to learn from Job's life. He stood firm and trusted God. With Job in mind, I felt I was ready to let down my guard and really trust God.

Brian's illness drained our finances. Our new mortgage payment had already stretched our budget. Though we never had credit card debt and our cars were older and paid for, we couldn't keep on top of the mounting medical bills that our insurance refused to pay. Instead of saving for our future, each paycheck went out to pay bills that were not covered by our medical plan. While the hospital worked to resolve the billing problems, private vendors were not as accommodating. They wanted to be paid now. Sometimes it would take six months or more before the insurance company processed a bill and made what felt like an arbitrary decision to pay or to deny payment. By then, most of the bills had already gone to collections. We were still waiting for a determination on many of the bills that stemmed from the first hospitalization. Some of those bills were topping out at over $30,000 each and our total income for the year at that time was only $18,000.

Sometimes people would try to encourage me by telling me not to worry about money or the cancer. They said our insurance would eventually pay for everything, but I could only envision losing our home. When people talked about new research that had found a cure for cancer, I knew they had not met the disease. My trust wavered. The threats of legal action and a cancer that would not give up kept me coming back to a place where I had to learn this lesson again and again.

Brian received his last treatment of the year in November. December's treatment would be withheld because Brian was having an umbilical hernia repaired. The medical team had convinced me that because the hernia had not closed, it would be important to repair the weak spot while Brian was still so young. I didn't like the thought of Brian having another surgery, but they assured me it was a simple procedure that only required an overnight stay at our local hospital. I was happy that Brian was going to get a break from treatment. The benefit from having the surgery and skipping chemo was that Brian would be able to enjoy Christmas that year.

Brian had been experiencing countless cycles of ups and downs. We started distinguishing between bad days and good days. I determined that on a good day, Brian would play outside and on bad days he had to stay in bed because he was so sick. But Brian saw all days as good. If he was in bed, he explained that "It is still me." Brian no longer wanted to hear any talk about the hospital or his cancer. He saw the extra attention that he was getting as something that was very loathsome and he had decided he wanted no part of it.

With Brian on the road to recovery it was easy to trust God to bring him through the next surgery. Brian's *third* surgery was scheduled for December 1. I stayed with Brian that night in Whittier and was able to bring him home early the next morning. He recovered quickly and never complained about having any pain from the procedure.

Brian only had three more months of chemotherapy left and everything was going so well. His hair came back and he seemed to have gained a little weight over the holidays and looked taller.

The rest of the month we celebrated the holiday with friends and family. There were so many things to do that it was an exciting and joyful time for us. There were programs at the school and at church. We baked cookies and decorated the Christmas tree. On Christmas day we visited both set of grandparents and watched Brian play with the other grandchildren without fear of exposure to diseases. It was a wonderful day.

6

1978

On January 27th, feeling confident that this journey would soon be over, I walked with a lighter heart down the corridors of Children's Hospital. We were coming into the home stretch, just two more treatments after this one. In March all of the tests would be re-done and the last dosage of chemotherapy would be given. I could see the light at the end of the tunnel. We were going to win this battle after all.

I was caught off guard when suddenly a series of unexpected events plunged us back into the darkness. The downward spiral began with Brian's accident. He had been running around the house with one of his favorite toys, a small blue and yellow radar gun—it was his weapon of choice when pretending to be a super hero. Suddenly, I heard a "Clump!" down the hallway near the bathroom. I ran to help but it was too late; Brian had already fallen on the floor.

So much blood streamed from his mouth, I thought the toy gun must have somehow split his tongue in half. I called our neighbor, who readily agreed to drive us to the emergency room. I was shaking so hard, I don't know how I was able to get Brian wrapped up in a towel and meet Cathy outside so quickly. She put her two little boys into the car while I held Brian in my lap and we started off toward the hospital.

Cathy realized suddenly that her car was out of gas; she had no choice but to stop at the nearest gas station. I don't remember stopping for gas or the twenty-minute drive to our local hospital. I only remember that when the emergency team saw Brian and all the blood, they rushed him into a room. I thanked Cathy for driving me and then asked her to pick up my daughter at school. Kevin could take us home after he got off from work.

A doctor talked to me briefly and said that they would have to do an emergency surgery to repair Brian's tongue. I anxiously sat in the waiting room. I didn't want to leave the area to call Kevin just yet because I believed that the surgery would not take long and I wanted to see Brian.

This was Brian's *fourth* surgery. It was several hours before the surgeon came into the waiting room to tell me that Brian was in recovery. He told me he had contacted Children's Hospital and had worked with them to make sure Brian's procedure followed the guidelines for a patient on chemotherapy. The surgeon told me it took ten sutures to save the lacerated tongue, but it should heal quickly. He also mentioned that there would be a significant amount of discomfort over the next few weeks. Brian would have a difficult time eating and swallowing. But they would not let me see him. I thought it was strange that the hospital forbid me to see my son.

Finally, a woman came in to get me, but instead of taking me to the recovery room to see my child, I was ushered into a small interview room. There were several people in the room, but only one identified themselves as a representative from Child Protective Services (CPS). I deducted that the doctor must have thought the injury was so unusual that they wanted to gather information about the toy Brian had been playing with. I was cooperative, but I was worried that Brian would be upset when he woke up and I wasn't there.

It wasn't until someone in the room said that they would be recording my answers during the interrogation that I realized I was in trouble. I had been so naïve—I didn't realize they had suspected me of causing the injury to my child. Oh, I don't have time for this!

I asked to be excused so I could call Kevin and tell him to pick us up at the hospital, but one of the men stepped in front of the closed door. I was being detained so they could ask me a few questions. I was told to sit down. Each member of the team asked me the same questions:

How did this happen?

- Did you harm your child?
- Do you hit your child?

I answered all their questions. "He fell when he was playing," "I would not harm my child," "I do not hit my child." I knew they thought I was guilty, but having no legal grounds to hold me against my will, they allowed one phone call.

As soon as Kevin answered the phone, I began telling him that Brian had been injured and had to have surgery. He said he could be at the hospital in thirty minutes. I forgot to tell him about the inquiry. I sat near the entrance of the emergency room and waited for his arrival.

When he arrived, the hospital ran interference and took him down the hall before I had a chance to say anything to him. In the interview room he was questioned separately.

- Do you know what happened?
- Would your wife hurt your child?

It had been hours since Brian's surgery, and I didn't know what to think. I was relieved when they brought Kevin to the waiting room but upset that they would not release our child to us until they had questioned him. A nurse signaled to the group that Brian was fully awake now and the group followed her.

I was angry. Were they going to interrogate a three-year-old, who had just had surgery? I had given them names and numbers of people they could contract on our behalf. Did they seriously think there was a connection between my child having a terminal disease and me wanting to cut off his tongue? They asked Brian:

- Did your mother hurt you?
- Did she hit you?
- Were you bad?

It only took a few minutes for the same nurse to tell us we could take Brian home. All the accounts of the accident had been consistent; however, the hospital would arrange a follow-up meeting so I could share "the weapon" with the team.

When I finally got to hold Brian, he had been crying. "Mom, have I been bad?" he asked. "Of course not!" I said as I flashed an angry look at the people standing in the hall. The ten sutures made his face appear so swollen. Kevin carefully picked him up and we walk out of the hospital.

Lesson 4: _Confident in Battle_

Two weeks later, taking up the shield of faith, I walked into the meeting with CPS. I was ready to extinguish all the false accusations that I would ever harm my child. God was working on me and I felt a renewed confidence. Brian had survived the cancer and we could see that our victory lay before us. This accident was only another distraction meant to take our eyes off of our blessing. I was no longer the weeping mother who had sat in a chair begging to see her child. I felt untouchable, yet CPS still did not believe our story. That morning, I had prayed that we would be strong and stay firm. The panel asked several questions and I showed them the small blue and yellow radar gun with small plastic wings coming out of all sides. I recanted the story, but still did not know exactly how Brian had fallen. He could have tripped over the long red cape he was wearing, or bumped into something. When Brian was questioned, he could not remember any details. He just looked at me and said, "Mom, I just fell."

I understood that calling CPS was a precautionary measure, but I was thoroughly disappointed that to my knowledge they had not expanded their investigation to the medical community that saw Brian weekly or the school system that I had worked with on a daily basis.

Before we left the meeting a woman spoke up, she wanted to ask Brian a few more questions. She warned me not to answer for the child. I rolled my eyes. How many times were they going to ask Brian the same questions?

- Was your mother with you?
- Did she hurt you?

Brian said "no" to both questions. Then he looked over at me and rolled his eyes. I had not expected him to model his mother's bad behavior, but regardless, we were finally free to go.

Several weeks later, Crystal had an appointment with our pediatrician. He told me he had been contacted by CPS, after all. He thought Brian must have hit his chin on the floor or on the bathtub causing him to bite his tongue hard enough for it to split. He didn't think the plastic gun had anything to do with the injury except for being in Brian's hand at the time of the fall. That explanation made perfect sense to me, so then why had CPS continued to grill us? He said they told him they would close the case because there was no supporting evidence. I wondered why that bit of information had never been passed down to us.

On Friday, March 10, we took Brian to the clinic for a series of tests and the final check-up at Children's Hospital. It was celebration day; Kevin had even taken the day off work! The doctors had been telling us for months that Brian was doing so well, it looked like he would be able to have a long healthy life.

Finally, the day had come when we would meet with Brian's doctor so he could tell us that the cancer was gone. We had arrived early and had completed all the tests before noon. But when the clock struck five, we still hadn't seen the doctor. We had sat solidified as a family in anticipation of hearing the good news, but now I was wondering if something might be wrong. The clinic was empty.

A nurse we had known for a long time led us into a back room. She did not smile or talk to Brian; she looked sad. An intern followed, telling us that the doctor would be in shortly to talk to us about a new treatment plan.

"A new treatment plan?" I asked. I told her she had made a mistake; this was our last visit. She looked at me before leaving the room and said, "I am so sorry." I was wrong when I thought that she was only apologizing for the error. My experiences at the hospital had taught me that it wasn't that unusual for an intern to make a mistake. We waited for the doctor to clear everything up.

But when the doctor came in, his posture was stiff, businesslike, and the appointment felt rushed. He hung the x-rays on the wall as he began talking to us. He said, "The cancer has come back. It has metastasized to both lungs. We believe that with more tests we will find that there are multiple nodes on the upper and lower lobes.

I was unable to speak; our cancer does not spread. It was the status we had so proudly held onto for the entire year. But the doctor kept pounding away at the fact that they had found more cancer and they did not know how extensive it was. He tried to show us the changes in Brian's current x-ray and pointed to the areas of suspicion. The cancer seemed to be everywhere. Kevin and I sat motionless, staring at all the evidence laid out before us that would sentence Brian to a premature death. Inside I was screaming, "No, No, No! Please God. No!"

Staying on point, the doctor explained the plan the medical team had put together, a plan to attack the cancer cells. They wanted to put Brian in isolation for three to six months—total isolation. If they isolated him for protection they could give him high dosages of medication and have a better chance of reducing the tumors. They hoped to avoid the only other option, two major surgeries back to back, one on the left lung and one on the right lung.

Then I heard him say that Brian would be taken from us and put into the isolation room in just three to four days. I looked over at Kevin and saw his head nodding in agreement with the plan. I mimicked his movements. When the doctor finished talking, he did not linger to answer our questions, but left abruptly. I heard deep, deep sobbing rising up in my throat. I could not contain it. The nurse that had led us into the room had stayed. She put her arms around me and told me she was tired of hearing about kids whose cancer had come back. She said she had recently resigned from her position and would be gone by the end of the month.

Every bit of my optimistic illusion had completely shattered. This type of outcome happens often? I can't go through this again. Defiantly, I petitioned the Lord, "I thought you didn't give your people more than they can handle!" Today we came to celebrate and we were ambushed. If only the doctor would have said those precious words that I had come to hear that day: "The cancer is gone!" That was what this last day was supposed to be all about. It was about winning the battle.

Still in shock from hearing the devastating news, I grabbed Brian up in my arms. I needed to get out of the hospital. I sobbed all the way down the long corridor. This had been the most diffi-cult year of my entire life, and Brian had suffered more than any-one I had ever known, and it wasn't over yet; this life was going to continue. I wanted our story to be about how we came through a difficult year and survived. When we drove up the driveway to our home, I could see that a little yellow card had been placed on our doorstep. The words inside the card read: "I am praying for Brian. It's hard to understand why Jesus permits things to happen and continue sometimes, but we just have to trust him, knowing that he loves Brian more than we can ever understand."

Who sent this? I wondered. How could anyone have known what we were going through at this very moment? Only God could send a message of hope when we needed it the most. Ashamed of my outburst, I went to my room and cried, "I know I need to trust you but Brian will never be healed, will he? He really is going to die from the cancer."

Saturday morning, I woke up feeling unremitting and was determined not to be broken and useless, I told Kevin we needed to celebrate, just like we told the kids we would. We had many things to be thankful for, we just had to dig a little deeper to find them. We spent the day at Disneyland.

On Sunday, a friend called and invited me go with her to a church in Costa Mesa where Corrie Ten Boom had been invited to speak. Corrie Ten Boom was well known in the Christian community because of a new movie based on her book called, *The Hiding Place*. Five months before her debilitating stroke, she had been touring several churches in Southern California, telling them how her Dutch family had been persecuted for helping the Jews during the Holocaust. She had suffered much, she lived in isolation, labored in death camps, survived with very little food and water. She had faced the constant threat of beatings and torture, and had watched her sister die at the hands of the prison guards, yet she never turned her back on God. Her horrific experiences only seemed to deepen her conviction that, *"However deep the pit, God's love is deeper still."* That Sunday, I listened to her give two sermons back to back on love and forgiveness. She told us that with God's help, she was able to forgive the man who had tortured her and her sister. At first she had told God that she could not go to the man responsible for her sister's death and offer him forgiveness. She did not want to forgive him. She hated him, but God made a way for her to accomplish his will for her life. She had such confidence about her walk with the Lord, she trusted him implicitly. She had a very human relationship with our Almighty God.

I wasn't anywhere near her level of maturity, nor had I suffered anything compared to all she had gone through. I had so much to learn. She talked as if she walked daily with Jesus and that no matter what she was going through he never left her side. When the service ended, my friend and I went up and sat on the second row and waited for the second service to begin. I needed to hear her message again. It was a great privilege to be taught by a person who had truly devoted her entire life to serving him. When the service started, Corrie turned around and greeted the people in the second row, and then she got up and stepped onto the podium.

I could see now, God did have his hand on Brian's life and mine. He had gotten us through the entire year by providing words of encouragement and comfort when we needed them the most. He had surrounded us with people who would pray for us when we were all prayed out, and he taught me how to focus by reading his Word every day. Had I known from the start that this cancer was not really going away, I would not have had the strength to help Brian through the first year. From the beginning, God had kept me from falling into depression or suicide or other reckless behaviors. His light drew me away from the darkness. I had found a hope in him; when I was weak, he was strong. When I couldn't take another step, he carried me. Who loves like that? Only Jesus could.

His message had opened my eyes to see that I wasn't in this battle alone. And like Abraham, Job, and now Corrie, I had to realize that this battle was going to cost me everything, but it would all be worth it.

I had grown enough to know what he wanted from me: a relationship with him, built on trust. I needed to become an obedient and disciplined believer, and a spiritual teacher to my young children.

"Lord," I prayed, "I surrendered my life into your hands. Use me to further your kingdom."

7

THE BUBBLE

Kevin and I sat down with Brian to make sure he understood the new treatment plan. We had to tell him that the cancer had come back and that he would be living at the hospital for several months. He would be placed inside a special room that NASA had designed called a "bubble." In the hospital's Laminar Airflow Unit, Brian would be protected from all kinds of infections. The hope of using such a drastic measure was that in the sterile environment chemotherapy could be increased to almost a lethal dosage killing a large percentage of the cells in the body. Presumably a good result would show that the cancer cells had been obliterated leaving only healthy cells with the ability to regenerate in his body.

I wanted Brian to know I would be with him throughout the treatment. He would be living inside the bubble and I would be staying just outside of his room. He would always be able to see me, but if I wanted to come into the room I would have to dress up in a space suit. I told him we thought it was the best chance we had to kill the cancer and avoid another surgery. He agreed that we should try it.

We wanted Brian to understand the benefits of the treatment, but we tried to explain the downside as well. Not only would he have to stay in the bubble continuously, but we would not be allowed to hug him or kiss him or have any direct contact with him.

I never told him about the other problems, the severe side effects that could cause permanent damage. Neuromuscular coordination problems, muscle pain, numbness, nausea, vomiting, difficulty with digestion, constipation, diarrhea, lack of appetite, weight loss, lethargy, hair loss, ulcers in the mouth as well as the urinary and digestive tracts, and inflammation of mucous membranes could all occur. His bone marrow would become depressed and decrease production of the red cells, causing anemia. His platelet count would drop, causing bruising and increased bleeding, and blood transfusions would have to be given. The white cell production would decrease, increasing the likelihood of infection. Bloody urine would result from the bladder irritations and his heart would beat irregularly and possibly fail.

My greatest fear wasn't so much the loss of life that seems to get distorted when you are dealing with a terminal illness, but again for me, it was the loss of self. If he beat the cancer, I wondered how he was ever going to recover from the battle scars. This battle could permanently change his bodily functions as well as his personality. Depression hits twenty to fifty percent of the children on chemotherapy. With the increased durations of pain and long periods of isolation, the risks were high for depression. I could only hope we were making the right decision.

The hospital called early on Monday morning to tell me the room would be ready on Wednesday. I would be driving down later that afternoon to show Brian his new living quarters and to drop off some of his favorite toys, clothes, pajamas, and pillows so they could be sterilized and in the room waiting for him when he arrived.

Inside Laminar, four small rooms that were linked together like box cars made up the unit. Each room was squared with two solid side walls that joined the units together, while the front and back walls were made of clear plastic. One of the solid side walls in each unit called the gray wall blew sterile air continuously through filters, keeping germs from entering the room. The specially trained nursing staff was able to access the units from the two long continuous hallways that ran parallel in the front and back of the units.

Once we saw what the unit looked like, Brian and I both thought it might not be as bad as we first thought. The bright yellow hallways, along with a cheerful staff, made our first visit very pleasant. Brian had hoped the unit would look more like a spaceship, but I consoled him by telling him about the spacesuits. The unit had been empty for some time and the staff was eager to get back to work. I would be allowed to sleep on the floor, in the hallway behind Brian's room.

Before I would sign the paperwork committing us to the treatment, however, we had some negotiating to do. Brian was to be admitted on March 15, but his most recent infusion, given by a person in training on March 10 already showed signs of a small infiltration. I insisted that from now on chemo be given only through the hand IV push, not injected into the veins located in the bend of the arm, the antecubital area. Both infiltrations had caused some permanent scarring and any further damage would put Brian at risk of losing his arm. The doctors agreed. No chemotherapy was to be given into the antecubital area of the arm. Brian's doctor gave me his word that they would not run the risk of damaging the arm further. We signed the agreement. The paperwork went into Brian's permanent file.

Brian was placed on oral antibiotics that would keep his digestive tract free from bacteria and fungi and he was bathed with special soaps and shampoos to make his skin germ-free. Brian did not mind all the extra inconveniences because he was eager to climb into the space "bubble."

Wednesday morning, the day Brian entered the unit, the nurses were already dressed in sterile paper space suits that covered their entire body. Staff began by explaining how the unit worked.

The only area of the unit not considered to be sterile was the floor. Anything that fell on the floor had to be removed and re-sterilized. The patient was not allowed to walk on the floor barefoot or sit on the floor unless a sterile blanket was put down. Anyone entering the unit had to wear the special space suit. They also had to wear sterile cloth boots and hoods, along with two pairs of disposable gloves and a mask. The first pair of gloves was to be put on outside the bubble. The second pair was to be put on over the first pair upon entering the unit. There were special techniques for putting on all of the items and it took instruction and a lot of practice to get it right.

Once Brian entered into the bubble, I was allowed to "suit up" and go in to help him get settled. I carefully pulled the suit over my clothes, not allowing the outside of the suit to touch the inside. The inside of the suit had contact with my skin and clothes and was considered contaminated. The first pair of gloves was worn while you were getting dressed. Once you were in the suit the gloves were considered dirty. A second pair of sterile gloves had to be worn over the first pair. It was a little tricky because the inside of the glove could never come in contact with the sterile outside. Once inside the unit I was not allowed to touch any part of my face and my mask had to be changed every hour.

Staff warned me that if any part of my body became exposed, I would have to leave the unit immediately. Inside the unit, I was to remain "downwind" of Brian so I did not block the airflow from reaching him. No one who was sick was allowed within the walls, whether it was a staff person or a parent.

Once inside Brian and I decorated his room with his toys. When I came out of his room, I removed the spacesuit. I hung pictures of Mickey Mouse and Superman that had been thoughtfully purchased by Kevin's cousin, Julie. I hung the large posters on the outside of the front and back walls. Brian never resisted any of the instructions he received that day and seemed to be mesmerized by the state of the art technology that was all around him.

The staff warned me that I should be aware of the fact that if I would don the spacesuit, Brian might have a negative reaction. But fortunately, I planned to stay for the duration of Brian's stay. And Brian thought the spacesuits were the best part of being in the bubble.

I did everything I could think of to relieve any anxiety Brian might feel. I must have done a fair job of it because the psychological evaluation report described him as "cheerful and cooperative." His mood stayed bright for the first two days.

On the 17th the intense rounds of chemotherapy started. High dosages of three drugs would be given for five straight days. The first two days went well and then he started getting so sick. It was hard to watch him from outside of the module. I couldn't hold him close or rub his head. He was alone.

Easter Sunday came early that year. On March 26, cousin, Julie surprised Brian by coming into the unit holding Brian's sister's hand. Julie and Crystal were both dressed up as pink Easter bunnies. Brian had been suffering with bouts of nausea that day, but managed to laugh when he saw a big bunny and a little bunny come bouncing down the hallway.

Later that night, after everyone one had gone home, several friends from church came by with guitars so that we could celebrate Easter in the hospital. The songs we sang literally made me forget we were in the hospital until one of the staff came down the hall and made a cutting comment. "Can you believe that?" she said, pointing at us. I don't know what she meant, but she sounded perturbed. We quickly wrapped up our visit and went to the nurse's station to apologize to the staff.

The following week, a team of doctors, nurses, school teachers, and therapists worked with Brian outside of the bubble using long rubber gloves that could reach through a plastic curtain into the unit. Most of the staff spent a lot of time with him, bringing him gifts, playing games and reading stories. He was still the only child in the unit. He loved the puppets and all the new books they brought to share with him. Whenever someone brought in something new, he would smile and say, "Is that for me?" He maintained his sweet disposition throughout the experience and continued to do whatever they asked.

One of the nurses, Cecilia, was young and single and joked about Brian being her "boyfriend" because she spent so much time with him on the unit. She was the one Brian looked forward to seeing most. She was never too busy to check in on him, even on her days off.

The school teacher, Patti, remained another one of Brian's favorite visitors. She appeared daily at the same time, Monday through Friday. She treated Brian just like every other student, even though he had not even turned four yet. She came with a lesson plan and tasks to be completed. He counted on her regularly scheduled visits even when he could not speak or move.

On Friday, April 7th, Brian had adjusted so well to his life in Laminar that the psycho-social team wanted to document his experience. Brian got so excited when all the lights, microphones, and cameras came into the room. He was not shy about answering all of their questions. When they asked what he could do inside the unit, he stood up on the bed and jumped up and down! I was shocked, because he had never done that at home. I had to laugh when he looked over at me shyly, hoping to get my approval. It would be his last good day in the unit and they had captured every smile, every laugh, and his good natured personality, all on tape.

Over the next few days the preparations were starting back up for the next round of treatment. Staff waited impatiently while Brian's blood work fluctuated, but as soon as it was high enough, the next round of therapy was ordered. The hydration process began the night before. The extra fluid made Brian feel uncomfortable so he was not able to sleep. On Monday, April 10, I told Brian that I was going to the nurse's lounge to shower and change my clothes, just like I did every morning. Brian was playing calmly on his bed when I left. When I returned, there was a man in the room pumping Brian's arm with chemotherapy.

I would learn later that this man was a physician associate, working under the supervision of Brian's doctor. I shortened his title to "associate" because it is how he signed the daily entries he made into Brian's medical chart.

It appeared to me that he had breached protocol; he was in the unit but he was not dressed appropriately and his skin was exposed. He was also rough with Brian, struggling with him. Then I noticed he was injecting a drug directly into Brian's arm. He was giving Brian chemotherapy.

I stared in disbelief, trying to understand what was going on. Finally, I said "No, please stop! I need to call Brian's doctor about the treatment. I have an agreement with the hospital." He would not stop. He continued pumping Adriamycin D into Brian's left arm. Then in what looked like a move of utter defiance, he pulled out the syringe and stabbed it into Brian's right hand. I freaked out and ran into the nursing station to get help. One nurse got on the phone and tried to locate Brian's doctor while the other one ran down the hall and asked the associate to wait, but he yelled at her. I stood outside the unit begging him to stop.

Devastated, I stood helplessly in front of my child, watching as the associate came out of the unit, screamed at me, and slammed the door as he left. I said a few calming words to Brian, but the ordeal had been too much for him, he was shaking. I ran to the nurse's station, hoping they had contacted the doctor by now, but they had only left messages. We all waited, but the return call never came.

I went back to the unit to check on Brian. By the look of his face, the swollen red eyes and tears still rolling down his cheeks, I could tell he had cried himself to sleep in my absence. The nurses stood by my side trying to assess Brian's current condition, but none of us could even begin to guess how extensive the damage would be. All I could do now was wait. I sat motionless, dumbstruck at what had just happened. Brian was supposed to be receiving treatment that would make him better, but this last injection felt more like a brutal attack. By night fall, Brian was so sick. I knew the stress of the day had not helped his fragile system.

On Tuesday Brian was already showing visible signs of infiltration. Unlike the last two burns, this time his entire left arm and right hand were involved. The arm was three times its normal size, and the skin looked like raw meat where the burn was starting to open up. I already believed that the highly toxic levels combined with the large amount of chemotherapy would cause Brian to lose his arm.

The associate ordered the second dose of treatment. I tried to stop the treatment but Brian's doctor still had not come to the unit to check on Brian's wellbeing. The nurses feared that another injection into the left arm would only do even more damage and moved the IV to the swollen right hand.

Wednesday, I got a hold of the nursing notes, looking to see if Brian's doctor had ever called back. There was nothing in the notes about the leakage or the burn. Another dosage of chemotherapy was ordered for today. I was so worried about Brian's arm that I called administration and left a message.

On Thursday, April 13, the therapy continued. Brian physically shook so hard as the toxins entered into his body that I thought his heart was going to stop. Now that I was in conflict with the hospital, the nurses stopped talking to me. I suspect they had been directed to simply follow orders and try not to get involved. I watched them move the IV to Brian's foot because he couldn't use his right hand anymore. In Brian's nursing notes the associate had written that "the patient suffered from an infiltration of the right arm." He had gotten it wrong–it was Brian's left arm! He went on to say in the notes that although the arm and hand were swollen, there was no fever. So treatment should continue.

The situation with the hospital was both emotionally and physically draining. I wanted to quit and pull Brian from the unit, but I feared any irrational action would only backfire and cause Brian even more harm. At times I could do nothing more in my prayers than to say the name of Jesus. I lived and breathed just that one hope. Finally realizing how much I needed the Word of God in my weakened condition, I turned to the Twenty-third Psalm. It's the psalm that Christians and non-Christians turn to for comfort. I read, "Even though I walk through the valley of the shadow of death, I fear no evil; for Thou art with me" (KJV). Covered by all the shadows, my deep, deep valley had become such a dark place.

Brian was suffering and I could do nothing without Jesus. I was a wounded warrior. I had become so beaten down that I had nothing else to give. If I could just focus I would be able to stand firm and fear no evil. I was so desperate to find higher ground that I had to just hold on and wait for him to lead me toward the light. This battle like all the others would draw me in closer.

> This is the message we have heard from him and declare to you: God is light; in him there is no darkness at all (1 John 1:5 NIV).

I needed a working faith so I began to pray for Brian. I prayed about the medicine, that Brian's heart would be strong, that his remaining kidney would not fail, that his liver would be able to process the high level of toxicity. I also prayed that the arm, hand, and now feet would return to their normal size.

The Lord is my Shepherd; I would need nothing else. The next morning, I stood in his strength.

On Friday, no treatment was given. I would not allow it. Brian's right hand was now swollen as large as his left. Brian was in such bad condition that even the nursing staff supported my decision. Brian would not receive any more chemotherapy. They started Brian on a medication that he had to take four times a day. No one would tell me what the medication was. I was told to refer my questions to Brian's doctor. I suspected it was an antibiotic.

8

THROUGH THE
SHADOWS

When members from the burn unit came in to evaluate Brian's arm, they told me that this time the damage that had been done was beyond repair. They ordered six weeks of physical therapy, but warned that they could not rule out the probability that Brian's arm might have to be amputated. The burn already involved a large portion of the soft tissues and had caused extensive damage to the muscles, nerves, and bone.

The physical therapist insisted that the toxic medication be stopped because it prohibited the body from healing naturally. He warned that any further damage would be irreversible. The team worried that even if the drugs were stopped now, when Brian's count bottomed out in the next few weeks they might not be able to stop the raging infection from spreading throughout his entire body.

The physical therapist took out a goniometer to assess Brian's range of motion, but the arm could not be moved. I could see that the white core of the burn was about the size of a fifty cent piece but was reminded by the team that the wound would grow larger each day.

To help ease some of Brian's discomfort they alternated hot and cold packs for fifty minutes, applied a salve, and then covered the burn with a temporary sleeve. Before the therapist left he told me that they would use drainage tubes to relieve the pressure and have to design a permanent cast that would encourage some movement with the arm. On the way out he ordered an increase in fluids to prevent further dehydration.

All I could think about was that all the progress we had made over the last year to retain the use of Brian's limbs had been lost. As I watched Brian struggling to find a position to sleep in, I could only see the damage that the medication had caused. His arm and hand and his feet were swollen and badly deformed. I fought hard not to fall into a state of total despair. At night I cried excessively.

It was Friday and the weekend staff was always a challenge because they were often unfamiliar with the unit, but the group that came in that weekend showed little patience for a child who was so sick. Brian required an exhaustive amount of care because he could do little for himself. The IV's running from his hands and feet made him completely immobile. They called him a baby because he was unable to get up to use the toilet and threatened him with diapers even after I had asked them to be more sensitive. When they tried to force him to retake medication that was mixed in his own vomit, I sought help from the R.N. overseeing unit, who quickly remedied the situation.

On April 17, Monday morning, I stepped away from the unit to get something to eat because Brian had finally fallen asleep. It had been almost a week since he had slept so soundly. When I returned, a lab tech had stuck Brian repeatedly trying to draw blood. I began counting the marks on Brian in his presence. He had even unwrapped the bandages around the wounded arm looking for a good vein. Generally, after three failed sticks you hand the needle to another tech. I knew it was important to get a blood sample that day but I wondered if they might have considered sending someone who had a little more experience when the child is so fragile.

At the nursing station the associate had written that Brian had "some" pain and "some" swelling. Some? It sounded callous; to me the pain and swelling looked excessive. Then I noticed he had ordered that the chemotherapy be put back onto the schedule: "He is scheduled to receive . . ."

Again I objected adamantly to the chemo. "Absolutely not!" I told the nurse that hematology was still in disagreement with the Physical Therapy Department. "It was time that everyone was on the same page!" I could not allow any more toxic chemicals to enter Brian's body until the two departments came to an agreement.

Later that afternoon, notes indicated that they "could not continue with the chemotherapy because of the high level of pain and the impending damage to the arm." He forgot to add that Brian's mother had gone ballistic and was not backing down.

The nursing staff still struggled with keeping Brian hydrated. The lab results showed a low blood count, and because of the nosebleeds there was talk about a blood transfusion. Since transfusions are very dangerous in Laminar, my anxiety peaked again and I began praying.

Blood work was ordered three times a day for an entire week. Brian was in serious trouble. His count kept dropping, and his oxygen level dropped. All of Brian's limbs were so swollen that Physical Therapy increased their visits to two to three times a day.

Because Brian had so many needs there were many people coming in and out of the unit; but most of them had to do with physical therapy. Once, I overheard a student who was working with Brian, tell him that if he did not bend his arm he would break it. When I intervened, the student insisted he was only kidding. I told him his joke was inappropriate and I was not kidding!

Without warning, the hospital held a meeting to address Brian's burn. I had been waiting a long time for this meeting and had hopes of getting our issues resolved. I felt the hospital had breached our contract. When I entered the room, I noticed that Brian's doctor and the team of nurses were conspicuously absent. The associate walked briefly into the room and claimed that he had acted appropriately and had followed protocol. When he left, the officials blamed me for the damage Brian had suffered. There were no advocates and I felt that the testimony was one sided. The meeting had been a waste of time. I suddenly realized that I could not afford the level of stress that this type of distraction brought, when my child needed me. I was sure the hospital was banking on that kind of response.

Late in the day, the associate came on to the unit right after I had gone down to the cafeteria for dinner. I did not think the timing of his visit was a coincidence. I believed we had an "informer" in our midst, probably one of the nurses, letting the associate know when I was away from the unit. He and I both knew that he had not seen Brian since the incident.

When I returned to the unit, a staff member told me that he had come into the unit to assess Brian's situation. When he realized how much pain Brian was in he gave Brian a large dose of Thorazine. "No!" I ran to Brian; he was already heavily sedated. Brian was asleep, his breathing slowed. I sat and watched him struggle to breathe for the next four hours.

Later that evening I felt a small victory when the hospital administrator finally sent a message to the unit nurses saying that the order for Vincristine had been rescinded, but then felt defeated when Brian had to be given a blood transfusion despite the high risk of infection.

That night the associate came back into the unit and added yet another dose of twenty-five mg of Thorazine into Brian's IV drip. I woke up in time to see him leave. This time Brian was in real trouble. He couldn't breathe. His respiratory system was shutting down. Before I could call for help a medical team arrived out of nowhere. The nurses must have realized what had happened. More IV lines were run and after several hours Brian was stabilized.

Nursing staff stayed close to Brian's side while I rode the elevator down to the cafeteria to get some coffee. I overheard two interns making light of the death of a little girl they had been treating. They made no effort to lower their voices, apparently disregarding the fact that I was also the parent of a child in treatment. In that instance I felt I was losing the battle.

On April 18, once again the morning brought a new order for chemotherapy. The associate, no longer using passive language, wrote "he will receive" chemo and also that oral fluid intake would be increased. Brian would not get chemotherapy, and I didn't know how his oral intake could increase when he had been unable to eat or drink for days. All of the nursing staff knew how strongly I felt about stopping the chemo because Physical Therapy had already written orders stating, "All treatment must stop." I read the rest of the day's notes and I wondered if I even had the right chart. The child in the report only suffered with a mild condition. None of it made sense to me.

Late that afternoon, about the time Outpatient was shutting down for the day, a nurse from the infusion center came into Laminar with Brian's doctor. The nurse stood by while the doctor talked to me about how the burn had put them behind schedule and that he felt a sense of urgency to get back on track, and Brian just needed one more injection. In the end I agreed to it. It helped that Brian had calmed down immediately when he recognized the kind nurse from the clinic who would be performing the injection. The medication entered into his vein quickly and Brian completed the second round of intense chemotherapy. Everyone seemed pleased with the results, but it did not relieve my anxiety about the unforeseeable damage that yet another toxic injection could cause.

I let the conflict continue to pull me into a dark place until I finally recognized that I was falling into the valley again. I quickly turned my thought to praises of gratitude. What could I be thankful for? God was doing great things for us. The injection had been given correctly, it had been one stick given by the hands of someone Brian trusted. It had been uplifting when the nurse from Outpatient told me that after hearing about all Brian had been through she had volunteered her time that day to help him. The way things were going, that day had been a miracle. I could finally see that we really were surrounded by people who cared about Brian's well-being.

I was also thankful Brian's doctor had finally come to the unit and had seen the aftermath from the infiltration, and that Brian was able to fall into such a deep peaceful sleep just minutes after receiving his treatment.

Notes on April 19 and 20 continued to upset me, yet I could not stop myself from reading the associate's account of the day. The chart read that Brian was "alert" with "good oral fluid intake" and that his pain medication had been reduced. Yes, Brian was awake, the IVs were pumping him up with fluids, and the pain medication had finally been reduced to eight mg, the correct dosage for a child his size. But where were the notes addressing the ongoing heavy nosebleeds, dehydration, and the need for drainage tubes?

When the evening came, we experienced another small victory. The nosebleed stopped temporarily.

On April 21, after Brian's fifty-minute session of physical therapy, the entire burn unit came in to present Brian with their new custom made "half" cast for his arm. The design of the cast had been a team effort and every member came to see if their effort fit properly and allowed the arm enough freedom of movement to function.

I could tell by the look on Brian's face that it was painful getting the swollen limb with open sores into the right position, but Brian whispered to me that he was okay. After the team left, Brian had violent bouts of nausea followed by a very bad nose bleed. He wasn't okay; the ordeal had been more than he could handle.

Late that night when he was finally able to fall asleep, I went to bed too. Sometime in the middle of the night a nurse came in and gave Brian Thorazine. She woke me up when she realized that she had mistakenly given twenty-five mg instead of the corrected amount of just eight mg. I calmed her down and told her I didn't mind staying up all night and keeping an eye on Brian. It had been an honest mistake and I was able to forgive her so quickly. Yet I still had not forgiven the associate. Each new day he continued to do something that made me angry; but God was working on my hard heart. I was learning that the associate didn't make me angry. Anger is triggered by our own response to the actions.

I wasn't too worried about the overdose this time because there would not be a cumulative effect. It was just a single dosage at a time when Brian could use the extra sleep. He was passed out for twelve long hours and experienced some slow labored breathing. I listened to him moan and watched his body jerk and twist in pain. Sometimes he held his hand up and tried to bite it. At times, tears ran down his cheeks, alternating with heavy sobbing. Watching him, I wondered if he felt pain or was having nightmares. It had been nine grueling days since the infiltration.

The associate remained out of touch with what was happening to my son. His notes for the day said there was a "decrease in swelling in the right arm and hand." It still was the left arm and right hand, and if there was any decrease in the swelling it was because of the drainage tubes. I could not wait for this man to rotate out of our lives at the end of the month.

Brian's hand was showing signs that it was starting to heal now that the drainage tubes had removed some of the excess fluids. Physical Therapy had determined that they no longer needed to work with his right hand but would concentrate only on the left arm now.

The previous day, Brian had suffered through several tomograms so the team could take a closer look at what was going on with his lungs. The imaging allowed the doctors to view the lungs by sections. It was difficult for the techs to take x-rays through the long rubber gloves that protruded into the bubble. But I knew it was harder on Brian to position his body with the new cast, swollen limbs and all those tubes.

I had been eager to hear the results, but it was just more bad news. Tumors in both lungs were unchanged. I couldn't believe the discussion in the morning rounds when I overheard students arguing whether or not they should keep Brian in isolation for three or six more months. I had already decided we were just wasting precious time. Brian's tumors had not decreased with the chemotherapy; it was time to get him out of the bubble.

At this point, my priorities for Brian were changing. In the beginning, I had prayed for the cancer to be healed, then for Brian's body to recover from the chemotherapy. When his suffering became great, I had even prayed that God would take him to heaven. But Brian was still with us. As I pondered all he had been through, I knew I had to turn my thoughts and prayers toward Brian's salvation. Brian needed his own personal relationship with Jesus. He could not depend on me to cover everything he needed. Being physically separated from my son while he had been in the Laminar unit had driven this point home. There was only so much I could do for him. But Jesus could be with him all the time. I could not do for Brian what Jesus could.

Kevin came to the hospital on Sunday and stayed with Brian so I could attend church. When the entire church prayed for Brian, I felt refreshed and able to get back into the fight.

The next morning Brian woke up and looked into my eyes. "You look so sad," he said. Back on the unit and faced with so many harsh realities, my hopes were easily shattered. Brian was right. I felt the weight of the battle. With the cancer growing inside Brian's body, his impending death became so real. I didn't want his last days spent in that plastic bubble that barred him from all human touch.

Brian was so concerned about me that he wanted to draw me a picture to cheer me up. It was the first sign that my child was still in that frail little body. He had initiated the activity and his words were sweet and sensitive to my needs. My child was back.

I provided him with crayons and paper that were on the bookshelf in his unit. He began to draw a silly looking bird with a big smile on his face, and even though his left arm was in a cast and his right hand was restricted, the picture was perfect.

I sat back to enjoy Brian's revitalization when the team from Physical Therapy entered the room announcing that they had come with very bad news. The arm was frozen. They explained to me that once the burns completely healed they would have to try to break the arm and re-set it. The pain would be excruciating.

Trying to weaken their argument, I told them we had been through all these warnings before with Brian's last burn. And he had recovered! But the therapist assured me that our past experience had nothing to do with where this process needed to go. I knew this was the same message God was sending me too. What I had been through was nothing compared to what lay ahead. It just felt like everyone was beating me to the ground. I felt like a punching bag. Inside I was yelling, "Go ahead; hit me again! Give it your best shot!"

I had to get out of Brian's room and go for a long walk. The cancer was growing, the arm would need surgery, and Brian was still stuck in the bubble; it was just too much for me. I sat next to a woman listening to a small radio. Pastor Chuck Smith of Calvary Chapel was shouting "Don't lose sight of your goal, the difficulties are for one purpose and that is to reign with Him . . . you must trust even when things are so difficult and you can see no good through the affliction. God promises that the outcome will be perfect peace." I went back to the room. I knew the words had been God's way of catching me before I fell.

For the next few days it was the prayers of our friends, our own Christian warriors who lifted Brian's needs to God's ear, while I read the Word and began to heal from the intense battle. Brian's arm began to loosen up. The therapists were so gentle when they worked with him that he had little pain. All day long I encouraged Brian to use his arm and stretch to pick up toys and crayons. Soon the arm was working again. The therapist thought the improvement was miraculous, and I could not disagree. Although the arm would never be normal again, it would be functional. There had been nerve damage and they thought the bone had become deformed, but there would be no amputation, no surgery, no breaking the limb and resetting it.

That night Brian suffered yet another severe nose bleed. The doctors thought another transfusion would be too risky at this point in his treatment. I prayed as we waited. The nosebleed stopped and Brian woke up feeling thirsty and wanted to eat. This was another miracle. I could finally see that Brian's pain was starting to decrease.

On April 24, I was so grateful when staff allowed me to move into the empty unit next to Brian. I believed that it was Brian's doctor who had taken pity on my dreadful sleeping arrangements. I would be allowed to sleep in a real bed again. Just that act of kindness lifted my spirits. Even if I had to continue to sleep fully dressed, I would not complain. It was such an improvement from being on the cold floor, constantly in the way when staff had to perform their duties.

On April 27 Brian turned four, but we waited until Sunday afternoon to celebrate his birthday and share our good news. At first, the staff was divided about whether or not we should be allowed to have friends and family members come to the unit, but as the weekend drew closer everyone got on board with the party. One of the nurses surprised Brian with a "sterile" cake and let him frost it. Other staff members thought to sterilize presents days before the big celebration. The day shift decorated the walls with balloons and Happy Birthday signs. Everyone was very accommodating once people started dropping by the unit to wish Brian a Happy Birthday. Only my parents stayed with Brian for the entire two hours because they had brought Crystal with them.

Brian and Crystal played with all the new toys inside the bubble. It was the only time a child's spacesuit would be provided so Brian's sister could visit. The kids built cities with the blocks, put puzzles together and even tried out the toy typewriter. Brian enjoyed the day but that night he was miserable. He had too much activity for one day and it had taken a toll on him. The nurses had to medicate him so he could get some sleep.

At the end of the month, it was decided that the treatment would be stopped. Our only option now would be surgery. The report read:

Pulmonary metastasis showed no decrease in size and because of this lack of response to high dose VAC therapy it was decided he should have surgical removal of these (pulmonary) metastasis.

On May 4, the treatment phase ended and the recontamination process began. Recontamination meant preparing Brian to come out of the bubble. He received several dosages of a powerful antibiotic to help him fight off any infections while his body readjusted to the non-sterile outside world. This time the antibiotics seemed to help accelerate the healing of Brian's feet, hand, and arm.

When the psychotherapist came in to talk about Brian's discharge, I had to run interference before she made our happy day into something frightful. She told Brian that kids in isolation could suffer from psychological or social problems. I told her we were planning a trip to Disneyland and that Brian was eager to get out. Shocked and in disbelief of my reaction, the psychotherapist brought in her team to help me understand the process.

The team of psychologists, social workers, and child activity specialists came in the next day to provide us with information and help Brian work through his fears. They told him he would be stepping into a germ-laden world. I smirked at the idea that Brian would have any trouble leaving. The therapist told me that I clearly did not understand the impact of social isolation.

They really believed Brian was going to need more therapy before he would be comfortable enough to leave the bubble. They thought we would have to go in and bring him out against his will.

The team also frowned on the idea that we would take a child directly out of isolation and place him in a very public amusement park. When they all left, I thought I better have a heart-to-heart talk with Brian in case he really did have any fear about leaving the bubble. He told me he wanted to go to Disneyland. I asked him if he was sad to leave the hospital and he looked at me like I was crazy. "Mom, I am just going to walk out." I assured him it would be just that easy. I promised to tell him as soon as it was time to leave. We waited patiently for two more days while the antibiotics kicked in.

Meanwhile, a representative of the National Aeronautic and Space Administration (NASA) provided paperwork and a short informative lecture on how to prevent outside contaminates from entering our home. There were so many things I had not thought about during our first year of chemotherapy.

He told me that clothes worn out in public were not to be worn inside the house; they were to be placed into a hamper with other soiled items. This procedure was just one of many ways we could fight infections. He also noted that "outside" items such as shoes, purses, and coats should be kept separate from the items that we wore inside the home. We would need to buy a dishwasher that sanitized the dishes. He reminded me that no personal items could ever be shared, and that included even hairbrushes. They also warned us to limit eating out in public.

On May 9, at 10 AM, it was time to go. Brian asked, "May I come out now, Mom?" I said, "Yes," and he walked right out into my arms, without any sign of being traumatized. A small group of people who had been working with him throughout the ordeal came in to say goodbye. He hugged all of them and then waved goodbye to the therapist, the social worker, and child activity specialist. We giggled all the way out to the car and then we drove straight to Disneyland, just as we planned.

We were there just a few hours, but the park was empty so we didn't have to deal with any crowds or long lines. We rented a stroller so Brian would not get overly tired, but that didn't stop him from climbing the tree house and riding the teacups, Dumbo, the Jungle Boat, and driving the antique cars. It was a very special day because we were able to do so much in such a short amount of time. We were feeling truly blessed!

9

A WAY OF ESCAPE

Seven days after his release from Laminar, Brian received the operation we had expended so much time, effort, and money to avoid. I hated the fact that we had misled our son into believing surgery could be avoided when in fact we had only combined the surgery with two long months of torture. Even though daily I had pushed aside my worst fears, here we were. Victory lost.

As I drove Brian to the hospital my heart was so heavy. I understood now how the gravity of a situation could lead you into a deep pit of despair. I had no strength to fight and didn't know how to get my faith into a position so that I could move forward once again.

My growing conviction that all Christians experience overwhelming anguish helped with some of the feelings I was having about being singled out. I thought to myself, *Who doesn't suffer?* Everyone faces a crisis at some point in life. We struggle when there is a death, or a serious illness. We struggle when we lose a job, face disappointments, experience painful divorces or the loss of a limb. Some struggles were emotional, others physical, but the struggle really wasn't about the circumstance we experienced. It was always about the struggle its self.

As we sat waiting to be admitted, I opened my Bible and went back to the Book of Job:

Though he slay me, yet I will I hope in him . . . (Job 13:15 NIV).

The Word expressed how I felt. I remembered that Job had not been granted a quick victory. God had permitted incredible suffering in his life, and then he permitted the suffering to get even worse. Job resolved to follow God even to the point of death and as a result God restored him.

I had reached a point where I knew I could not go on without him, but I had not fully understood how far-reaching his power and love was for us. I wondered why we all fight so hard to control our lives when we need simply to place everything into the hands of our loving Father. Once you realize how much he loves you, there is a joy and a peace that cannot be explained. And yet each time I was faced with difficulties, I tried to take back the control over my life without any regard for the commitment I had made to him. When I came across this scripture, I wondered if God had written the words just for me at that very moment.

> God is faithful, who will not allow you to be tempted beyond what you are able, but with the temptation will provide the way of escape also, that you may be able to endure it (1 Corinthians 10:13 NASB).

Paul's letter to the church at Corinth is not a promise that God won't allow more trouble in our lives than we can bear. Paul only promises that God will make a way for us to get through the temptation. In other words, however much pressure we are under, however unbearable it may seem, we still remain free to choose our response. We can give in to temptation and respond by becoming hardened. We can fall into despair. We can curse God, as Job's wife told him to do.

But we are also free to choose another way—to cry out to God for the wisdom to respond according to his will. And God in his faithfulness will answer by providing a way to escape.

It had always come down to choosing to walk with God. Why would anyone choose to walk this road alone, when only God promises to take you through it? When Kevin and I turned to him, he gave us confidence to endure the trial, peace to heal our hearts, and a joy to embrace life once again.

Lesson 5: <u>Unspeakable</u> Joy

After several hours of waiting at the hospital, I signed all the admission paperwork and Brian was assigned a room upstairs. Kevin worked that day but would be at the hospital for the surgery on Tuesday. I found an extra blue chair for sleeping and Brian and I settled in for the night.

The next morning, May 16, Kevin and I watched as they wheeled Brian into the elevator for his *fifth* surgery, a thoracotomy with excision biopsy of the right upper lobe. We prayed that Brian would have a quick recovery—and he did.

Brian tolerated the surgery well. He was awake in the recovery room and in good condition. Once he was wheeled into ICU, I waited to read the chart notes:

There was only one gray tan firm metastasis located on the right upper lobe. The remainder of the lung felt perfectly normal. No other nodules were seen or felt on the right side.

In less than twenty-four hours Brian was out of ICU and his drainage tube was pulled. Brian seemed to be unscathed from all that had happened to him. The next day he was walking the halls of the hospital pulling his IV pole behind him. On May 18, he felt well enough to visit the nurses in Laminar and go to school. That day he told his teacher, Patti, that one thing he especially liked to do when he was home was to read. I smiled to myself, wondering what that was about. He was still too young to do much reading at home; he must have been trying hard to make a good impression.

On May 19, the pathology report came back. The nodule was made up of "closely packed tumor cells consistent with metastatic Wilms' tumor." Brian was discharged late that Friday afternoon.

Since the hospital was just minutes from the Los Angeles Zoo, I surprised Brian by asking several family members to meet us there. All of our kids were out of school, so I thought they might enjoy having corndogs for dinner at the zoo. When everyone arrived, we made up a large group of twelve. We rented a stroller for the day, but Brian preferred to be carried by his dad. He did not want to look like a baby in front of all of his cousins, but he laughed when the older boys pushed each other around in the stroller.

At home Brian was healing quickly and getting stronger, but the hospital contacted us sooner than I had expected. It was May 25, and Brian's surgery was not scheduled for five more days. The hematology nurse was calling to say that Brian needed to come back to the hospital; he had been exposed to chickenpox.

Two children had already died, both of whom had been in the same wing of the hospital where Brian had been, one recovering from heart surgery, the other on chemotherapy. I knew chickenpox is a deadly disease for someone with a weakened immune system. Many of the parents at the outpatient clinic talked about their growing fear of being around unvaccinated children. I had heard that chickenpox attacks our children from the inside out, killing by attacking the vital organs: the liver, kidneys, heart, and the brain. Fortunately, Brian's blood count was high enough for him to receive the varicella vaccine.

On Monday, May 29, Brian was readmitted to the hospital for his *sixth* surgery, a left thoracotomy. I don't know how Brian found the courage to return to the hospital time after time without a fight. I struggled to tell him about this upcoming surgery when he hadn't fully recovered from the last one. He was feeling so good until I explained the next procedure. He sat in front of me, listening to my words; I watched his dark brown eyes grow dim and his spirit go dark. He fell into a state of complete silence. He didn't want to have to go through it all again and neither did I. I tried to bribe him, promising that I could give him the world when it was over, but nothing could touch the harsh reality of our situation.

I prayed with him, but wondered if his little thin body could really take two major surgeries so close together. The next morning as Brian was wheeled into the operating room; I was confronted by a hospital representative and summoned to the billing department. I was told that there had been problems with payment from our insurance company. I was aware of the delay in payments, but there was nothing I could do about it even though I had tried. It was frustrating because so often the information I received over the phone did not match the paperwork I had in my hand. I had tracked several outstanding bills that had been paid to the wrong vender. I knew that there had probably been many mistakes and that our financial situation was a bigger mess than any of us suspected.

The hospital's financial department tried to help me by working out an agreement with Crippled Children's Services (CCS). CCS would sort out our bills and we would make monthly payments directly to them. I was grateful for the help. It all sounded so easy. I signed all the paperwork that the hospital put before me and left. My child was in surgery and I needed to find out how he was doing.

Lesson 6: _Mantle of Love_

As I sat waiting to see Brian, my thoughts went back to how difficult this surgery was for Brian to face. I remembered Corrie's words: _"God's love is deeper."_ At her weakest point she had known profound intimacy with God and found the greatest strength in his love and presence in her life. I found courage and comfort from her testimony.

I knew that, like Corrie, if I just looked around, I could see how God had enriched our lives with his love. I wrapped myself up in that love, hoping that Brian felt it too.

Brian went from the recovery room to ICU in two hours. Three pulmonary nodules had been removed from the left lung. He had lived through the surgery but his little body always looked so lifeless in ICU. His breathing was shallow. When his lungs filled up with fluid I did not care that staff complained that I was in the way. Nothing would keep me from being there by Brian's side. This second surgery had not been anything like the first one. His body was not bouncing back like it had two weeks ago. It did not look like Brian would ever be able to leave the hospital and yet I didn't lose hope.

Multiple nodules meant that the cancer was not retreating. It seemed like the harder we fought against this disease, the stronger it came back. Brian was in ICU for several days. Even with care twenty-four hours a day he suffered.

That first morning in ICU they took many x-rays because the drainage tubes were blocked. Later in the evening, there was another concern; the drainage in the tube was dark red. On the second day, a respiratory therapist worked to get Brian to blow into a glove to help inflate his lungs, but Brian was too weak. The third day Brian started to recover. The x-rays taken that morning were good and the chest tube was pulled that afternoon. Brian was moved downstairs into a semi-private room, and I finally felt some relief that he was out of trouble.

On June 1 Brian was asking for a McDonald's hamburger so I snuck him out of the hospital the next day and we purchased a Happy Meal. He was breathing on his own and the last x-ray showed that his lung had fully expanded. He was discharged on June 2. God had made a way for us to endure the entire ordeal.

Just five days from the date of discharge Brian had to return to the hospital for the second part of his varicella vaccine. Chicken-pox continued to be a problem at the hospital.

On June 9 I felt very optimistic going to the follow-up appointment with the surgeon. Each day Brian was showing signs of making a good recovery. But when we sat down to talk to the surgeon, he told us that Brian's future looked bleak. The pathology report had come back and even though the surgeon had taken out all of the cancer, there was little chance that Brian had long to live.

The first metastasis, left lower lobe, consisted of a large triangle of lung tissue with a core in the second superior segment; in the left lower lobe were two small sections and the last left upper lobe there was a soft nodule.

The cancer had spread throughout the entire lung. Brian only had six weeks at home to recover before radiation therapy began. The surgeon told me the therapy would be difficult. Brian could experience problems with swallowing, sore throat, and possibly more burns.

Compared to what we had been through with the chemotherapy, radiation was far less intrusive. Chemotherapy had kept us tied to the hospital. There were long infusion days followed by bouts of nausea. Brian had to carry a bowl with him everywhere he went because even the smell of food could make him throw up. I dealt with the risk of depression, damage to vital organs, and the high risk of infection, but it was the senseless errors that made the process so hard to bear. Brian had been through so much. I was relieved the hospital had offered a different type of treatment.

Like chemotherapy, radiation was used after surgery to guard against cancer recurrence. According to the hospital's manual:

Radiation therapy is treatment by high energy X-rays (gamma rays from cobalt 60 and other ionizing radiation). The interaction between the radiation rays and the cellular tissue damages the DNA within cells (the genetic code that directs development), causing the cells to die as they are about to divide. The doses used kill the cancer cells but have a minimal effect on the surrounding normal tissues. The result is a reduction of the tumor's size. The side effects are skin damage and nausea. There are more serious effects if the radiation is given to the head or stomach.[8]

Unlike the outpatient clinic, our first visit to radiation therapy was very quick and easy. The team was very personable. They introduced themselves by name and explained every step of the process. The radiologist mapped out the area to be treated by making permanent ink marks on Brian's chest. There were no long waiting lines; everyone that came into the clinic had a designated appointment time. After about thirty minutes, we were free to go. Brian wanted to go to school, so we visited the hospital classroom for a whole hour that day.

On July 10, I took Brian to his second visit at the radiology clinic. Brian climbed up on the cold table and was told to lay very still. Once the marks were double-checked for accuracy, the thirty-minute treatment began. The first and second treatments went well, but then Brian began to develop a radiation burn. The inflamed area looked like a bad sunburn. The dosage of radiation was reduced and treatment continued. We were able to continue with the same routine throughout the whole process: radiation, school, and lunch at home. With radiation, the only down time was a quick nap after lunch and then Brian was up and wanted to play. With the help of the nutritionist, I was able to make a few changes in Brian's diet to accommodate the suggested soft food menu.

A month into the treatment, the financial department set up another appointment. At the meeting I was asked if I was taking the significance of our financial situation seriously. I understood that the accountant was concerned about the hundreds of thousands of dollars we owed. Of course I was taking it seriously; the illness had taken both a physical and emotional toll on me. I asked her what I could provide to help the hospital feel more comfortable with our situation.

I had come prepared for the meeting. I had all of our insurance information with me and had proof of monthly payments to CCS.

Kevin had job security and we had no reason to believe that the company insurance would not take care of us. They suggested that we agree to an Extraordinary Medical Expenses Coverage because our bills were mounting with no end in sight.

Radiation therapy was supposed to end on August 25 but stretched on into September. We had missed a few days because of burns and equipment failures, but Brian was doing well. His mop head hair was back, and his activity level was good. Brian didn't seem to mind radiation therapy; he never complained. The past few months had been the closest thing to a normal life that Brian had experienced since he had gotten sick.

Crystal started second grade and I signed up for room mother again that year. Brian entertained himself by playing with neighborhood kids during the day, and he even had a best friend. People didn't stop and stare at him, and he didn't feel like a sick kid anymore. He still liked to play Superman or ride on his Big Wheel. His only visible battle scar was the way he held his left arm, but none of the kids he played with seemed to notice it.

In October, we celebrated the end of treatment with a trip to Disneyland. In November, Brian and Crystal accepted Jesus as their Lord and Savior. It was a circumcision not done by the hand of man. Although the cutting away of the flesh does not make you a believer, circumcision of the heart does. Deuteronomy 30:6 says, "The Lord our God will circumcise your hearts and the hearts of your descendants, so that you may love him with all your heart and with all your soul, and live" (NASB).

We celebrated Christmas all month long, starting with a trip to Big Bear to play in the snow, a visit to Santa's Village to see Santa, and we even squeezed in a trip to Knott's Berry Farm.

Family and friends who had kept their distance for months remembered our children at Christmas time. We spent Christmas day with the grandparents, and afterwards we had a quiet celebration at home. At my parent's house, I was so proud of my dad for ending his addiction to cigarettes so that he could spend more time with his grandson. The doctors had wanted Brian to stay away from cigarette smoke because of his diminished lung capacity. Upon hearing my request, my dad simply quit smoking. I knew it could not have been easy for him, but he never smoked another cigarette.

When we arrived at Kevin's parents' house Kevin's mom gave Brian a toy guitar, the size of the ukulele she had learned to play when she was young. All the kids wanted to play it, but it was Brian who was taken aside as she began to teach him how to hold and play the instrument. For once in his life, Brian was the center of attention for all the right reasons.

10

1979

In January, the doctors told us that new tumors were growing in Brian's lungs. More surgery was suggested, but we felt like Brian had been through enough. We prayed about our decision and then we talked to Brian. Chemotherapy was our only other option.

It was a turning point for us when we decided to choose chemotherapy over surgery, but in April we faced the same junction. The tumors were growing and interfering with Brian's breathing and his rapid decline was affecting all of us. Did we stop treatment, refuse to go forward with the surgery, and watch him die, or did we continue to fight knowing it might only prolong his suffering? I didn't know the answer.

Brian was happy that we had been able to save his hair from falling out with headbands and hats. Putting pressure around the scalp helped to stop toxins from reaching the hair follicles. Having hair was important to Brian. It didn't matter how many times we told him that being bald was cool, he still wanted hair. I think in his mind being bald was the only thing that separated him from being a normal kid. Pain was just something that he had learned to live with.

I went to church each Sunday and prayed daily about what direction we should take. While I did not question God's provision for us, my emotions vacillated between being hopeful and feeling defeated.

In his book *The Problem of Pain*, C.S. Lewis writes, "We are rebels." He says we can only take up the true armor of God when we die to self, but that requires a complete surrender. After all we had been through; I hadn't realized I was a rebel, still fighting with God for control over Brian's life. But the words hit home. It was true, I wanted Brian to live.

Lesson 7: _Complete Surrender_

There is really only one battle and that is the battle that lies within. Five years ago, it had been easy to give my life to Jesus. But after watching Brian go through six surgeries and the threat of having him go through another one had raised the cost of surrender significantly. So here I was, learning the same lesson again, but at a much deeper level. I would seek things that were eternal, resting in confidence that God was watching over Brian.

Jacek Bacz, in a commentary on *The Problem of Pain*, writes that "at the highest level, pain, through trials and sacrifices, teaches true self-sufficiency: to rely on God, to act out of heavenly strength, out of a purely supernatural motive."[9] It was true; the pain of our circumstances had killed all other distractions in my life so that my focus was on God. I had come to know him as my only lifeline. I surrendered to his will, believing that he had a plan for Brian's life and I stepped away from that fight.

One evening on television, as Brian struggled to breathe, I heard the testimony of Joni Erickson at a Billy Graham Crusade. Paralyzed from the neck down after a swimming accident, she had asked God to heal her, but no physical healing came. Confined to a wheelchair for the rest of her life, she believed that her daily struggles had driven her into a closer relationship with God. The accident took away all distractions; there was no place else to go but to God. By sharing the joy and love of life she had discovered in the midst of tragic circumstances she has touched many lives.

It was the first time I had heard of a daily struggle with suffering. So often suffering had been linked to a temporary situation.

It was encouraging to hear that a physical healing was not the goal we were striving for. Our goal was a closer walk with our Lord and Savior. I believed God wanted to use our sorrow to drive our heart and mind to him. Brian's illness had caused us to pause, to turn from the life we had known to a new life with him. Each day he was teaching us how to live life more abundantly. What a privilege it was to walk with him.

The belief that God's abundant life is about material wealth and perfect health seemed to be one-dimensional; neither of those things will keep you happy or render an eternal reward. Ed Stetzer clearly defines the abundant life.

> The abundant life is about the gifts we receive from him (mercy, peace, love, grace, wisdom, etc.) and share with others.[10]

The more I read my Bible, the more I began to see that God's desire for his people wasn't simply that they live lives that were safe and prosperous. His desire was for them to become like him so that they might reflect his love in every circumstance, even in persecution. He wants our lives to be a reflection of who he is.

> To this you were called, because Christ suffered for you, leaving you an example, that you should follow in his footsteps (1 Peter 2:21 NIV).

On April 15, Easter Sunday, we celebrated the resurrection of Christ in church as a family. We still had no direction yet on whether Brian would have to face another surgery, but we continued to hold our focus on him, living one day at a time.

Two weeks later, on his fifth birthday, Brian was into the nadir. His, grandparents dropped by for cake and ice cream, but Brian was having a very bad day. He had no energy and his hair was falling out in large clumps. Before everyone left, I carefully unwrapped the gifts in front of Brian. He wasn't interested in anything except our sheltie dog that day. We brought Toto inside where Brian sat next to him quietly consoling him.

Eight days later, just before the next round of chemotherapy, we tried again to celebrate Brian's birthday. I invited two of his closest friends to Disneyland. It was Saturday, Cinco de Mayo, and the park was packed full of people but all the Disney characters were out too. Mickey greeted us when we walked into the park. Donald Duck strolled down Main Street and stopped to steal Brian's hat. When he realized Brian was not a well child, he simply patted the hat back on to Brian's head. When the three little pigs went after Brian's hat, Brian had held on tightly, but Goofy pulled his baseball cap completely off and exposed Brian's bald head.

After the hat was replaced, Goofy hung around for a while until he was sure that Brian had recovered. It was the thing that Brian had feared the most, that people would see him as that child with cancer. The incident shook him to his core and yet he tried to brush it off as if nothing had happened.

Back at home, he cried. I had wanted his birthday to be special and was so sorry about his hat. He tried to cheer me up and told me that he had had "good day." But I didn't know if he would ever find the courage to go out in public again.

In May the Los Angeles smog made the air so heavy that Brian's damaged lungs could no longer pump air through them. Although I had been complaining about the smog for months, it was the first time I had realized how much the smog affected Brian's breathing.

Smog had been a problem for the city of Los Angeles since the increase of automobiles back in 1943.When the number of cars tripled in the seventies, their exhaust caused a heavy cloud to sit over the LA basin. Brian's breathing was already compromised by the cancer in his lungs, the scar tissue from the surgeries, radiation, and chemotherapy; and now we had to deal with poor air quality. As the summer months drew closer, Brian was confined to the house. The children spent the entire summer indoors.

Then we encountered another problem. Gasoline rationing made it difficult to get to the hospital. In 1979, an oil crisis decreased the output of oil, only by four percent, but global panic drove prices high, up to $39.50 a barrel. The result was long lines at the gas stations. In California, gas could only be bought on an assigned day. Even though we had an official "Statement of Exemption" because of Brian's medical treatment, we couldn't find a station that had any gas available. The gas stations could not purchase enough tanks to keep up with the high demand. Brian's cancer treatments took six visits to the hospital each month, requiring three fill ups.

On May 11, when Brian went in for his physical, it was only because a gas station owner from church allowed us to fill up our tank on the weekend. When we returned for another fill-up on Wednesday, the station was closed. We scrambled to borrow cars from friends and family to make it through the entire week.

Brian's treatment continued throughout the months of June and July and so did the gas rationing, but that wasn't the only problem. The summer temperatures soared, causing the city to issue smog alerts. Without the typical Santa Ana breezes blowing through the valley at night the air became stagnant. School-age children, seniors, people with lung disease, or those who had suffered a heart attack were told to stay indoors while employees were urged to carpool. Every day the air seemed to get thicker.

With the kids locked up inside, they had no choice but to play with each other. Most of the time they were the best of friends, but some days they were each other's worst enemy. It seemed cruel to keep Brian inside when his days on earth were limited. Playing outside was the only thing he ever asked me for. It was such a simple request. I began to loathe the dirty air that hung all around us.

I started thinking about a time when life was easier; the air was clean and I didn't have to deal with cancer. I remembered when I had only heard about people having cancer but was not personally affected by it. Now two people in our family were suffering from breast cancer and receiving chemotherapy, my mother-in-law and my dad's sister.

On June 30, one of Kevin's cousins in Placerville was getting married. Kevin's mom bought a new wig and wanted to wear it to the wedding. She was feeling good and begged us to drive up north and meet them in Placerville. I felt anxious about leaving the kids with my parents, but it was just for the weekend. It took seven-and-a-half hours to get to Placerville. We arrived at the farm late in the afternoon.

I had forgotten how clean the air was in Placerville. It was such a contrast from the grey soot we were breathing in Southern California. At the farm, we could still see all the way to Mt. Diablo, more than 100 miles away. Kevin and I decided that this was where Brian needed to be.

After the wedding, Kevin's uncle, the father of the bride and now a local real estate broker, drove us to see three homes. The homes were too secluded for a city girl like me. But when he took us to see a house that was being built on a two-acre lot, it stole our hearts. With little consideration about medical care for our son, the local job market, the financial impact of our purchase, or even the fact that moving here would put 450 miles between us and our families, we placed a bid on the house.

When we returned home we were eager to get our house on the market, so I set up an appointment with a realtor. Kevin spoke with his supervisor at work who suggested that we put in for a medical transfer. He told us that all we would need was a letter from Brian's doctor. It sounded like an easy task. I would talk to the hospital when Brian had his next appointment in July. We were in no hurry because the new house still had to be finished and then we would have to wait for a final inspection before we could actually move in.

Crystal's birthday party at the end of July was a small get together with family and friends on Tuesday, followed by a visit to Disneyland on the weekend. Brian was set on going because his hair was growing back and he didn't have to wear a baseball cap.

He still remembered Goofy's hat attack and he didn't want that to happen again. It was a very short trip, because it had been exactly two weeks from the day of the last chemotherapy treatment, but overall we had a nice time there.

When we arrived at the park, it was hot and crowded. We took our time greeting all the characters. Minnie and Mickey were on Main Street. By the time we got to the Castle we counted that we had seen all seven of Snow White's dwarfs, and that was good enough entertainment for us. A trip to Disneyland in the middle of summer really isn't about the rides, unless you don't mind standing in long lines in the heat. We stayed just long enough to see the parade and then left before 4 PM, the hottest part of the day.

In August, the doctors were telling us that more new tumors had been discovered and the existing tumors had continued to grow with the treatment. I could tell that Brian's condition had deteriorated over the last four months. Now along with the labored breathing he was having trouble sleeping at night. The scar tissue restricted his lungs so much that he would wake up in a panic because he could not catch his breath. I still had not put our house on the market. I wasn't thinking about the move anymore; all those dreams had faded away. I only cared about what was happening to Brian. It didn't matter anymore whether there was smog or no smog because Brian couldn't go outside anyway. I wondered if we went ahead with the surgery if it would only be a last ditch effort to help Brian breathe on his own. I prayed and believed God's hand would lead us in the right direction.

A few days before the surgery my mother called, asking me to go see my aunt in the hospital. Her breast cancer had spread to her colon and she didn't have long to live. I went to the hospital and asked her if she wanted to accept Jesus into her life. She was receptive and prayed the sinner's prayer. She died eleven days later in the hospital.

On August 12, it still took more than five hours to be admitted to Children's Hospital. After a series of testing on August 14,

Brian underwent his *seventh* surgery, another thoracotomy-wedge excision of nodes of the left lung.

When the surgeon came out to talk to us, he said things had not gone well. He told us he had removed a section of the lung but it would not help Brian's breathing. Brian was in ICU for a week. When he finally woke up, the hospital still had problems keeping his pain under control. He struggled to ask me, "Will the pain stop soon?" I kept telling him it would, but that wasn't true. We almost lost him twice when his lungs filled up with fluid and collapsed. My poor little precious boy could not breathe without the surgery and he almost died with it.

As Brian left ICU on August 18, I heard rumors that Gary Coleman had been admitted to the hospital. He was a young actor on a new television show called *Diff'rent Strokes*. He played the role of Arnold Jackson. He would have been around eleven years old at the time of his hospitalization. He had a kidney transplant in 1973 and suffered from an autoimmune kidney disease, which kept him short in stature. I never knew why he had come into the hospital, but it did boost my confidence. He was such a big star then. He was constantly in the news. Children's really was the best hospital in Los Angeles because even celebrities, who had many options, chose to receive their medical care at that facility.

That evening, when I took the elevator down to the cafeteria, I had a chance encounter with the associate from Laminar. He recognized me immediately, even though it had been over a year since the incident. Seeing him again allowed me to reflect back on months of spiritual growth. I was no longer a rebel. He apologized for the damage he had done to Brian and it was so easy for me to forgive him. God covered me with his love that evening and reminded me all he had done for me so that I might be forgiven. I also apologized for my actions. We had both harbored ill feelings for too long.

Brian was discharged on August 19, just a few days before Maria, a dear friend, had sent these words of comfort:

Valleys are low, but not lower than my hand. Mountains are high, but I reach them.

Look not down on the valley, but up onto the heights which I inhabit and you shall see daybreak.

You shall see the sun like never before. That which is seen is seen to be, is not what it is. That which you see is an illusion, but that which I grasp is reality.

Weary not my child. Hold, stand fast, and lean on me, so I can carry your load and show you that which I have planned before time began.

I believed that these were God's words, spoken to comfort us. Brian was on his way to another quick recovery. God had helped Brian through the low places and now he would linger for a time on the mountaintops.

Brian and Crystal stayed with my mother while my dad and I attended my aunt's funeral. She was the first person in our family to die from cancer since Brian had been diagnosed.

In September the air quality in Los Angeles made history when the city faced a smog attack. The air had become so toxic that the news reported they had never seen anything like it. Everyone had to stay inside. The kids and I stood at the patio door and stared into a thick layer of what looked like fog. Even I could feel the burning in my lungs and chest.

11

LEARNING HOW TO FIGHT

The hot temperatures and stagnant air hung over the basin for weeks. There had already been over 169 smog alerts that summer. Brian's cancer had become more aggressive and I felt we had little time to make our move up north. I would have a lot of work to do to make it happen but first I needed to go to the doctor and get myself checked out.

After a brief consult I was admitted into the hospital for an exploratory surgery. The local doctor dismissed the need for a hysterectomy because, "I was too young for that." He suggested that my symptoms were all in my head, caused by all the stress in my life. I agreed that I was under tremendous emotional and financial stress; but fearing it was something more, I wanted a second opinion. I made an appointment with the OB-GYN who had delivered my two children.

When we picked up the children that afternoon, I had a chance to spend some time with Kevin's mom. I was surprised by how much she had deteriorated since we had last seen her. I bought her a Catholic Living Bible and made a commitment to call her every day. Her illness was simply one of many reasons why we should not move, but I felt that Brian's health had to be the priority. That night I called our real estate agent. I was tired of the smog and all of life's struggles. We were ready to sell.

I called Brian's doctor to find out where we were with the letter he had written to Kevin's employer, he sent us a copy. The letter read in part:

September 21

As results of the surgical procedures, chemotherapy, and radiation treatments, Brian has a definite compromise of his lung function. This is causing him some difficulty with relation to the build-up of air pollutants and the deterioration of the air quality in the Los Angeles area . . .

I understand there may be a possibility that Mr. Perigan could relocate in his work to an area that would reduce the possibility of Brian having these problems in the future.

The next day our house sold and we signed all the paperwork. Everything had fallen into place so easily that I thought the only thing I had left to do was to sit back and wait. I called Kevin's uncle excited to tell him about our sixty-day escrow, but he had bad news for us. There had been another offer on the house in Placerville. That offer didn't have a contingency clause, like ours, and the seller accepted it.

It was just a house; I didn't need to worry about it. There was nothing I could do about it now. I couldn't fly back to Placerville to look for another house; Brian was still struggling and I was too sick. I wondered if we had gotten ahead of God's will, and I quickly un-invested myself in the question of where we were supposed to go. God knew our hearts; something would work out.

I could not even begin to understand the events of the coming weeks. First, Brian's grandmother died on October 5. Brian and I were at Children's Hospital when I got a call saying that she'd had a stroke. By the time I arrived at the hospital in Arcadia it was too late. She had already entered into the death throes. The doctors thought the chemotherapy treatments had triggered the massive stroke. I called Kevin and told him to meet us at his parents' house; there was no need for him to come to the hospital now.

Losing Marie was difficult. Over the past few months, we had spoken many times about life and death. I had prayed with her; she had been open to receiving Jesus as her Savior. I knew she was at peace, but still the funeral was so sad. She had always been so supportive during Brian's illness and enjoyed picking out new toys for him to help ease his pain. She had always dressed Crystal up like a little doll in clothes that we could never have afforded.

A week later our real estate agent called to remind us that we would have to be out of the house in less than six weeks. We had nowhere to go and moving heavy boxes around wasn't helping my condition.

On Monday, October 15, I met with my doctor to review the results of my exploratory surgery. He said I had an advanced case of endometriosis. He talked to me about several options but I chose a total hysterectomy. He wondered, given my current situation with Brian, if I had considered having any more children. My answer was no. Both pregnancies had been difficult. And besides, my family was complete.

On Tuesday, October 16, I had surgery and was able to return home Thursday. I felt so much better that I started packing up boxes again. I was doing too much too soon. Several days later, when I found myself in an emergency room it took less than an hour for my doctor to call in strict orders: "Stay off your feet!"

Meanwhile Kevin's position at the phone company was in jeopardy. We had completed all the paperwork for the job transfer to Sacramento but there were no job openings. As a last resort the company offered to place him in an operator's position; it was the lowest paying job in the company. I didn't know how we could pay our mortgage with less money, but I couldn't worry about that too. I suppose all these attacks were just more fiery missiles, but this time I stayed focused.

Brian's next round of chemotherapy was canceled when his blood count dropped. Nothing like that had ever happened before. I guess I had not realized what a toll the last few weeks had taken on him. Everything in his life was chaotic. We were moving, but we had no place to go. Nothing at home looked familiar anymore. There were boxes everywhere. His mother was hospitalized and his grandmother died from cancer. I knew that all of those things had to be hard on him.

It was an emotional time, and I cried many tears. Brian, who was always at my side, tried to reason with me. He would grab my face and remind me that it was a good day. Worried, he would ask, "Why are you crying?" I only wish I could have handled it better.

We were just seven days away from the move; still no place to go and no job in place. I turned to God. "Lord, what do you want me to do?" I couldn't panic because Brian needed me to be strong. I called Kevin's uncle to ask him about rentals, but his uncle wouldn't let me talk. He had something very important to tell me. The potential buyers had not qualified for the loan, and their offer had fallen through. The house was ours for the taking. It was just the right timing. There had never been a reason to worry. God's got this!

I called Kevin at work to tell him my good news, but his news was better. The company had found a job that would suit his skill level and he could stay at the same pay scale. It was a miracle!

Just five months ago we had started down a road that we hoped would give Brian a better quality of life and now we were just days away from our destination. We did not realize how many twists and turns there would be, but our blind faith had pulled us through. We had no time to agonize over each road block, and we didn't worry when it looked like the plans had changed, we just readjusted ourselves. In my former life the move would have been impossible, but now, it was a piece of cake because God had taken the lead.

I had so many things to be thankful for. We were really going to move to the foothills after all. I was finally free to walk away from everything that reminded me that my child was sick. I was free to start over.

In the morning, on November 17, we left the children with my parents and we flew to Sacramento to finalize the paperwork on the house in Placerville. On the way back to the airport we drove by our new home. It was only the second time we had seen it. It was perfect. We had never moved into a brand new home before. The paint was fresh and the carpets were new. We couldn't wait to move in. We flew back to Los Angeles that evening, feeling good about our new purchase.

While we were gone, the hospital had tracked Brian down at my parents' house to tell them there had been another exposure to chickenpox. My mom and dad had panicked, thinking that Brian had to get the vaccine immediately. I reassured them the clinic would wait till Monday to set up our appointment. On November 19, the doctors wanted to check Brian's blood count before he got the next vaccine. His count was high enough but the nurse thought she heard something irregular in Brian's heartbeat. The electro-cardiogram (EKG) revealed that Brian's heart was a little weak but nothing to be concerned about.

The chickenpox exposure and the condition of Brian's heart would have been disturbing news if I had not already had a full plate. I simply reassigned the threat as yet another spiritual attack, a minor interference. I went home to finish packing. All the drama was over.

The last few days in Southern California, I spent time with the people who meant the most to me. While Kevin was at work, I picked up my nephew and took the kids to the zoo. That evening the whole family sat by the lake near my parents' house and fed the ducks. On Wednesday, we spent the day with friends, the kids rode their horse in the morning, and we all ate at McDonald's in the afternoon.

On the last day, while Kevin was loading up the U-Haul Truck with boxes, the kids and I drove to Children's Hospital to say good-bye to everyone. Brian and Crystal visited the classroom, Laminar, the social worker, and all the staff at Outpatient. It was sad leaving the hospital and all the people we had grown to love.

Early the next morning, while many people were preparing to celebrate Thanksgiving, we had friends and neighbors over help-ing us load the heavier furniture into the truck. We had celebrated

Thanksgiving early that year at our house with the grandparents. We wanted to get everyone together so we could tell them about our move to the beautiful Sierra Foothills. We felt very blessed to be so supported by our friends and family.

The move went smoothly. The kids and I took the dog and the fish while Kevin drove the moving van. We had been lucky that the entire contents of our 1,400 square foot house fit nicely into the small moving van.

It only took eight hours to get to the new destination and four hours to get everything out of the truck. Our best friends had driven up for the entire weekend to help us get settled into our new house. All three of our kids ran up and down the stairs while the adults worked to set up our new living space. It felt so good to see how readily Brian adjusted. It was just another confirmation that the decision to move had been the right one.

On Saturday night, our last evening together, we treated our friends to dinner at a nearby restaurant called Sam's Town. It was sad to see them leave on Sunday morning but it didn't take us long to get used to living in the country. Our new three-bedroom home had a large stone fireplace in the living room to keep us warm at night. Nestled among large golden oak trees, the lot gently sloped down from the road into a heavily wooded area. The neighborhood was filled with children and at night we could see a million stars.

We lived among wildlife, where everything looked so natural and rustic. It was the perfect place to live. The white-tailed deer ran free throughout the foothills and ate up most of the new vegetation that we planted, but we didn't care. We didn't mind the diamondback rattlesnakes sunning themselves on the front porch, the bats that lived in the upstairs balcony or the tarantulas that migrated across our yard each October. We were so happy there and were thankful that Brian could spend his remaining days on earth playing outside.

In December, Brian started kindergarten. He was motivated to attend school because he wanted to ride the big yellow school bus that stopped in front of our driveway every morning. He was growing up, but was still thin. He had enough hair to look like we had buzzed it off short for the new school year. Wearing a heavy sweater and a coat, he looked like any normal five-year-old.

Brian was so disappointed when I drove him to school rather than letting him ride the bus on that first day. I introduced him to his new teacher and talked to him about how he could get in touch with me if he wanted to come home early. But Brian also had a few things he wanted to tell me about school. I was not to tell any of the kids that he had cancer and we weren't ever going to talk about the hospital. I told him that his teacher knew he was on chemotherapy, but that she wasn't going to tell anyone. On the way home, we followed the bus route so Brian could see how long the bus ride would take, but he told me he didn't care. He had his heart set on riding the bus regardless.

After I had done all that I could think to do to prepare him, I watched him walk out the door, up the driveway, and get on the bus all by himself. When he came home he was so happy and wanted to tell me all about his day. I didn't tell him how I sat near the window anxiously awaiting his safe return. I was so happy that he fit in. It wasn't long before he had many friends dropping by the house after school. Word had spread quickly: it turned out that we had the best long, sloping driveway in the neighborhood for riding Big Wheels.

By the second week of December, the weather turned unseasonably cold and it snowed. The kids went sledding down our driveway landing in the garage. Whether it was summer or winter our driveway drew many of the neighborhood kids to our house.

Coming from Southern California, we did not have any idea how to combat the cold. Long johns, heavy socks, and flannel lined jeans were things that our neighbors told us we needed. They also told us about Christmas Tree Farms and where to go to find Santa.

On the weekends we went into the El Dorado Forest and gathered free wood for the fireplace. On Sundays the local churches had evening concerts with new up and coming Christian groups. There was so much to do that I didn't even feel homesick around the holidays. We were enjoying everything our community had to offer.

On December 17, Brian completed his next round of chemotherapy in Sacramento. The hospital, University of California, Davis Medical Center (UCD), was a forty-five-minute drive from our house. UCD had just started operating in the city of Sacramento in 1977, but the hospital buildings were made up of a small Medical Center built in the 1950s. The clinics were outsourced to old metal trailers spread around the grounds.

Although Brian had been treated for cancer for almost three years now, because he was new to the area, the staff acted like he had never been to a medical facility before. They explained the difference between the hospital and the clinic. Then they talked to me about the specific type of cancer that Brian had and how he would be treated with a new experimental drug. I was very interested in learning about the new drug until I realized that it was really just one of the drugs that Brian had been taking for some time now, Adriamycin D. The nurse told me that it was the most effective agent in the treatment of cancer, but that the cardio-toxicity that manifests is irreversible and leads to heart failure. I told the nurse that Brian had been on the drug for some time and already showed signs of having some damage to his heart. She continued on point to remind me that the drug could kill him. Then she told me that Brian's treatment course had been adjusted so that it would be given over an eight-day period.

Brian was very unhappy about missing so much school. The doctors tried to reassure him that he would be able to return in January, but I had already told him he could go to the Christmas party on December 19. The local newspaper was coming to take pictures and all the kids were going to talk about what they wanted to be when they grew up. Brian wanted to be a doctor.

At the clinic, Brian's new doctor continued to explain more about the side effects of the drug. He told Brian he would lose all of his hair with this round of therapy. Again, Brian looked at me to fix it, but I couldn't. Even the tightest bandana could not stop hair loss with that many dosages. Brian gave a heavy sigh and said to me, "Mom, everyone will know."

When we got to the infusion clinic, it was clear to me there had not been much money put into the building or the equipment. The system was antiquated but the staff was exceptional. They were kind to Brian and we had no problems with the treatment.

We celebrated a quiet Christmas at home on Tuesday, because Brian was so sick. On Christmas morning Brian opened up his new Star War toys, while Crystal played with her new plastic Snoopy dog.

It was feeling a little too quiet because all of our neighbors left town to spend Christmas with their families. By the weekend, Brian was feeling better and so we decided to drive down to Los Angeles to see the grandparents. My parents had sent presents already, but when they heard we were coming they scrambled to buy new gifts for the kids so they would have something under the tree. We enjoyed all day Saturday with them and left right after lunch on Sunday. I hadn't realized how much I missed them and it had only been a little over thirty days since our move.

There was snow on the ground when we got home that night. The kids woke up early to play in it the next morning. Kevin had already shoveled the entire driveway so he could get the car out and drive to work. That was the only downside to having a very long driveway.

On New Year's Eve we sat around the fireplace and played games and ate s'mores. At the stroke of midnight, the kids came up with an idea for the new house. They decided the house should have rules. I wasn't sure why we had to have rules, but I thought maybe the idea had been inspired by one of Crystal's school projects. I wondered if the rules made the kids feel more in control of their lives. As we sat in a round circle each person had a chance to come up with their own set of rules. Since I couldn't come up with a single rule I wanted to implement, I volunteered to be the one who wrote the rules down and would later be responsible for posting them near the front door where they could be read by all. The rules went like this:

House Rules
- No smoking—Crystal
- No hitting—Brian
- No yelling—Kevin
- No playing on the stairs—Crystal
- No alcohol—Brian
- Everyone cleans up their own mess—Kevin

The rules solidified the fact that this was our house, that each person was an important part of the team and that we had come together to build a new life here in Placerville.

12

1980

Brian was eager to go back to school but the doctors had told him he would have to wait until his blood count came up. Every morning after Crystal got on the bus, Brian would say "Pretty soon I can go to school; right, mom?" When I didn't turn around right away, he had the habit of grabbing my face and pulling it toward him, so he could ask, "Right, mom?"

On January 14, Brian ran up the driveway and hopped on the bus. He was returning to school, unafraid of what lay ahead. He liked his new friends and his teacher, but every afternoon when he returned home, he was so tired. He continued to persevere. He never wanted to slow down or even allow himself to take a brief nap. He always took the time to report that he was having a good day so that I would not interfere with his forward march in life. He had finally entered a place where he was comfortable in claiming his own destiny in life.

As his mother, I only could see how he struggled and it broke my heart. Physically he was unable to keep up with the other children. He worked so hard to fit in, even after we had explained to him that everyone was unique in some way. His response had been dismissive and he looked at me as if I didn't understand. He would never be like the other children, but he still hoped that they wouldn't notice. Emotionally he had learned to keep his feelings in check. He gained some confidence in just knowing that he was a good student and loved by his teachers, but when his uniqueness separated him from the other students his nights were filled with tears.

Nevertheless, with the return of the cancer, all of the surgeries, and monthly chemotherapy, like a good soldier he just kept fighting the fight and returned to school. I appreciated Brian's kindergarten teacher keeping a close eye on him and informing me of any problems. She was older and had years of dealing with children with many types of disabilities. She always included Brian in newsworthy photos and encouraged him to participate in all the activities. I knew Brian was in good hands at school and it was where he wanted to be.

Brian had been asked to be a ring bearer in two upcoming weddings. The first wedding took place on January 26 and went extremely well. He walked down the aisle in a little black velvet tux bearing the ring. He was accompanied by a beautiful little flower girl dressed in a white gown. They made a striking couple as they walked down the aisle side by side. For a brief second, I saw a young man in love with the woman he was going to marry; it was the closest thing I would ever have to visualizing what Brian's future might have looked like. The image quickly faded.

Brian didn't mind all the pictures or even the stares during the ceremony. I don't know how he learned to be so bold in public. I had been the doting mother that morning, and he had to remind me that we were not going to talk about the hospital. I didn't know what to say when a member of the wedding party asked me how he was doing. I turned to him for a response and he answered casually, "I'm fine." He refused to be defined by his illness.

His next chemotherapy round ended on February 15, and the second wedding was held the next day. It was the wedding of Brian's Laminar nurse, Cecilia, who used to joke about Brian being her boyfriend back when she was single. I knew Brian loved her but he had been so sick, I just assumed he would not be able to attend.

On February 16, Cecilia's wedding day, Brian's blood count was already starting to drop, his hair was falling out, he was nauseated, and then it started raining. I tried to talk him out of going, but he did not want to disappoint Cecilia. It was a very long drive to Los Angeles, but Brian kept telling me that he could do it. We arrived at the church early, and I dressed him up in the same velvet tux but this time the cap on his head wasn't just for looks. I held my breath when he walked down the long aisle of the beautiful Catholic Church and stood next to the bride. He stood very still during the formal Mass and then participated in the ceremony doing whatever he was told. After it was over there were a few more pictures and a forced smile. We gracefully bowed out of attending the reception and made a quick exit to the car. Brian barely made it to the car before he got sick. I told him how proud I was of him. He had made it through two long hours and had done a wonderful job. He had so much self-control for a five-year-old.

After the wedding experience, I decided I would no longer let the doctors dictate what Brian could or couldn't do. He had earned the right to make his own choices in life. He had shown great control at the both weddings and was able to accomplish his goals even during a time when he felt his worst. That day I realized that I really did need to step back. God was driving Brian's life. I had been demoted to the back seat and was only allowed to go along for the ride.

As soon and we got back home, Brian told me he wanted to go back to school. I think he was just testing the waters, I let him go. I reminded him that I could be at the school in ten minutes if he needed to come home. On Monday morning, he rode the bus by himself. I sat near the phone all day but he never called me.

A few weeks later, the kindergarten class had a share day. Brian asked me to go with him to help carry our two black cats. I was thrilled that I would actually be able to attend an entire day at the school and watch him interact with his classmates.

I felt a little nervous for him when it was his turn to speak, but he did a good job and the cats stayed in his lap. He started out a little shy when he told the class that the cats were brothers and that he'd had them since they were kittens. He also shared how one cat had been bitten by a rattlesnake, and how large its head had swelled. When one of the kids asked why the cat didn't die, he thoughtfully shook his head, like it was a miracle that the cat lived, and said, "I just don't know." I thought to myself how true that statement was. We will never know why one lives and another dies.

We could not hide the fact that Brian had cancer from his classmates anymore. There were too many doctor appointments, play restrictions, and we had gone to the principal's office to override the dress code. Brian needed to wear a hat all the time now. When classmates began to protect him from the remarks made by the other students, he was embarrassed. But his teacher, Mrs. Carpenter, told me I should not be alarmed. She sent a progress note home with Brian that month.

> He is showing good growth and gaining confidence. He is well liked by all the other students.

In March, Brian had more x-rays, and once again the results were disheartening. We still wrestled with choosing a practical response to this disease. How did trusting God and surrendering to him translate when it came to decisions about medical care? Once again we seriously questioned whether to continue with the so-called life saving measures. Brian was receiving the best treatment the hospital had to offer, but it was having little effect on the cancer. When I turned to the medical professionals, they always wanted to continue with the treatment. They hoped that the next month would bring good results, but that was rarely the case.

I couldn't help but think how many times the chemotherapy had failed us. Even when the therapy had been intensified in Laminar the tumors grew. I thought we had probably seen more results with the surgery and radiation therapy. But even with that I was not sure that all of the cancer could be removed. Regardless of what everyone was doing to help Brian get better, the cancer just kept coming back. So why should we let the chemo continue? Wasn't it only prolonging Brian's pain and increasing his suffering for whatever time he may have left?

Brian was so tired of the chemotherapy and all the surgeries. He was tired of the cancer interfering with the life he wanted to live. I didn't believe that stopping treatment or continuing it would give him the results that he wanted. Yet it was heartbreaking to think that we would simply just give up.

That afternoon I sat and listened to the doctors at UCD explain to me that there was evidence the cancer was still growing. My response was not the one they wanted to hear. They wanted to use more drugs to try and knock out the cancer, but we had done that before. After three long years, Brian's vital organs were being impacted by the toxic drugs, and we knew the chemo could kill him, just like it had killed my mother-in-law. Wasn't it just more humane to let him die? Isn't going to heaven our ultimate goal?

After ruminating for several hours about what our options were, I realized I was taking control back again. This wasn't my problem. I did not hold Brian's life in my hands. I was not the Creator nor did I have any power over life and death. I heard Katherine Kuhlman, a television evangelist, once say that she had to die to self a thousand times daily. I handed it back to God. "Lord," I prayed, "not my will but yours."

How many times would I have to go back to that same lesson? I answered my own question. Probably until I got it right. It was pride that kept me turning away. It was repentance that got me back on the right road again. Sometimes I would catch myself going down the wrong road right away. Sometimes it would take weeks or years before I got it right but that didn't mean sin would not pop up again in an entirely new situation. But I did see some progress. God was transforming all of us, little by little, to be more and more like him, but a complete transformation would take a lifetime.

A friend at church said she received this word for Brian on March 15, 1980. It gave us all hope, but Brian believed the words had come directly from Jesus.

Brian my son, we love each other right!
I am with you every minute. I never leave your side, even in your sleep.
I love you, so I died for you, Brian, and I would die again.
That's how much I love you.

We are a team me and you
And a team is stronger and better than one.
Remember that I love you!

Brian loved thinking about having Jesus on his team. He was so encouraged by the words that I made them into a plaque and hung it over his bed. The words continued to encourage him until the day he was able to meet Jesus face to face.

On March 19, we agreed to continue the chemotherapy at UCD. For months, we had sat in the little hot trailer along with all the other sick pediatric patients. The cancer kids sat and played with children that were coming into the clinic with many different diseases including chickenpox and measles. All the children shared one bathroom. The staff ushered sick children into rooms, but the viral diseases were airborne. Other hematology patients and their parents seemed to be unaware of the presence of danger but I was hyper-alert on the issue because of my talks with NASA.

I talked to Brian's doctor about what I could do to help change the situation and make it safe for all the kids. I told him I was willing to go to administration. He was grateful for the support but said the hospital was launching a building program and it would be a long time before any changes could be made. I decided to write a letter anyway.

We were almost ready to leave the doctor's office when the doctor told Brian he would have to miss school for several weeks again. It was a touching moment when the doctor took Brian's concerns seriously. He told Brian about a new study that used vitamin supplements to reboot the immune system. In the study, the vitamins had increased strength and shortened patients' periods of down time. Brian was eager to take the vitamins. The extra time the doctor spent with him that day made a big difference in Brian's outlook. It was the first time he actually had a say in his treatment plan. He was excited that he could do something for himself to get better.

After the infusion the doctor wanted to set up Brian's next appointment in April. He wanted to hospitalize Brian for an entire week for tests. I was opposed to admitting Brian to the hospital for so many days. That was when he said we had only one other option.

On April 6, after church, we celebrated Easter with Kevin's uncle and his wife and their four kids on the farm. It was a beautiful day in the foothills, and there were eggs hidden all over the thirteen acres.

On Sunday, April 13, I was excited about driving down to Los Angeles so Brian could have all of his testing done in one day. My best friend, Bonnie, and her daughter, who lived in LA, were going to travel back home with us and stay through the weekend.

On Monday morning at Children's Hospital, Brian started the testing. There was a slight snag in our plans when the doctors thought they had found yet another problem with the heart. Further testing revealed that the damage was still well within a mild range, so the treatments would continue at UCD.

We all drove back to Placerville on Wednesday. I could not wait to show my friend all the improvements we had made to the house. The four-day visit went by quickly and on the weekend all four of us, Kevin, Crystal, Brian and I, drove her and her daughter to the airport to say goodbye. I was surprised at how excited my children were to watch the planes land and take off. I had forgotten that neither of the kids had ever been to an airport.

The next week, I read a book I had picked up in Los Angeles called *Don't Waste Your Sorrows,* by Paul Billheimer.[11] Paul and his wife had a television show on Trinity Broadcasting Network (TBN). Their ministry started late in life, right after they had written two best sellers in their late seventies. The notoriety from Paul's books gave the couple an opportunity to teach a seminar in San Diego in 1977. When televangelist Paul Crouch heard their message, he asked them to move out to California and host a television show on TBN.

Their book was a breath of fresh air to me because Paul and his wife understood human suffering. Faith healing ministries had become so prevalent in our Christian circles and across the country that it was becoming unpopular to talk about adversity. The new role of the church was to market Jesus in a way that was more appealing to the masses. The thought was if Jesus promised wealth and good health to church members, then pastors would see their membership numbers and income increase. Today the church markets an even wider message that just makes people feel good about themselves; they don't even need Jesus. Nobody wants to talk about a deeper walk with God because it comes at such a high price. He demands sacrifice and new heart.

In his book Paul Billheimer talks about the benefit of suffering. He claims that the deeper the suffering, the greater the spiritual comprehension and love. He states:

> Those who are not healed may not need to accept second class citizenship after all, but may be nominated for enhanced rank and eternal glory. Instead of relapsing into discouragement, resentment and defeat—which is a waste of their sorrows—it is their privilege to take advantage of their suffering and cause it to work for them. When the soul undergoes this deeper death of self, it enters into a great wideness of spiritual comprehension and love; a state of almost uninterrupted prayer, of boundless charity for all people; of unutterable tenderness and broadness of sympathy; of deep quiet thoughtfulness; of extreme simplicity of life and manners; and of deep visions into God and the coming ages.

I wrote to Paul to let him know what this word of encouragement had meant to me. I never expected to hear back from him. I sent the letter to TBN, the largest Christian broadcasting network in the world.

Meanwhile, progress reports came in from the kids' school teachers. Crystal was still set to graduate despite all the days she had missed at school and had even been chosen as a finalist in the county's spelling bee. Brian's teacher sent some extra homework with her report, telling me he just had to complete a few more pages of homework to get into the first grade. Brian's quarterly report card read:

> Brian appears to be happy about school and has shown much good growth since he entered last fall. He has been exposed to a wide variety of activities and seems anxious to be involved in all that we do. Making his own choices and decisions are not always easy for Brian, but he is gaining confidence and seems more relaxed and comfortable. He seems interested and excited about reading and math groups. He is hearing rhyming words. He enjoys books and should do well in first grade in the fall. Brian is well liked by his peers and he seems to enjoy working and playing with them. He is really delightful and I am pleased to have had him in my class.

It was a good report. I was thankful he was doing so well. On the weekend, family and friends came over to celebrate Brian's sixth birthday. Brian's blood count was high that day, his hair had grown back in and he felt good. It was a beautiful warm day, and we were able to have a barbeque outside on the deck. We had lots of help that day putting up the new swing set.

The next day, Monday, April 28, we were back at UCD for chemotherapy. That morning I came ready to address some of the concerns I had over the treatment of pediatric hematology patients. It had been more than a month since I had sent the director a letter and had heard nothing back from him. I marched up to his office suddenly realizing that I had not even thought about making an appointment. I was quickly humbled when the man agreed to meet with me on such short notice.

The problem, as I saw it, was simple. We needed to separate children with inhibited immune systems from the normal population. The exposure to colds, flu, and any number of contagious diseases was potentially a life-threatening situation for our cancer kids. The director was very receptive and shared pictures of the plans they had for a new clinic. He said he took my concerns seriously. Several weeks later I was happy to hear that a few changes had been made. Cancer Clinic and the Pediatric Clinic would now be held on different days until the new building was completed. Only the infusion clinic with its own private waiting area would be open daily.

Brian's treatment ended after just three days because again his blood work showed that his count was dropping too fast. The doctors were concerned, but Brian was pleased about the shorter treatment because it meant he would be able to return to school a little quicker.

On the annual picture day at school, I dressed the kids up in matching outfits, unbeknownst to them. I don't think they ever realized that Crystal's blue dress matched Brian's blue shirt. Only I appreciated the extra effort I had taken that day. My children looked perfect!

Brian was becoming more independent and wanted to spend more time with his friends. I started letting him attend birthday parties and visit a few selected friends in their homes. It was time for me to let go of my fears and let him live his own life; and I had to start living mine.

I took a temporary part-time job with County Mental Health that year doing medical transcription. One of my cousins facilitated my hiring. I was just a fill-in until a permanent employee could be hired but it was the first time I had worked in more than nine years and I enjoyed the experience.

On May 28, I received a notice from a law office that represented Children's Hospital. They were demanding payment of $12,173.05. I called the hospital immediately. My parents had just paid out a settlement on this bill in April. The hospital rescinded the request.

In June Brian completed an entire round of treatment at UCD, but the EKG showed mild but permanent damage to the heart. The term the doctors were using now to describe Brian's condition was cardio-toxicity. Research warned:

> Mortality, as a consequence, is quite high once clinical signs and symptoms occur. Cumulative dosages are especially lethal in mice and rabbits and children.[12]

We were referred to the hospital in Los Angeles in July for the next round of treatment. UCD sent this communication to Children's Hospital:

> Just a quick note to indicate the enclosed information referable to Brian Perigan. Clinically, he is doing well without any major problems. Since January 1980, he has continued on his 1.6 weeks cycle alternating Adriamycin, Vincristine and Actinomycin-D (2/4, 3/19, 4/28, 6/19). I also initiated 200mg of Vitamins a day as of 3-19-80.
>
> As I indicated in our phone conversation, because of the mild changes . . . we elected not to continue with Adriamycin on 6/19/80. I have suggested to the mother that she discuss with you whether further Adriamycin should be given.

While the doctors worked out the details, we bought the kids a doughboy pool to play in during the hot summer months. I thought the pool would encourage all the kids in the neighborhood to come to our house so I could keep a closer eye on Brian, but before the water could warm up enough for us to use it, we had to return to Children's Hospital.

The hot summer sun and the heavy layers of smog were like a death trap for Brian. When we saw the doctor on Monday, he told me Brian was suffering from the poor air quality but that we were also seeing, in his labored breathing, a deterioration caused by the disease.

Brian understood that the doctors thought he was dying. He told me we should just stop the chemotherapy altogether. He reasoned that if it didn't work then he shouldn't have to take it. He also told me he was ready to die. I could understand how he felt; I had been with him every step of the journey. If I had been him, I would never have endured that many years of treatment. He had been a fighter, but now he was tired. Suffering from intense respiratory distress he just wanted to give up. The doctor spoke to me about needing more time, but I told them it was Brian's choice. After some negotiation, it was decided that Brian would continue the treatment through September. Later that evening, not wanting Brian to feel as though he had been strong-armed into a decision, I assured him that if he wanted to stop sooner, we could still do that.

The hospital ran a series of scans that week and decided to try a different dosage of chemotherapy on July 28. On August 1, new x-rays were taken but the tumors had continued to grow. A decision was made by the medical team to skip chemotherapy in August and prepare Brian for his *eighth* surgery.

As a family we were all glad to hear that the medical team shared our ambivalence about continuing chemo, but now again surgery was our only option. I took a deep breath and asked Brian what he wanted to do next. I wasn't surprised when he said he wanted to go to Disneyland because after all it was Crystal's ninth birthday.

13

A SECOND CHANCE

It was Saturday, August 2, and for some reason that day, Disneyland wasn't crowded. The park was a refreshing round of therapy after another intense week. It seemed like we could never get away from the battle between life and death. It would have been so much easier if only Brian's life wasn't left hanging out there in the balance. Faced with yet another life threatening surgery, we were ready to have some fun.

We had gotten an early start that morning and met our best friends out in front an hour before the park was scheduled to open. The morning was cool and the Santa Ana winds were keeping the smog at bay. All three kids always wanted to go on the same rides: the cars, the train, It's a Small World, and The Mad Hatter's Tea Party, so that is what we did. We left after lunch and got back to my parents' house before the afternoon crowds arrived. We had a good day.

Bob, Bonnie, and Traci followed us home to Placerville Sunday afternoon. It was their third visit to the house. We tried to do something special every day they were with us. The visit helped us forget that this was probably going to be Brian's last summer. We went to Lake Tahoe to play miniature golf; we climbed the mountains to take pictures of the waterfalls. One day we went to the Sacramento Zoo. The five days went by so quickly. On the last night, we just stayed home and enjoyed the outdoors. The adults sat on the deck and the kids splashed around in the pool. It had been a great summer, but it wasn't over yet.

Kevin's cousin was getting a pilot's license that summer and came up with a wonderful idea. His instructor offered to take Brian up in his small airplane. Brian had always wanted to fly. None of us had ever been up in a Cessna. The plane flew around the San Francisco Bay. It was a clear day and the sky was so blue. Brian was so excited, but timid, when he boarded the plane. I hadn't realized that he actually felt scared. I wondered what drove him. How was he able to push on no matter what he was facing?

When the day ended, Brian was all smiles. I was so happy for him. He fulfilled his dream. He had been pretending that he could fly since he was three. Finally, at six he had a chance to see what it was like. Two weeks later, Kevin's cousin came over to the house with several handmade planes. He hung a motorized plane from the ceiling of Brian's bedroom. Every night Brian reminded me that he had been in a plane just like that one. It wasn't long before we had all the planes hanging from the ceiling.

On August 22, we attended the wedding when Kevin's dad got remarried in San Marino. I think all of the family was happy to see their dad find someone that he could share his life with; it just seemed that the timing was a little off. It had only been ten months since Kevin's mom had died and we were still mourning her death.

Kevin drove our car back to Placerville on Sunday morning and the kids and I spent five more nights with my parents because Brian had appointments at the hospital. Early Monday morning Brian began going through a complete medical work up in preparation for the next surgery. His blood work was good. His HGB, (Hemoglobin) was 12.7 and WBC, (the white count) was well over 4,000. The only thing we were waiting for now, was a surgery date.

Friday morning, my parents and I drove back to Placerville in their car. The kids were excited to travel with the grandparents, but I shouldn't have been driving. Emotionally drained, I struggled with whether or not we should go through with the next surgery. I was losing focus. When we first moved into the new house I couldn't wait for my parents to see it, but now the visit felt like something I needed to do for them when I could barely take care of myself, let alone Brian.

During the long ride, my parents confided in me about how sad they were that we were so far away. I had not realized how difficult it had been for them to watch their only daughter move, taking their grandchildren away from them. My parents looked old and frail and my dad had lost so much weight. I felt so conflicted about moving away from them, because while they missed us, it had given Brian a second chance.

When we arrived at the house, my dad tried to tell me how happy he was for us but I could tell that he was just trying to make me feel better. We took them to see where gold had been discovered in Coloma. Then we came back to the house for a home-cooked meal. My dad became very emotional when it was time to leave on Sunday morning. He was sorry that Brian had to face another surgery and slipped a few dollars into my hand to help with the expenses. I didn't realize then that my dad thought he might never see us again. He was that ill.

That evening I started preparing for the kids to start back to school on Tuesday. Everything seemed so uncertain because we did not know when the hospital would call with a surgery date. I didn't really think Brian could go back to school. Any sudden movement left him gasping for breath. Today he didn't even want to get out of his pajamas so his request to go back to school just sounded like wishful thinking.

Whenever Brian felt bad, it took every ounce of strength I had to turn my thoughts back to God. I wondered if this next surgery would really help my child or do more harm to him. I did not have time for constantly worrying about what might happen. With each surgery there was a risk that I might lose Brian, but fear and faith don't travel together in the same company. I turned to scripture. God's plan for our life was not about putting a Band-Aid on our wounds. It was about helping us change our perspective. God had a plan for Brian's life.

"For I know the plans I have for you [Brian]," declares the LORD, "plans to prosper you and not to harm you, plans to give you hope and a future" (Jeremiah 29:11 NIV).

As I tried to let the words sink in, I read a letter written by a dear friend who had become a missionary in Taiwan. She was always sending me something that would encourage me to grow in my spiritual walk. This time it was something written by Smith Wigglesworth called *Spirit Soaked*:

Be filled with the Holy Spirit. In other words, be soaked with the Spirit. Be so soaked that every thread in the fabric of your life will have received the necessary rue [regret; sorrow] of the Spirit. Then when you are misused and squeezed to the wall, all that will ooze from you will be the nature of Christ.[13]

I wanted to be so filled with the Spirit of God that when I was pressed to the wall, all that remained would be Jesus, and so that when Brian left us, God's glory would remain. I had to get this right this time—a complete surrender.

I sat back and reflected on the last few weeks. The summer was over now. As I gathered my thoughts I concluded that even if Brian died tomorrow, I would never regret the move to Placerville because it afforded him almost an entire year to make new friends, play outside, and even attend school. Those were the things that were most important to him.

I picked up the all the mail for the month of August and came across a five-page letter from Rev. and Mrs. Paul E. Billheimer. It read in part:

My dear, dear Penny:

I regret that your letter did not reach us until this week . . . our hearts our deeply touched with your situation. Our daughter had cancer all over. . . . So we know much about the battles you have been going through. I regret your suffering from a certain kind of teaching. I know all about that emphasis.

The letter went on to share more about their personal testimony. At sixty years old, Paul's own health had begun to fail. He had to quit working and move from Indiana to a milder climate. In their new home in Georgia, his wife suffered a massive heart attack, their granddaughter was killed in a head-on crash, and their daughter died of cancer. They endured their share of what they called "deep valley" years. They had truly lived through a life time of suffering. The letter continued:

I trust that the Lord has sustained your faith and enabled you to surmount the hurdles as you come to them. . . . We have had many, many healings in our family, as well. We have also had a lot of hospital experiences. We cannot give you explanations for all that has come. We are sure that Romans 8:28 (And we know that God causes all things to work together for good to those who love God, to those who are called according to His purpose) is absolutely true. . . . Our faith does not always triumph, but the Lord does not cast us off. He just keeps on patiently working with us. Helping us to learn step by step. Please let us hear from you again. In His glorious fellowship looking for His soon return.

On Tuesday morning, I gave in and drove both kids to school. Brian's new teacher met us at the door and assured me that she knew Brian's history and would make sure he was put on the right bus when it was time to come home. Crystal ran off when she saw two of her best friends. Everyone seemed happy to get back to their "real" life. I stopped at the grocery store on the way home and had just finished putting all the food away when the phone rang. The call came from UCD; they told me they could handle Brian's next surgery, but if I felt more comfortable at Children's I should call

Brian's doctor right away. I called Children's Hospital, and the surgery on his left lung was set for September 9. My parents had company coming during that week, so I made arrangements to stay with my father-in-law and his new wife, Helen. By the time the kids got home from school, I had the car packed and was ready for an early morning departure.

During the drive I talked to Brian about the next surgery. We had always tried to be optimistic, because we never knew what God might do next. There had always been the hope of an intervention or a new drug or new procedure, but in reality, most of the time we were only handed one option at a time. Brian never questioned me, God, or the doctors, but just resigned himself to the inevitable.

I thought about Job, when pressed to the point of being crushed, he called out to God, "Have I sinned? Have I erred in my ways?" Job never loses hope, but, finally, in so much pain he says:

At least there is hope for a tree; if it is cut down, it will sprout again . . . . If a man dies, will he live again? All the days of my hard service (struggle) I will wait for my renewal to come (Job 14:7, 14 NIV).

Job sent a clear message. Even when it looked like everything was going downhill . . . there was still hope. I too, still placed my hope in him.

Thursday morning, I took the kids to the Prayers and Share Meeting at Melodyland Christian Center (a Charismatic/Pentecostal church—1969-2003) located across from Disneyland. It had been a theater in the round until Pastor Ralph Wilkerson turned it into one of the largest and most influential churches in Southern California. It had over 10,000 members.

That morning, Rev. Ralph Wilkerson announced that they weren't going to minister to individual needs but that God would minister to the whole body of Christ. We were just one of the many broken people there, hoping to be prayed for. The last word the doctors had said to me was that there was little hope. My heart had sunk and I needed God's help today. Now, Lord! Right now!

The assistant pastor walked down our aisle and before I knew it we were on the stage. I did not know how we got singled out that morning. I had not talked to anyone about Brian. But however it happened, just the acknowledgement of our suffering was comforting.

When the pastors prayed to heal this stubborn illness of cancer, my son believed God would heal him. I only felt resolved because I had come to a place where I accepted an eternal healing, and not just a temporary physical one.

In the face of so much pain, knowing Brian was going home soon, death was something that I was growing to welcome. We have purpose, there is a plan, but when he calls us home to our final destination, we need to be ready to go. If Brian's earthly body failed him, he would be rewarded by having more time in the presence of Jesus than we had.

Lately, the songs we listened to at home had more to do with leaving this earth than living in it. The kids loved to sing a song entitled "I Am Only 4 Foot 11 But I Am Going to Heaven" by a young Christian artist known as Evie. The words raised my children's spirits and made them feel "ten feet tall." Watching them perform as they sang along with the music used to make me laugh, but the closer we got to yet another surgery; it only made me feel sad.

Evie Tornquist had introduced a new song on an album called *Never the Same*. The song, "Special Delivery," written by Carol and Ron Harris, was one that Brian picked up on the first time he heard it.[14] Brian sang the song with such conviction that I believed, even at such a young age, he knew where he was going and held no fear at all when it came to dying. In his honor, I hoped that we would choose to celebrate with him when God took him to heaven.

On Friday I called friends and asked them pray because the hospital had called with an unusual request; they wanted to re-do all of Brian's testing. I rallied my thoughts and hoped for a miracle. Maybe the new tests would show that the cancer was gone.

The day of testing was difficult to watch as Brian suffered through one grueling test after another. Finally, a group of interns came in to measure his blood gases to see if they were within normal range. It is a painful procedure, but done quickly. A sample of blood is taken from the artery located at the wrist. The site is numbed, the artery found and then a large tubular needle is inserted. However, the new interns could not find the artery. When they held him down Brian was frightened. They repeatedly stabbed at his wrist; blood was everywhere. He had three large gashes in his arm. He cried out and then whimpered, "Please, help me."

I struggled to make my way to my child. I cradled Brian when it was over. I was stunned when a student walked over and thanked me for calming Brian down, patting my back. We left the room and walked into the cardio clinic for the last test of the day, a stress test. Without Brian having to say a word, I knew it had been a very bad day. All day long he never asked to go to the classroom. I had to carry him back to Outpatient Clinic.

It was after 5 PM before all the results came in. The doctor dismissed signs of liver and kidney dysfunction, understated the "mild" damage to the heart but said that the x-rays revealed two tumors on the left lung. Two tumors were all they could see, but there could be more. Brian was cleared for surgery on Tuesday morning.

Once again I had hoped for an easy way out, but I knew if God had not made a way to skip the surgery, then he would make a way for us to endure it. He was still God; he had not forgotten us. I focused on all the times before when he had brought us through the battle.

Over the years there had been many miracles. Brian had lived for years, not just a few months. It was God who intervened so that we now had a beautiful home in the foothills. Brian's arm was functional, and his personality had been unchanged by the cancer. He was funny, sweet, and forgiving and he was still able to accomplish many of the things he wanted to.

I took some time to explain to Brian that the students were learning how to do procedures and sometimes they made lots of mistakes before they got it right. Then we had to talk about the prayers for healing. I had to tell Brian that although we always pray that God will make us whole, just like Jesus we must never forget that we want God's plan for our lives.

Early Saturday morning, Kevin flew into Ontario airport. The kids and I picked him up and then we drove straight to Disneyland. "Another trip to the park" was the prize we gave ourselves after enduring a very bad week. Brian didn't need a wheelchair this time and he wanted to stay all day. It was the highest his energy level had been for a while. Seeing him laugh and play was always good for me. At night we drove to our friend's house in Rowland Heights, and while the kids stayed with a sitter, the adults went to dinner. After much discussion and prayer, we went to bed believing God would provide all that Brian needed.

On Sunday morning, I did not want to attend church when our friends mentioned there was going to be a miracle service at Melodyland. "Lord," I prayed, "I only need you." I didn't think I could take going through the prayers for healing again. And yet under pressure, I surrendered, and we all went to church.

When Rex Humbard and Maud Amy took the stage they told the congregation that the Lord had told them not to hold the miracle meeting that had been planned for that morning. Instead, Rev. Rex Humbard simply talked about trusting the Lord in all of our circumstances. This was what I needed to hear.

Later in the service, though, Brian and I were called up to the platform for prayer. Rev. Humbard prayed for us individually, that we would have courage because God knew our pain and he cared. If I had not gone that morning, I would have missed the blessing. Humbly, I told the Lord I was sorry I hadn't wanted to come. When would I learn to *always* trust him? God had heard the cries of my heart. I was overwhelmed with gratitude.

The admissions office kept us waiting for a room until 11:30 PM on Sunday. Everyone was hungry, so Kevin drove to McDonald's just before they closed at midnight. When Brian saw the Happy Meals, it reminded him of parties we'd had at McDonald's. He thought we were having a party at the hospital. I wondered if we were celebrating Brian's last moments on earth. As soon as we finished eating, Brian went right to sleep and Kevin and I left the hospital.

On Monday morning back at the hospital, all of Brian's food and drink had been suspended. There had been an opening in the schedule for an afternoon surgery and our surgeon took it.

On September 8, the surgeon came into the room to tell us that he thought Brian's *eighth* surgery, a thoracotomy to remove metastatic lesions on the left lung, would only take an hour. We sat in the room waiting for the nurses to take Brian upstairs.

Brian was restless. It was after noon when he was wheeled into the operating room. He had been awake for more than six hours without any food or drink. The long wait had only elevated his anxiety level; all of his previous surgeries had taken place in the morning.

Kevin and I felt numb as we entered the ICU waiting room. We had been through this cycle so many times; hoping for a miracle, accepting the surgery, waiting to see if Brian lived through it. I sat on the bench, not praying, not searching scripture. I felt I could do nothing more than hold on until it was over.

It was at that moment I noticed that there was a woman sitting next to me reading her Bible. She took my hand. We talked for five hours about the fullness of Holy Spirit. The time flashed by. A nurse startled both of us when she came in to tell the woman that her son had been moved to the Intensive Care Unit. She quickly gathered her things and we hugged goodbye. I waited eager to hear something.

At 6 PM, a very tired surgeon came in to tell us that Brian had made it through the procedure, but they had found three tumors instead of two. The first two were removed easily but one was involved in the chest wall and they couldn't get all of it out. When he said that Brian had made it, I didn't hear anything else he had to say, I was just praising God that our son was still alive.

We didn't have to wait to see Brian. The nurse called us into ICU shortly after the surgeon left. Brian glowed and looked angelic to me. There were tubes everywhere: oxygen tubes, an IV, chest tubes and a catheter, but all I could see was that my child had come back to me. We sat with him until late in the evening, but the ICU was crowded so we went back to my parents' house to sleep. Their company had gone home and their guest room was more comfortable than the room at my in-laws.

Kevin and I were thankful Brian survived. That night we reflected on our spiritual journey. It wasn't something we did very often, but it was obvious that the attacks had only made us stronger.

The next morning, Brian was heavily sedated and struggled to breathe. For four long days and nights, we watched as Brian lay drowning in his own fluids. I didn't panic at first because we had been through this before, but when the intern added more fluid to unblock the drainage tube and did not pull the fluid back out, I went to get help. Unplugging the tube was finally accomplished when the surgeon came in during rounds, but the pain Brian went through was unbelievable. They had to take more than twenty-seven x-rays to determine the right position for the drainage tubes. Then fever set in, and the lung collapsed several more times. There were more blockages, and even with Brian heavily sedated, we could see his mouth move as he tried to cry out. No one thought at that point that Brian would be able to recover. Had we prayed that Brian would come back to us at any cost? Was this all our fault?

At the end of the fourth day, we were losing hope. The nurses moved Brian's bed to a far corner with two chairs so we could be with our son. All we could do now was to wait and see if he stabilized. We were feeling pretty low when Rev. Kemp from Melodyland and his wife dropped by to pray for us. Just a prayer and a few kind words eased our anxiety and we felt a blanket of peace falling all around us.

An intern came in to tell us the latest x-ray showed another blockage. I just sighed and watched him flush out the tube. The tube began to drain immediately and Brian's fever and pain went away. By nightfall he was able to take deep breaths and was moved into a semi-private room on the third floor. Everything turned around with a simple prayer to an ever present God.

I asked Kevin to stay with Brian while I went back to my parents to pick up a few things so I could spend the night with Brian. I had so much on my mind. The doctors were talking about keeping Brian hospitalized for the next three to four weeks, so that they could start him back on radiation therapy. Some of the interns had mentioned that they would be combining the chemo and radiation together. Brian was so frail that I thought these were drastic measures. I needed a break so I could have time to think about what our options were.

It was after 10:30 PM before I left the facility, too late for me to be alone in the parking garage. I walked quickly to my car, but there were two men leaning against the driver's door. "Oh, Lord, what is this? Am I in danger?" One of the men grabbed my arm. He demanded to know what I thought of the hospital. "Is this the best one?" As he held me in place I didn't feel scared, I just felt drained. I told him "Yes, it is the best hospital." He asked me the same question again, shaking my arm this time. By now I was having a serious conversation with the Lord. I was thinking that, *I'm too tired for this!*

When the man finally let go I unlocked my car and got in. I put my Bible on the passenger seat. And I heard God's voice. "That man has a problem. Won't you help him?" "Ok," I said, and got out of the car. "Do you have a baby here?" I asked. The man's friend looked so surprised; how could I know that? I ignored him. I talked directly to the man who had so much pain. He cried when I asked him if I could pray for him and then I hugged him and got in my car and left. Had God used me when I had nothing to give? I praised Him for letting me bring some comfort to that man's heart.

As a new Christian I had praised God for the basics: food, shelter, and clothing. As I grew in faith, I learned to praise him because he walked with me through the valleys. But just as I had witnessed in Corrie ten Boom, there was a deeper praise that rises up in the midst of our suffering that took Corrie to her knees, had Job cling-ing to hope, and caused Stephen to lift his eyes to heaven.

Lesson 8: *Instrument of Praise*

There is praise in all of us even when we feel isolated, suffer in pain or face our toughest enemy. This praise is not limited by our circumstances because it goes beyond that. When our eyes are on him and we stay focused, our soul rises up to meet every battle and only then do we begin to learn that it is the battle itself that causes all the distractions to fall away and leaves you naked before him. And as you approach the throne of glory the only thing left is praise; in the purest form.

It no longer mattered what our circumstances were, praise wasn't really what we did when we received a blessing. God never had to earn our praise. He had always been worthy to receive it no matter what our situation was like here on earth.

I got to my parents' before 1 AM and fell asleep as soon as I hit the bed. I didn't return to the hospital until early the next morning. As soon as I arrived, I told Kevin how sorry I was about my long absence, but he said he thought I had needed the rest. I told him to take the car and spend the rest of his time in Los Angeles with his dad; I could handle whatever the day brought.

14

THE RONALD MCDONALD HOUSE

On September 14, Brian was discharged to the new Southern California Ronald McDonald House (RMH). It would be our home for the next four months. The House was originally scheduled to open on that day, but because the project had experienced some delays, the grand opening had been pushed out to October 1. RMH was beautiful and looked finished to me. The House was furnished, a manager had been hired, but I soon learned there would be many final touches that needed to be done before the official opening.

The Ronald McDonald House was built for families who travel long distances and need a place to stay while their child is treated for cancer in the hospital or at Outpatient. The pamphlet described the facility and its purpose:

The Southern California Ronald McDonald House is a two story "home away from home" . . . for a minimum fee of just $5.00 a night. The home-like atmosphere not only provides a safe and affordable alternative to hotels, but it also provides therapeutic benefits, as parents are able to co-exist with other parents who have children with terminal diseases.

The first floor is made up of common areas, which include: a large sunken atrium, a den-library with a fireplace, a living room, a large kitchen, laundry room and an outdoor play area. There are sixteen private quarters located on the second floor with attached bathrooms, closet space, telephones and a television set. All of the private bedrooms have two twin beds and a small sofa bed.

In 1980 Children's Hospital was seeing over 700 children for serious diseases. Since the hospital serves as a base for the treatment of childhood cancers, many families must travel great distances and across state lines for care.[15]

The house manager, Jan, explained that each family was responsible for cleaning their own living space. Upon check out, the bathrooms had to be scrubbed down, rugs vacuumed, and sheets washed and put back on the bed so that the room would be ready for the next occupant. In the kitchen, each family was responsible for purchasing their own food and labeling items before they were put into an assigned storage area. In the play areas, all toys had to be returned to the toy boxes each night.

Our brand new room was completely furnished and very comfortable, but the common areas still needed some organization. Jan, a single mom, lived with her son on the first floor in a small apartment. Crystal and Brian looked after her child, while she and I worked on the House. One morning I wanted to surprise Jan by having everything in the kitchen clean and put away. My efforts backfired; I had used the wrong type of soap in the commercial dishwasher. Bubbles were cascading down to the floor when she walked in. Jan laughed and handed me a mop. She had the perfect personality for the job. The long days and nights that we worked tirelessly on the facility helped me to heal.

Once the House was finished, I sent the Billheimers a quick update on Brian's condition. They had sent me a picture of themselves in their first letter, and in return I sent them a picture of Brian in his blue shirt so that they would remember him in their prayers. I also told them about Brian's renewed commitment to Jesus, and that he was reading his children's Bible daily.

I never heard back from the Billheimers and remain doubtful about whether or not they received my letter. Shortly after they had celebrated their sixtieth wedding anniversary, Paul and his wife, Jennie, ended their television ministry. I later heard that Jennie died in 1982 and Paul died in 1984.

RMH officially opened with a media-covered ceremony attended by Mayor Thomas Bradley and many others. I attended the ceremony and appeared on the six o' clock news to discuss what the opening of the House meant to parents like me, who had children with cancer.

I learned that the idea for the RMH had been pioneered by NFL Philadelphia Eagles player Fred Hill and his daughter, Kim Hill, in 1973. Kim was receiving treatment for leukemia and her parents had no choice but to pay $80 a night for a room in order to be near her. Fred and Kim thought there needed to be a better solution, one that kept the family together.

The Hills were at the facility that Wednesday afternoon to cut the ribbon that officially opened the third RMH facility. Today there are over 338 RMHs in more than thirty-six countries around the world that allow families the option of staying just a block away from the hospital for a minimum fee.

Dr. Stuart Siegel, the Head of the Division of Hematology-Oncology, and Brian's doctor, wrote this about the House:

I can say without hesitation that having the Ronald McDonald House is going to help us give some children the chance for survival that they would not have had otherwise. I really think it will be as important to some children as the drugs or the medical attention I and my colleagues give, because it is going to mean they can get to that treatment and that is just as important as the treatment itself.

It was true that the House meant everything to us. It provided us a place to stay and it protected us from the outside world. As more new families settled into the House we became a very close knit community. It felt good to talk to parents who had faced the same fears and struggles I had experienced. There was a commonality in the way that we talked about and treated our children. Many of us faced the same insecure future, ever hindered by mounting financial pressures.

This new environment also had a healing effect on the children. Crystal had the opportunity to be around other siblings dealing with similar issues. It was important to her to have a peer group that fully understood what it was like to be the "other" child.

But the experience was most important to Brian. He was finally surrounded by children who looked just like him. All the kids bonded instantly. It didn't matter if you were five years old or twelve, you knew what it was like to look different and act different than the other kids at school. They all had experienced the dark side of the disease. They talked openly about blood transfusions, chemotherapy, and surgery. Brian had never had anyone who really understood that part of him. The very best part about being at RMH was that the kids didn't even care whether he wore a baseball cap or not.

The next day, it was time for me to talk with Brian about the next round of radiation. He would be starting treatment that afternoon. I dreaded telling him, but I had already put it off till the very last minute and couldn't delay the confrontation any longer. Brian responded with relief. He was so happy to hear that he was not going to have to re-start chemotherapy. Brian knew the routine at the radiation clinic. He reminded me each time they asked him to do something that he had done it before.

We had been living in the RMH for almost a month and had met many new families. I was surprised to learn that Brian was among a very small group of children who had lived more than three years with the Wilms' Tumor disease, although I did remember we had met one child, in the beginning, who had survived for five years.

Some of the stats I had read said that only two out of ten kids actually make it, but I remember that "make it" only meant they lived a couple of years. When Brian was first diagnosed, I thought we would have a different journey from the little boy with Wilms' Tumor that we had met on our first admit. When he died, Brian's cancer was still considered Stage 1. I was so hopeful back then, but now all I saw was lots of sick kids, living fragile lives with very short timelines.

One day a friend sent us a word from the Lord that said, "Spring will come again." It should have revived my spirit, I wanted to believe it was true, but it was fall now and we still had to go through all of the winter months. Spring was so far away.

During the week the kids and I ate soup and sandwiches, but every Sunday we drove thirty-two miles to church and then stopped by my parents' for a home-cooked meal before we returned to RMH. It was a nice way to break up the week and it gave me a chance to check in on them.

In mid-October, Brian's radiation was delayed. He was healing slowly and the risk of more treatment was too great. I decided to take the kids home so they could enjoy Halloween with the kids in our neighborhood. UCD would follow up with blood work and echocardiograms on October 19. We would celebrate Thanksgiving and a late Christmas at home that year despite the radiation treatments.

I was so happy to be home—but it was short lived. I was back in Los Angeles on November 8. On Sunday I went to church with friends in Anaheim. The message was on financial responsibility. I never heard one word of the message, but when people started going up to make a weekly commitment, I went up to the altar and gave the last $20 I had. It was my way of giving God control of our financial situation. We had been tithing since we became Christians, but I could not manage the stress of unpaid bills, the fights with vendors, and pressure from the hospital. We were starting to receive more and more threats of lawsuits. On that day my giving wasn't about the church or their building fund, it was about me letting go.

Kevin was still working long days and on the weekends. We hadn't bought anything for the new house except for the small pool and swing set. We all wore the same clothes each week. It was my mother-in-law who had always loved shopping for new clothes for the kids, but now she was gone. The trips to Los Angeles took a full tank of gas each way and I was still living on less than $20 a week at RMH. Disneyland was our only splurge. We went shamelessly every chance we got. I hoped the trips would offset any feelings of stress or deprivation associated with our otherwise frugal lifestyle. It was a concern that year when Disneyland raised the cost for one adult and two kids from $15 to $25, but we managed to get free passes on occasion from our church and the community.

At RMH, a few of the original sixteen families were still living at the facility. When we returned, I was disappointed that "our" room had been rented. Sixteen rooms filled up so quickly that we were lucky to have any room at all. I brought in my own cleaning supplies and prepared our new room for another long stay.

On the weekend I worked with the manager to "refresh" some of the unoccupied rooms. Families that stayed in the House were responsible for cleaning their own rooms, but depending on the circumstances and on people's individual standards, there was always more to do. Often when a child died, the House manager and I would just tell the families to leave and we would take care of everything.

One afternoon all the families in the House were given free passes to Disneyland. It was fun going out as a group because for the children there was strength in numbers. It was a great day for my two kids because they knew so much about the park and could tell the others about their favorite rides.

When we got back to RMH that evening we couldn't wait to plan the next trip. The Los Angeles Zoo was just minutes away from the hospital, and for the next trip after that, there was an Arboretum in Pasadena.

I went home for Thanksgiving because I didn't want Kevin to be home alone on the holiday without the kids. When I returned to Los Angeles I stopped by my parents' house. I decided that it was time to start helping them with outside chores, when I saw my mother pushing the lawn mower out in the front yard. They had supported me my entire life, now it was their turn. Neither my dad nor my mother was in any shape to do any kind of yard work or paint the house anymore. I could help them with those things because my visits were so frequent now.

In December Brian started back on radiation treatments. The radiologist adjusted the dosages as needed so that Brian would not have any more problems with burns. But as the treatment continued there were no changes in the size of the tumors. Treatment was stopped. At some earlier point, this might have been devastating news. But at this point I saw the break in treatment as an opportunity to spend Christmas at home. We still had time to decorate a tree and exchange gifts with neighbors.

I was so excited to celebrate Christmas at home and got busy right away writing a Christmas letter to send to all of our friends and family so I could update everyone on Brian's condition and thank people for their prayers and support. On the weekend we cut down a Christmas tree and brought it home to decorate.

But on Monday, December 14, the hospital called and with just a few words dashed all our plans. They wanted us to return to the hospital the next day to redo Brian's x-rays. The team had decided to resume treatment in six days. I was so disappointed because I knew that we would not be able to squeeze in another trip home with the treatment ending the first of the year.

Back in Los Angeles, I tried to make the best of our time at RMH, but most of the families had gone home for the holidays. School was out and there were no other activities. Someone brought in a small carousel ride for the children, but the facility was so new that no one had really given much thought to organizing a Christmas Party at the House.

When the radiation therapy restarted on December 21, the treatment days were sporadic because the staff members had their own holiday parties to attend. Brian had to have therapy on December 23 and on Christmas Eve. Kevin drove down that Thursday and met us at my parents' house late that afternoon.

Brian was not feeling well enough to enjoy any part of the holiday. On Christmas Day, our mood was low. Brian just wanted to be held all day long. We had to help him open the gifts. All he could do was to stare at the new toys all around him.

The next day Kevin and I went to his dad's for an "adults only" Christmas dinner. There would be no gift exchange. The dinner party felt a little stiff, but it was over in an hour. It was good to see Kevin's siblings. We hadn't had a chance to see his brother or sister since the wedding.

Kevin drove back home on Sunday and the kids and I returned to RMH. Brian resumed daily treatments on Monday, December 28, that continued through New Year's Eve. When the treatment ended, we didn't stick around even though the traffic on New Year's Eve was heavy. We wanted to start the New Year at home.

The kids brightened up as soon as they walked through the front door and realized there were presents waiting to be opened, underneath a very dried up Christmas tree.

Brian made a belated birthday card for Jesus the next morning. He wrote:

God is good
Jesus We Love
Happy Birthday Jesus!

15

1981

Both of the kids went back to school on January 14, but Brian's attendance was infrequent. The long bus ride compounded by longer days at school made him so tired; yet he wanted to continue.

With all of his daily struggles, Brian became very upset when he found out that chemotherapy was re-starting in February. He hated missing school.

On the first day of chemotherapy, a cold, rainy Wednesday morning, the roads were icy. We had left the house early, and I wasn't too concerned about getting back home before the big storm hit. I envisioned a very short day with no surprises at the clinic.

The first test at UCD found high levels of toxicity around Brian's heart. The doctors were already talking about stopping the treatment altogether after just two sessions. I suggested that with the absence of chemo, Brian would be able to spend more time in school. The doctor looked at me with disbelief; he thought I had clearly misunderstood Brian's prognosis. He said, "When we stop treatment next month, we are sending Brian home to die. There is nothing more we can do for him." He continued, "If Brian wants to keep up with his school work we should consider a tutor."

I already knew Brian didn't want a tutor; he liked going to school. I tried to explain how workable the school district had been and how his teachers allowed him to graduate each year. Then I said, "Brian wants to feel normal. He wants to ride the bus, sit in class, do homework, and play with his friends." The doctor did not think I was being realistic. He told me Brian's condition would only worsen, his days would become difficult, and he would probably never even get to return to school. The words hit me in the face. They were so harsh. I hadn't realized that this was what the end of life looked like. I relented a little, not wanting to fully give up all hope. I told him that on "bad days" we would agree to have a tutor. Brian looked stunned. Was I fighting with his doctor? He shook his head in agreement with me, a little too enthusiastically. He would agree to have a tutor only on "bad days."

On February 11, 1981, Brian's doctor wrote this note to the school district and handed it to me to give to them when I was ready. He had always been so kind and just wanted me to hear the truth. As he left the room, he smiled and said, "I'll see you next month."

> I have seen and examined Brian. I feel that it is necessary and helpful for Brian to be tutored. I understand that the school's teachers and parents are trying to work out a program, in having him in part-time school attendance. I feel that this should be encouraged. Thank you.

When we had finished with the infusion clinic and walked out into the parking lot, I could see thick white clouds sitting just above the foothills. I didn't know they were snow clouds.

I was quiet on the way home thinking about what the doctor had just said. "We are sending him home to die." Brian is dying! I knew that! But it hadn't registered that he was dying right now. Was the doctor trying to tell me it was time to give up?

At an elevation of just over 1,000 feet, outside of the city of Cameron Park, the light covering of snow was beautiful. As we got closer to home, I thought it was strange that there were no cars on the road. Then suddenly, my car slid into a ditch. I was traveling with a sick child, who had just gotten a dosage of chemotherapy and had a weak heart, in below freezing temperatures. I got out of the car and checked for damage. The car was fine, but it was embedded in the snow. We were stuck on the hillside of a back road, ten miles from home. We were not prepared: no heavy coats, no boots, no blankets or water. I didn't own any tire chains or have snow tires on my car. I didn't even realize that in this type of terrain I needed front wheel drive.

In minutes, a fire truck pulled up and took us to a local fire station. Brian was so excited about the rescue and couldn't wait to see the fire station. As soon as we arrived at the station, I called my neighbor and asked if she could come pick us up. She had lived in the area all her life and knew how to handle every situation. I was surprised when she told me the roads were blocked and even she couldn't get out. At home we had six inches of snow. I had just called Kevin at work to ask him to pick us up when a fireman flagged down a school bus to take us home. The storm had been so severe that it closed down the town for the remainder of the week; no one went to work or school or had treatment for the rest of the week. It was the last trip I took in the snow without the proper equipment. From then on I traveled with chains in the trunk year-round. We weren't in Southern California anymore.

Over the next few weeks the doctors' prophetic words came true. Brian started growing weaker each day. He tried to attend school on March 2. Determined to ride the bus, I let him make his own decision about returning to class. He assured me he would be okay; but he wasn't. His teacher told me that Brian had begged her not to call me, but she knew something was wrong. I got in the car and drove straight to the school to pick him up. He was smiling when he saw me, but we both knew he was just pretending that nothing was wrong, saving face in front of the other children. I told his teacher we would be working with a tutor for the rest of the school year.

Brian held his chest all the way home. It scared me to see him like that. I kept telling myself that this is what it is going to be like. He will not be able to go outside, he will stop eating, and he will lose control of his body functions and will probably get to the point where he doesn't even recognize me. I had to wake up and realize that this was my new reality.

Two weeks later UCD made one more attempt at treating Brian's cancer with chemotherapy. When the x-rays came back and it looked like the cancer had continued to grow, they called Children's Hospital and told them there was no benefit in any further treatment.

Brian did well once he recovered from that last round of treatment. We fell into a normal routine of having his classes at home. I was finally able to catch up on a few things that we had ignored since Brian had gotten sick. The kids got their first haircuts and dental exams in a long time. I was surprised when the dentist told me that most kids with cancer lose their teeth because the drugs are so toxic. I felt very thankful that Brian and Crystal had no decay.

Each week we followed the same pattern. We did grocery shopping on payday Fridays, trips to Tahoe on Saturdays so the kids could play briefly in the snow, church on Sundays, and during the week days after the tutor left, they played indoors with the neighborhood kids.

We were just settling into a life that embraced death by cancer when I got a letter from my mother. It was odd to get a letter, when I was just a phone call away. The letter was depressing. She was at the end of her rope. My dad had gotten very ill and she was taking him to the VA Clinic in Long Beach several times a week. He had told her that he wanted to die at home, but she was a nurse and would not allow it. Toward the end of the letter, she said she had not been feeling well either. She blamed her lack of energy and recent falls on the fact that she was so worried about my dad.

When I called home, my dad answered the phone and in a cheery voice said he was fine. My mother got on the phone and told me he was going in for surgery on the May 26. He had Stage 4 colon cancer. She also mentioned that she was going to delay her own biopsy, which would confirm that she was not just overly worried about my dad but in fact had non-Hodgkin's lymphoma. I told her I would come home on May 28. Brian had become so weak that Children's Hospital wanted to run some more tests.

Inundated with so much bad news, I again felt the power that cancer had over all of our lives.

Brian's first grade teacher sent out a quarterly report card that month. I was apprehensive about showing it to Brian before we left, but he had already noticed that the mail was for him. We opened it up together. I explained to him that since he had not been able to attend school every day like all the other children, I was sure his teacher would take off some points for that. He dismissed my explanation because he was used to getting good grades no matter what was happening in his life. Brian just wanted to read the last few lines, where she had projected that he would "pass into second grade without any problems," but I started at the beginning. His teacher wrote:

Brian is a very high achiever academically. His skills in all areas but language are above average. His language skills show steady progress. He is showing good improvement in developing peer relationships and will take part in group activities. He has adjusted well in all areas.

He was so proud of the good report that he handed it over to his new tutor, Nancy, as soon as she walked into our house. Nancy had made an easy transition into Brian's world, even though he gave her a hard time on the first day, reminding her that she could only come if he couldn't make it to school. Nancy understood and was willing to come only when he really needed her—which turned out to be every day.

Nancy worked with Brian's teachers so that he completed the same tasks as his first grade class. He was able to run through most of the weekly assignments in a day or two and spent the rest of the time doing art and crafts. Brian still loved homework and begged Nancy to leave him an assignment. He also loved that his homeroom school teacher remembered to call and invite him to parties and field trips despite the fact that he never felt well enough to go.

As we waited to hear from the hospital, I started experiencing feelings of ambivalence again. There were moments when I felt relief at the thought that if we really stopped all the treatment, I could put all my energy into making Brian's last days comfortable. But just like all the crossroads we had been forced to face in the past, thinking about doing nothing and letting Brian die left me feeling like I was giving up the fight. I prayed that the "breastplate of righteousness" might guard my heart in this battle too.

We spent three long weeks at Ronald McDonald House. It was all too much for me to handle. Brian's testing during the week continued to confirm that he was nearing the end of his journey. On the weekends, I took my mother to Veterans Hospital to see my dad. He was not eating and losing massive amounts of weight. The thought of losing my father was too much for my mother and she needed so much support that it was physically and emotionally exhausting.

My last Sunday in Los Angeles happened to be Easter, but none of us stopped the routine to go to church. It was only my mother who remembered to mark the occasion by stopping at the store to purchase two small Easter Baskets for the kids after we had spent the day at the hospital with my dad. The kids had to stay outside my dad's room in a waiting area and entertain themselves. Those long days were hard on everyone.

Brian had started to play around with words that rhymed and wrote this silly poem about Easter:

I think Easter is nice.
I want to know, do mice?

He and Crystal had entertained themselves that day by drawing several Easter pictures to give to their grandparents.

Monday, Children's Hospital finally determined that in fact the tumors in the lung had not grown since the last chemotherapy treatment. They were not sure why Brian's pain had increased but thought that scar tissue might be involved. The doctors wrote out a prescription for painkillers. Brian needed them daily now.

I stopped by my parents' house before we headed back home to Placerville, because my dad had been released from the hospital. He had lost more than sixty pounds and his black hair with some gray was now pure white. He was angry with me because I had not come to the hospital to see him. When I told him I had come every weekend, he could not remember my visits. My mother tried to tell him that he was heavily sedated and sick from the chemotherapy and simply could not remember, but he still insisted I never came. I was pretty shook up when I left. I believed he would never forgive me for not being there for him, even if it wasn't true. It was a terrible way to end the visit. I had never known my dad to be confused about anything. When I started to leave, he tried to tell me not to worry about it; he knew I had a lot on my mind. In tears, I hugged him and said good-bye.

On April 21, I was heading home to plan Brian's seventh birthday party. I only had a week to plan the "last" party. Torn in so many directions I tried to focus on all I had to be thankful for. Dad was back at home, Brian was feeling better, and the party came together with little effort.

I invited Brian's first grade class and all the neighbors to the party, but I was shocked when they all showed up! I had ordered ten pizzas, but it wasn't enough. I could only hope that the ice cream and cake would fill everyone one up.

On Brian's seventh birthday the change in his appearance was remarkable. He looked good—tall with a full head of dark brown hair. Even on pain medication, he did a great job as the party's host at Chuck E. Cheese. He and his guests played games and won prizes. It was a great day thanks to the party planners at the pizza place.

On Sunday the party continued. Brian was all smiles when our Placerville family and friends came over for a potluck and birthday cake. Brian loved all the attention he received.

When Kevin's cousin Julie arrived, she came prepared with notebook and camera. She had called several days earlier to see if it would be okay for her to take a few pictures of Brian and ask him some questions for a death-and-dying project she was doing for one of her classes. Normally a birthday party might not have been the best time for such a grim subject, but we were rarely home.

I had checked in with Brian to ask him if he minded answering a few questions about dying. The topic had become so common place in our home that he thought nothing of it. He acted like a ham during the pictures and talked casually about his life experiences. And Julie kept the conversation fairly light. The discussion about death with my seven-year-old was probably harder on her than it was on him.

Brian never liked to spend much time talking about how sick he was. After fifteen to twenty minutes he was ready to do something else. He started looking for a way to excuse himself. He finally ended the interview abruptly by saying, "I am very sick and will probably die from cancer, but today is a good day, so I am going to go play."

When Julie talked to Crystal, she just repeated what Brian had said: "Everyone dies." When Julie asked how she felt about it, she answered "I don't know" and also ran off to play.

The pictures taken and answers gathered from both kids made Brian's seventh birthday that much more memorable. When Julie asked Brian to fill in the blanks, he said:

Brian, what is your favorite color? _______*blue*_______

What do you want to be when you grow up?___*a doctor*___

What do you like to do?_____*ride my bike*_________

What is the worst thing that has ever happened to you? _____*fighting with my sister*____________

Who is the strongest person you know? ____*Jesus*____

Who do you want to meet? ___*Jim Bakker and the guy that plays the American Hero*_______

Who is the luckiest person you know? _____*me!*_______

I was amazed by Brian's strong character and ability to cope with his hardship. What we learned from that day was that Brian had indeed, embraced the life he was given.

16

MY HERO

In May, I let Brian go back to school. His blood count was within normal range now, and it was surprising how much energy he had. Thankfully, Brian's experience that month was straightforward. I know because that year, after he turned seven, he started keeping a journal. His first week's entries went like this:

- **Tuesday, May 26**—Went to the store and bought food and clothes. My favorite shows are: *The Jeffersons, Little House on the Prairie, Love Boat, Family Feud, Sesame Street, and Mister Roger's Neighborhood.*
- **Wednesday, May 27**—Ate breakfast and my sister and me were playing together.
- **Thursday, May 28**—Couldn't go to school. Saw Big Bird on TV.
- **Friday, May 29**—Rode the bus to school. It was a nice day because the sun was shining. I had a fun day at school.
- **Saturday, May 30**—Had a fun day.
- **Sunday, May 31**—Outside playing on my swing set. It was sunny.

Two weeks later Brian graduated from first grade with his class. He even attended the school's picnic and played a game of kickball. I had to laugh at my own insecurities about how he would do back at school. He was doing just fine! O ye of little faith!

When Brian brought friends over to the house, it was usually to play with Star Wars action figures. Over the years, he had been drawn to several superheroes that could fly. First there had been Superman and the red cape, then Batman with the radar gun, which ended up with a CPS intervention. Then he fell in love with Star Wars. It wasn't until the following year that Jesus became all he needed.

Early in 1981, a hero was born when a new television series began on ABC called *The Greatest American Hero*. The series chronicles the adventures of a man named Ralph after a group of aliens gives him a red suit that grants him superhuman abilities. Unfortunately for Ralph, he loses its instruction booklet and thus has to learn how to use the suit's powers by trial and error, often with comical results.[16] Brian liked watching Ralph turn his failures into victories, but the most important part of the show was the cape and the music. He no longer used his red cape to transform into Superman; now it turned him into an American Hero. The theme song from the series became one of his favorite songs. *Believe It or Not* hit the top forty music charts in June.[17] We heard the song everywhere we went, even in grocery stores. By the end of summer, it was number two on the top 100 song list, and Brian knew all the words, including the line, "Flying away on a wing and a prayer."

Brian became my hero that summer. He did not walk passively through life, he embraced it wholeheartedly. Nothing ever held him back. And the most incredible part of all of it was that he always expressed so much gratitude about being such a lucky kid.

On June 10, we made the long trip to Children's Hospital for one full day of testing. They knew the cancer wasn't really growing anymore but because there had been so much damage to the lungs, the doctors were still baffled about how he could still be alive. The only thing we had changed in Brian's life had been his diet. We had gone back to eating normal meals. We had tried several new healthy diets, vitamins, and food supplements that were supposed to discourage the growth of cancer cells, but in the end, our experience had been that all the natural cures only encouraged the cancer to grow. I withdrew all the sugar restrictions and we stopped trying every new product that came on the market.

That year, summer brought an incredible sense of freedom. For months there were no daily trips to the hospital for radiation or chemotherapy treatments, we had no pending surgery dates, and there was no need to sequester Brian due to a low blood count.

We left Children's Hospital and started our first three-week long vacation. We were taking a road trip across the United States. We had never been able to take a real vacation, but now that Brian was feeling better, our priorities changed. Having little money was not going to stop us from enjoying the last vacation we would ever enjoy as a family, I would just have to be creative with our finances.

We left from Los Angeles and drove eleven hours to Henderson, Nevada, and spent a night with one of my friends from high school. Then we had two overnight stays in motels, one in Wilcox, New Mexico, and one near the Alamo in San Antonio, Texas. We rested three full days with my cousin and her family near Houston.

The kids were having a great time. They didn't even mind all the driving. They sat happily in the backseat, making up stories, playing games, and writing songs. It felt like everything a family should be.

Of all the songs the kids composed, "Spankin' Spoon" was their favorite. They sang it for the entire 5,200-mile trip. It didn't make a lot of sense, but parts of it did rhyme. I think they loved to sing it because it targeted me and their dad, even though discipline at our house had long been reduced to a raised eyebrow.

<u>Spankin' Spoon</u>
There once was a little girl who had a big giant pear.
She threw it up in the air and it landed in mommy's hair.
So mommy got the spankin' spoon.
She got a spanking spoon, she got a spanking spoon
   and she ain't gonna spank too soon.

There once was a little boy who bought a neat toy.
   It was a water gun.
And he squirted daddy and boy did his daddy run.
Then daddy got a spankin' spoon.
He got a spankin' spoon, he got a spankin' spoon
   and he ain't gonna spank too soon.

For some reason the kids thought it was hilarious when I pleaded, "No, not again." And much to my chagrin, they would sing it again and again.

As we continued to drive through Texas, a news reporter on the radio kept repeating a tragic story using words that rhymed. Brian decided to write about it in his journal:

<u>El Paso</u>
There was a fire in downtown El Paso at 10:45 this morning.
Eight people were killed.
A baby died,
The parents cried.
But it was hot outside, so it would have died anyway.

On the trip he wrote several poems:

<u>Vacation Time</u>
Vacation time is fun. Fun for everyone.
You see trucks that go by. You see mountains that are high.
You see a horse and see a cow. Soon I gotta go. Bye now.

<u>A Family</u>
Can be a mother, son, and a daughter,
Or a mother, a father, and a son, and daughter.
God made it so any kind of relative of yours would
   be one happy family.
And don't forget God is part of our big happy family too.

And a short story:

What Was That?

One cold winter night baby bear snuggled down under the bed covers and shut his eyes to go to sleep. Then right in his room he heard a eek and a creak and a squeak. Baby bear sat straight up in his bed. What was that?

From Texas, we took the southern route and drove for twelve hours to Gaylesville, Alabama, to stay with my aunt for seven nights. The long hours in the car seemed to go by so quickly because we were in vacation mode. We arrived at our final destination in Charlotte, South Carolina, on June 22, and spent three nights near Heritage USA.

Heritage USA was a Christian theme park built by televangelists Jim and Tammy Bakker. In 1981 Jim and Tammy dominated Christian Television. Watching their show had become part of our daily routine. Their variety show provided Christian entertainment and helped us fill the gap when we couldn't go to church. They had many popular guests. We heard from Bill Bright one day and Mother Angelica the next. Music was provided by a wide range of up-and-coming Christian artists like BJ Thomas, Andre Couch, and Michael W. Smith.

In 1965 a very young and humble Jim and Tammy Bakker started out on Pat Robinson's *700 Club* doing a children's show. In the '70s they joined Paul and Jan Crouch, creating *Trinity Broadcasting Network* (TBN). The split in 1972 was the beginning of the *Praise the Lord* (PTL) Program.[18]

When they bought Heritage USA, formally Fort Mills, it was over 2,000 acres of raw land. In 1981 it housed a television station, a store, gift shop, and a Christian campground. The fall of PTL happened after the Grand Hotel and theme park were built on the property years later. Jim Bakker famously resigned in 1987 after being charged with selling securities and he spent time in jail before a federal jury dropped the charges against him in 1996 and he was released.[19]

But back in 1981, Heritage USA brought Christian families together around a campfire. We rode a trolley car around the property, and sat through two tapings of the television show.

We left Heritage USA and stopped at a Six Flags amusement park in South Carolina before spending the night in Birmingham, Alabama. Then we drove fifteen hours to spend two nights in Dallas, Texas, with my cousins. We spent our last night in a hotel in Flagstaff before heading for home.

On the morning of June 30, we enjoyed a beautiful clear day at the Grand Canyon. Gazing across the ravine was almost as calming as being by the ocean. It was so expansive. How could anyone fail to see God's handiwork? The entire vacation had cost $700 dollars, but it was well worth it. For twenty-one days the Perigans had been completely pain-free for the first time in four years.

Once we were back home, Brian's pain returned. I tried to keep him busy by planning back-to-back activities because that had seemed to have worked so well while we were on vacation. I thought there was some connection between daily distractions and feeling better. Too much stimulation could wear him out, but just enough could take his mind off the disease and give him a break from the pain.

So, that summer we had many distractions. One weekend, Cecilia, Brian's favorite nurse from Laminar, came up and spent the weekend with us. Brian loved the giant shiny blue dump truck she brought with her and felt good the whole time she was there. Throughout the entire month we had an array of company. It was working. During the visits Brian seemed to forget he had cancer, but when they left he was in terrible pain. I tried taking the kids to the park, roller-skating, and miniature golfing, but nothing worked until the trip to the movie theater.

He caught another break when *The Great American Hero* movie came out that summer. The timing was perfect. Brian pretended to be his new hero for an entire week after seeing the movie.

At the end of that week the pain came back and two days later, we returned to Children's Hospital. On the drive down to Los Angeles, Brian suffered bouts of labored breathing. I was afraid he wouldn't make to the hospital. I turned my thoughts over to the Lord. He had given us a great summer. We had taken a road trip and not had a care in the world during the entire trip. Now it was time to focus on what Brian needed. I knew what my priorities were.

Once we drove into the Los Angeles basin it was no surprise that they were still having smog alerts. When we left in 1979, there had been 234 days with poor air quality. Two years later, there had been little improvement; they had 220 days of poor air quality in 1981. It would take decades to clean up "the dirtiest air in the world." Brian's pain intensified so much that he asked me to pat his back, to help relieve his pain.

On Friday, July 17, Brian's doctor said he thought it would be best if we stayed at RMH until the "team" decided what the next step should be.

17

ALTERNATIVE TREATMENTS

I was feeling anxious when I entered RMH. Brian's situation was so volatile. I ignored the loud voices coming from the kitchen. I checked in and got the kids settled into a room. It was late, but I let them stay up and watch television while I went downstairs to label our groceries. I heard several of the parents mention alternative treatments during their heated discussion. It was something I knew little about. I stayed in the kitchen and emptied the dishwasher.

Years ago one of my cousins was diagnosed with an inoperable brain tumor and sought alternative treatment in Mexico in the form of injections from embryonic sheep cells. His condition greatly improved with the treatment, but I also knew his family had money, so I never considered that there might be similar options available to us. At the hospital there had been some talk about a drug called Laetrile but the general consensus was that the drug did not work.

Laetrile/Amygdalin PDQ/B-17 was a highly controversial (*alternative*) treatment in the late 1970s. Derived from apricot kernels, it was tested in the United States in 1973 and was found to have stopped the spread of cancer in mice but there were rumors that it elevated levels of cyanide in the blood. In 1981 the National Cancer Institute determined the drug to be ineffective; however, Mexico continued to use it as a noninvasive therapy to treat cancer. Today the drug is still known for being an alternative treatment.[20]

After finishing in the kitchen, I decided to join the conversation with the parents in the other room and found that the discussion was actually centered on an article in *The Candlelighter's Foundation Quarterly Newsletter*, a handout for the parents who have children with cancer.[21] In an article written by Scott Berman, "Pediatric Informed Consent Rights," Berman refers to the very high profile case of Chad Green as an example of when Child Protective Services had stepped in to remove a child from the parents' custody.[22] I was shocked to learn that the court had ruled that the Greens had failed to meet their legal responsibility as parents simply because they chose to try Laetrile, an alternative treatment. But even today parents who wrestle with using solely nutrition, prayer, vitamins, or nothing at all run the risk of legal intervention. Talk of the Greens' struggle took me back to four years before when I was questioned about Brian's fall. I had been unaware of the legal authority CPS held during our irritating inquiry.

Chad Green developed acute lymphocytic leukemia at the age of two and began chemotherapy treatments in Nebraska. When his doctor wanted to add radiation treatment, his parents, Jerry and Diana, a deeply religious couple, moved to Boston to check out other options. The parents believed that their child only had a fifty percent survival rate if he continued on traditional chemotherapy. Laetrile was a promising new drug with fewer side effects.

Once the media became aware that the Greens were seeking an alternative treatment, CPS was alerted and the court gained medical custody of Chad and restarted chemotherapy. The Greens fought back and took Chad to Mexico where his condition temporarily improved with special diets, Laetrile, and chemotherapy.

For the Greens, Laetrile may not have been the wonder drug that they were looking for, but in our case neither was "traditional" treatment. Chad Green died on October 12, 1979.

Chad died in Tijuana with both his parents at his side. He was three years, ten months old. Three months before,

Diana Green had stopped the chemotherapy treatments (Laetrile) Chad had been receiving at the Tijuana clinic, believing that God would heal her child. Chad's Mexican doctor had tried to persuade her to resume the treatment, but she would not.[23]

I understand the difficulty the Green's faced in determining how to best treat their child. I, too, had been willing to do anything for my child. If I had heard of an alternative treatment that worked with Wilms' Tumor that might have greater benefits and fewer side effects than chemotherapy, nothing would have prevented me from trying it.

At the end of Chad's life, the Green's chose to stop all treatment and put their faith in God. Many people condemned the parents for this decision, but I understood completely. It is a dire situation because you want to provide the best possible care for your child and yet in faith you must ultimately leave him in the hands of God. I believe that such heart-wrenching decisions are a very personal matter—not a legal one.

Brian was scheduled to have a number of scans the next morning. The doctors had talked about starting him back on chemotherapy to ease the pain but the team had not made a final decision yet.

As Crystal's tenth birthday approached, it did not look like we were going to be able to plan a big summer party for her after all. There was just too much going on. We had been at the hospital for more than a week and more tests were being scheduled. I had hoped it might be an opportunity for me to match the now famous Chuck E. Cheese event that we had in April. But that wasn't going to happen.

On Crystal's birthday, Patti, the school teacher, tried to cheer me up by getting us away from the hospital for a while. She invited us to her beautiful home in the Hollywood Hills for lunch. Brian and Crystal seemed to enjoy the day, but I sulked, hating that cancer had spoiled my plans for a party.

On August 10 through 14, Brian received low dosages of chemotherapy. Then on August 22, I took Brian to another healing service. Kevin told me about a card we had gotten in the mail from a Rev. John Wesley Fletcher. I did not know who this man was at first, but then I remembered seeing him on PTL. My friend, Bonnie, and I went out of curiosity. The address on the card led us to a small unfurnished building in a strip mall where people were lined up all around the parking lot so that this guy could touch them. Everything about it seemed wrong. At one point, Rev. Fletcher walked toward us but I held Brian behind me. After a thirty-second standoff, we left. Brian didn't need a human touch; he had Jesus. What was I thinking!

In September, we were back at home when we heard evangelist Mario Murillo talk on the evils of a game called Dungeons and Dragons. We knew nothing about the game, but the kids were intrigued by the talk of an underworld.

By mid-September, most of Brian's days were bad again. He begged to attend a birthday party one day and I let him go, but he nearly collapsed when he entered the front door of our home. He was in so much pain.

On Wednesday, October 14, when I took Brian to UCD for his monthly checkup I knew something was terribly wrong. Brian's body was cold and grey. His test results revealed that his red blood count had dropped to a dangerously low 6.9. A normal reading was 13. He was sent to the emergency room and given a transfusion. The doctors said he was losing lots of blood but they did not know why. I called Kevin and asked him to come to the hospital, and told him that Brian's condition was grave. I thought the lung cancer had advanced and Brian was going to die that night.

The doctors were convinced that Brian had developed cancer somewhere else in his body but they could not find it. They decided to keep him in the hospital until they could figure out what to do next.

It was happening again. Brian was dying and we seemed to be looking through a glass window, unable to do anything to help. Why couldn't this bleeding just be something simple this time, like an ulcer or the result of a nose bleed? I wondered. Why was it always cancer?

On Monday the doctors ordered a CT scan, followed by a full body scan. Brian had to drink preps and was injected with dyes. The tests found that there were new tumors in his lungs, and that his one remaining kidney looked abnormal. They gave him another transfusion. There were calls back and forth with Children's Hospital, and yet they could not stop the bleeding.

On Sunday, October 18, 1981, Brian lay in the hospital bed bleeding excessively and I was asking God to take him. I feared that the cancer had invaded every organ. He had already suffered through so much. In my glimpses of the future after Brian's diagnosis, I could never imagine what this much suffering would look like.

"Hasn't he been through enough? God, he is only seven!" I tried to bargain with God. "Lord, take me and let him live." I calmed down when a nurse came into the room and finally gave Brian enough pain medication to put him to sleep. I needed a break; I hadn't slept in four days. All of a sudden, living one day at a time had become impossible.

The doctors didn't know what to do and Brian was quickly fading away. All the cancer treatment, tests, emergency visits, and hospital stays were proving to be a treadmill I couldn't get away from. It was time to really let go; I wondered what would happen if I stopped the chemotherapy. What if my decision triggered a legal action? Totally exhausted I could not take this cup too. By the time I had arrived home, I was worn out. God, what do you want me to do? Every pathway looked dark and I couldn't see where any of them were leading me. I fell asleep, wearing the same clothes I had worn all week long.

On Monday morning, I woke up because the phone was ringing. It was one of Kevin's friends, calling to say he had a word for us. He said that God wanted us to trust in his word. Before I left for the hospital I picked up my Bible and read:

Because of the Lord's great love we are not consumed, for his compassions never fail. They are new every morning; great is your faithfulness (Lamentations 3:22–23 NIV).

In the book of Lamentations, Jeremiah expresses that there is still hope in the most difficult of circumstances. God still wants us to go on with purpose. This word told me that God still loved me and had not deserted me. I was thankful for Kevin's co-worker's words of encouragement but sensed there was something else that the Lord wanted to tell me.

Lesson 9: _Sweet Communion_

Being in the presence of God was something that I felt all day long. It was important for me to stay in fellowship with the Lord. I came to him in sadness and with praises. Recently there had been a new level of intimacy in the relationship as I was learning to be still and wait for the Holy Spirit to reveal God's words.

It was October 19, 1981, and we were just one year away from Brian's homecoming when I heard the words that God wanted me to trust. As I sat quietly in Brian's room I felt a presence I had never felt before. Then a lesson was given. If I was going to buy a car, I would not want just any car; the car would be a specific model and color. I realized that when I prayed, I must be just that specific. It was the only way that I would know when the answer that came had been given by the hand of God.

I took Brian's hand in mine and prayed for healing in the name of Jesus. This new cancer was coming to kill and destroy; but it would be stopped. This cancer would come but it would not stay.

I could feel the indwelling power of the Holy Spirit. Opening my Bible. I read:

> If you, then, though you are evil, know how to give good gifts to your children, how much more will your Father in heaven give good gifts to those who ask him! (Matthew 7:11 NIV).

Not even the doctors knew what was wrong with Brian on that day but God had told me that Brian would not die from it. He had given a gift. Ultimately, Brian's life would not be saved. Cancer would kill him, but this new cancer the doctors believed was developing would not be the thing that took his life and it would not take our faith.

Brian received another transfusion on Tuesday and started to feel better. When Kevin came by the hospital after work, I still had not heard anything about the last test results. It was late when the social worker came into the room and sat down to talk to us. It was never good news when the hospital sent in the social worker to talk to the parents. I braced myself because I had already sensed in my spirit that the tests would show a new cancer, and I felt she had been sent in to tell us there was nothing they could do.

But the social worker only talked about her allergies, told me about growing up in Southern California and about her job. My stomach was in knots. She said she thought Sacramento was too polluted and she was thinking about moving back to Los Angeles. I smiled because we had done just the opposite, having moved from Los Angeles to escape the pollution. But I was still waiting for the bad news. Debbie had never skirted around any issue with us so I wondered why it was taking her so long to tell us the truth. We sat quietly, waiting. Finally, she excused herself, and said she was heading home. No bad news. She had just dropped by for a friendly visit.

Kevin left and I settled in for the long night. I wasn't feeling anxious because I believed that God had told me he had already won this battle for us.

After eight days, Brian was discharged from UCD and admitted to Children's Hospital in Los Angeles. Before we left, Brian's doctor in Sacramento told me we were probably looking at a surgery to stop the bleeding. He felt we would be able to make the forty-five-minute flight to LA without a problem, despite Brian's rapid blood loss. Staff made all of our arrangements for the flight. We were scheduled to leave at 7 AM, the next morning, or so I thought.

We had one night at home before we had to head back to Los Angeles. I anticipated a very short trip because I knew God was going to intervene. I packed lightly. I went over to my neighbor's house and asked her if she would donate blood in Brian's name because he had used up so many transfusions when he was in the hospital but she came up with a much better idea. Eager to help, she decided to contact the Red Cross and have a community blood drive. I was grateful that she was willing to take on such a feat but was sure that I would be returning home in a few days to help her.

When we arrived at the airport in the morning it was chaotic. Inadvertently, the hospital had written down our arrival time on the medical flight request and not the departure time. We had missed the flight. Dazed, I handed my paperwork to the woman at the check-in counter. When she saw that Brian was going to Children's Hospital for an emergency surgery; she held a plane that was already on the tarmac. It was an unprecedented call made by United Airlines. When we got on board, the airline flight attendants treated Brian with great care. Brian asked for a pen and paper; he wanted to write in his journal. His entries don't reflect his physical condition, because he was so focused on the flight.

October 24: I am going on an airplane. I might be a little scared but pretty soon I'll be fine. I am going to L.A. because I need to go to the hospital there. I wish I didn't have to do it today but I have to. I don't know how many days I'm staying there. I am 7 years old.

The day after we arrived in L.A., he wrote:

<u>October 25:</u> I went on an airplane, I am fine now. When I got in the airplane I was a little bit scared. My mom's friend picked me and my mom up. I am at my friend's house and I woke up because I went to sleep on my trip from Sacramento. I think I'll be just fine the flight that I took yesterday was my second flight. The first one I went on was a little airplane and I don't think it went as high.

After an overnight stay with friends, and a night at my parents, on Monday morning I borrowed my mother's car to drive into Los Angeles. We checked into Children's Hospital on Monday, October 26, where Brian would have to endure five more long days of testing. Brian suffered through more scans, dyes, and enemas and still the new cancer had not been located. Finally, on Friday evening, October 30, the doctors said that the results from the barium enema confirmed cancer in the colon. I was saddened by the news, but still believed God was working it out.

Brian was released from the hospital that evening. He looked pale and was despondent. I worried his heart would give out while his doctors worried about whether the last transfusion would hold him over until they could get him scheduled for surgery. We spent the weekend with my parents.

I was still baffled by Brian's cancer. Wilms' Tumor follows a specific path, from one kidney to the next, then the lungs, the liver, the bones and finally attacks the brain. I wondered if we were still dealing with Wilms' Tumor or an entirely different form of cancer. I hoped that God would spare Brian from yet another surgery but it was in his hands. I had to focus on what I was promised; that Brian would not die from this cancer.

The next day Brian jotted down some more notes.

<u>November 1:</u> I am at my grandma's house. I ate breakfast a few minutes ago. I'm going to church in a few minutes then I am going to come back to my grandma's to eat some things and then I'm going to the Ronald McDonald House to spend the night.

*   *   *

Now I'm at church, I keep wondering how many days I'm staying in L.A. I'll tell you how I got down here you see when I lived here I had a doctor and he still is my doctor, so how it happened is the doctor called and said me and my mom had to go there. So my mommy ran around the house and packed then we hurried to the airport and we flew to L.A. and that's how it happened.

18

MY BEST FRIEND

We checked into the Ronald McDonald House late Sunday night on November 1. It was quiet and peaceful in the house that evening. I sat in the kitchen and talked with a woman who had recently arrived. She had a son Brian's age, Tony. The boys had many similarities. They were the same size, had mop head haircuts, and both had been diagnosed with terminal cancer. Brian and Tony became inseparable that very first day, and so did their mothers. By nightfall the boys proudly announced that they were "best friends."

On Monday, before I left for the hospital, the House Manager met me in the kitchen with suitcases in hand. She asked if I could cover for her while she was away on vacation. I had some concerns about Brian's hospitalization, but she just handed me a pager and told me not to worry about it. She said Tony's mother, Pauline, could be my back up.

Brian and I endured the admission process, but when the surgeon came to our room he was angry that the surgery had not been put on the schedule. He issued a pass and told us to return to RMH until everything thing could be straightened out.

While the surgeon seemed upset about the delay, I was elated. Anything that was out of the norm caused me to wonder what God was going to do next. I still had peace when the surgeon told me he would have to do not one, but two, surgeries. I did not panic when he explained that the first surgery would be exploratory to pinpoint where the bleeding was coming from and the second surgery would be to fix the problem. I was fasting and praying and believed God for the miracle he was performing in Brian's life.

When I returned to RMH I called my neighbor in Placerville to find out how the blood drive had gone. I had planned to help organize it but she had already done all the work to make it a success. She had made many phone calls to the schools and churches and even handed out flyers. Kandee told me that hundreds of people from the community came out. It was the largest turnout that the American Red Cross had ever seen in the foothills. I was deeply touched by the support of so many friends and strangers. I just wished Brian had been there to see all the people who had turned out to help.

In the morning I called my friend Bonnie to tell her God was going to heal Brian's colon cancer. I caught her completely off guard; Brian's cancer seemed to be everywhere and yet I was only focusing on one spot. I felt certain that God had spoken to me. She suggested that we take Brian to the elders of the church for prayer. I told her I would come by and pick her up.

I had cried out to God at my weakest point unable to endure this next journey and he answered me. I thought about the time when Jesus cried out to God. It was because he was facing something so unimaginable: the cross. He wasn't giving up. He was choosing to do whatever God had planned for him, no matter what it cost him. While I knew that it was not going to be easy I had come too far to allow yet another attack from the cancer to cause me to stumble. God would be our God in our victories and in our defeats. Either way he was still God.

When we got to Melodyland, Pastor Kemp called the staff together to pray for Brian. He anointed Brian with oil and believed that the doctors would work a miracle. Afterward, the pastor took Brian aside and sat with him, talking quietly for a long time.

When we returned to RMH that afternoon, the house was still quiet. There had been no new admits and everything was running smoothly. The hospital called and notified us that Brian needed to be re-admitted so we returned and were in a room in less than an hour. As I was starting to settle in for the long night staff told me that they did not know when Brian would have his surgery because it still had not been placed on the schedule. We waited.

The child in the bed next to Brian was legally brain dead, but the parents had insisted on keeping their son on machines that would simulate life. It was sad because the child had drowned in the family pool. Just hours before he had been a vibrant two-year-old and now he lay on the hospital bed lifeless. His arms and legs were extended due to the lack of oxygen to the brain. I felt that his abnormal posturing made the situation even worse. It might have been easier to accept if his body had softened and he looked like he was resting peacefully.

The parents sat at the bedside of the small boy and wept uncontrollably. They seemed totally unaware of anything else that was happening in the room. I felt bad asking the nursing staff if we could be moved to another room, but the hospital did not find our request unreasonable.

The only room available was a private room. I felt like we had been elevated to a place where Brian would receive special treatment. It was a blessing to have the room to ourselves, but the hours spent in it would not be pleasant ones.

Kevin and Crystal had flown down for the surgery. Crystal stayed with my parents while Kevin and I were at the hospital. I did not want to believe that this surgery would ever be on the schedule, but once again every step that was being taken seemed to bring us closer to the operating table.

The nurses came in to tell us that Brian would need two enemas before midnight, and he would be receiving medication and bowel prep throughout the night. It was a lot for a little guy to go through. He already had limited air capacity in his lungs, a damaged heart, and was weak from losing so much blood. The medicine made him nauseated and he threw up all night.

Kevin left the hospital at 1:30 AM to get some rest. I stayed with Brian until he fell asleep. Again, I wavered, was God preparing my heart for the ultimate healing. I left the hospital to shower at RMH and to put on some clean clothes. At 6:00 AM Kevin returned to the hospital, I came in an hour later. We had fasted for two days, standing firm that this cancer would not take Brian's life. But that morning the doctors reiterated that in Brian's delicate condition we could easily lose him during the surgery. As I paced the halls of the hospital, my emotions were all over the place and yet I knew God had spoken to me.

I was beginning to feel some peace about the surgery when the nurse came in to take Brian upstairs. Brian did not want to go. He looked at me and said, "Mom, we prayed." His words pierced my heart. Then as we were riding up to the sixth floor, he screamed, "Mom, I don't have to have this." I had never told Brian that he would have to endure another surgery. His final words left me broken.

The nurse offered to give him Valium to calm him down. I nodded to her in agreement. I had been so absorbed in my own spiritual battle that I had not given Brian the tools he needed to work through this surgery. Each surgery brought some uncertainty. I never knew what God would do, but I did know that he would take care of us. Like Brian, each time I had hoped that God would intervene and stop the surgery. But unlike the case of Isaac when God provided Abraham a substitute sacrifice, Brian was always the sacrifice. Not even God's loving arms of grace could stop my tears.

Brian underwent his *ninth* surgery that day for colon cancer. The laparotomy for abdominal tumor/probable bowel resection of the right back intestine, lower bowel, took five hours. I stopped the thoughts that ran through my head. There were doubts about a healing and questions of a second surgery but I denounced them. I prayed, "Lord we believe that you are doing something very different this time." I opened by Bible and read:

Turn to me and have mercy on me; grant your strength to your servant and save the son of your maidservant. Give me a sign of your goodness, that my enemies may see it and be put to shame, for you, O Lord, have helped me and comforted me (Psalm 86:16–17 NIV).

I turned to Kevin and he read the words out loud. "And save the son." I praised God, "because Thou, O Lord, has helped me and comforted me." We waited. Quietly, I thanked the Lord that this cancer would not take Brian's life.

Although they had taken Brian upstairs at 7:30 AM they did not actually start the surgery until 10 AM I shuddered when I thought about all the time Brian had spent through the years waiting for the next surgery. He was alone and afraid. This time he was older, he knew the pain the surgery would bring and in his heart he must have felt God had failed him by not taking this surgery away. He had been alone with his thoughts while he waited for two-and-a-half hours.

We had been in the waiting room for seven-and-a-half hours when the surgeon walked in at 3:00 PM. Brian had tolerated the resection well, but they only removed eighty percent of the cancer. Minutes later a nurse came through the double doors to tell us that Brian was awake and was being transferred to ICU for post-operative care.

When Brian arrived at the ICU unit, he was still sleepy. I sat by his bed and waited for them to bring in his medical chart so I could read what happened in the operating room. There was still twenty percent of the tumor in Brian's body and I knew our miracle would not be complete until that cancer was completely gone. At every intersection I still expected a quick fix. I don't know why it took me so long to learn that my way was not God's way.

I sat near Brian's bed reading his chart:

Preoperative Diagnosis: Recurrent Wilms' tumor, right flank, with involvement of abdominal wall and bowel. The operation would be an excision of recurrent tumor in the right flank, with small bowel resection and resection of terminal ileum and right colon, with two anastomoses (connections).[24]

It was felt on physical examination that it was unlikely we would be able to remove the entire mass (an area of approx. 5-6 cm diameter)[25] because it had apparently invaded all layers of the posterior abdominal wall in addition to involving the bowel, (which was left in place).[26] Furthermore, in his preoperative workup a nodule was seen in the right lung which had not been seen previously and is presumed to be metastasis.

The next day, we met with the surgeon to discuss in "layman terms" what he had found. He told us that the tumors had been located above the area where they had removed the right kidney. Two sections of the intestine had been removed, and they only removed a portion of the tumor that had penetrated through the skin into the back.

There were many new terrors this type of cancer would bring to my seven-year-old. Colon cancer had killed my aunt when the breast cancer spread to her colon, and it was killing my father. At the end of life people with lung cancer feel like they are suffocating, but the colon cancer would bring with it more surgeries, forced feedings, and a colostomy bag. Nothing about having cancer was ever easy.

I stood firm believing that God had stepped in and provided us a new morning. When we had become too weak for this battle he said, "Be still." And then he stepped in and fought for us. Some friends insisted that because Brian had the surgery, he wasn't healed. I understood how it looked. But I knew in my heart that when the cancer was gone, even Brian's doctors would confirm that there had been a healing. When others pressured me about an explanation why we were not praying for a complete healing, I knew that Brian's ultimate healing would come when he went to be with Jesus. God would press us so that our oil became pure, but he would not crush us.

Within twenty-four hours, Brian was stable and he was moved out of ICU. For the next six days, doctors, residents, and interns talked about the colon cancer. I listened but continued to resist doubt about where this disease would go. I had heard a message about temptations weeks ago that helped me get through the coming days. The minister said, "Just because thoughts fly over your head doesn't mean you have to let them build a nest in your hair." With all that was going on around me I could have easily wavered with uncertainty, but those doubts were just random thoughts flying over my head. I didn't have to believe they were true. I was standing alone, holding on to what I believed to be true, with a grateful heart.

Brian looked so good just two days after the surgery. All of us waited with anticipation to see how his digestive system would react to the resections. When the nurse came in later that day to change the dressing I got a good look at Brian's wound. The surgeon had re-opened the scar from the first surgery. Four years ago that scar had stretched across his entire body but now it was less than half that size.

On Sunday when the surgeon made his rounds, he was very pleased with Brian's progress. He told us that as soon as the secretion began to run clear from Brian's nasogastric (NG) tube, the plastic tube used to remove contents from the stomach, it would be a sign that Brian's intestinal tract was working again. Before Kevin flew back home, we prayed, thanking God for the healing that was taking place in Brian's body. Right before our eyes the cloudy liquid turned to a clear fluid.

A few minutes later a new resident came by to check on Brian. I asked him to check the vital sounds, but he said he heard nothing from the abdominal cavity. I ask him to try again because the secretions coming from the NG tube were clear. He listened again, and this time he said that everything seemed to be working. He signed the paperwork for the NG tube to be pulled.

It wasn't long before Brian's doctor dropped by to discuss the next step, radiation therapy. They wanted to start destroying the cancer cells that remained as soon as possible. He went on to say that the side effects of radiation to the digestive system were concerning. The nausea and vomiting would be severe, resulting in a loss of appetite. If Brian became too thin it would put an additional strain on his heart. He suggested using medical marijuana (THC), as it had worked so well with other patients. I was open to the idea. It sounded like a better alternative than the opiates that Brian was currently using to control his pain.

I asked the doctor about an order for Brian to have fluids. Brian had been asking for water and the surgeon had said that once the NG tube was pulled, sips of water would be okay. He checked the chart, but realized that there was no order for fluids because the tube had not been pulled yet. We would have to wait.

My parents arrived at the hospital at the same time that Bob and Bonnie did. Brian was looking somewhat cheerful when he saw Traci and Crystal walk into his room. Prematurely, I told everyone how well Brian was doing and that I was expecting that an early discharge would be forthcoming.

My parents stayed with Brian while the six of us went to dinner and then dropped Kevin off at the airport. I knew Brian was in good hands because my mother had been a nurse in the Navy. Nothing bad would ever happen on her watch. As we left, I turned to wave goodbye to Brian, my dad, and my mother. I would bury them in that order. Each one fought a battle with cancer that they could not win.

When I got back to the hospital two hours later, everything was calm and Brian was sleeping. My mother said there had not been any follow-up from the surgeon. Brian would have to wait another day before the tube could be removed and liquids started. Feeling safe, surrounded by people who loved him, Brian had fallen asleep as soon as his grandma started to read him a story.

After a rough start, we were sailing though this ordeal. I knew that not every prayer would be answered in the way I had hoped; but this time I could see God's handiwork. Although my faith in God was not based on signs and wonders, he was faithful. I had learned to recognize the enemy's attacks and knew to stand firm. I believed that he would provide for us, not realizing that even at this level what we really needed and what we thought we needed were two different things.

19

___

A NOT SO
EASY FIX

As Brian slept, I did a little research on the use of marijuana; I talked to staff and a few of the parents. The consensus was that it helped some people with the nausea, but had been especially helpful when radiation targeted the stomach or intestines. Radiology said that the real problem was the wait time to get approval for it; it could take up to thirty days. They also thought that because THC (tetrahydro-cannabinol) was approved on a case by case basis, it was going to be especially difficult for us to get approval for a child so young.

THC was synthesized from the cannabis (marijuana) plant by Israeli scientists Dr. Raphael Mechoulam and Ychiel Gaoni in 1964.[27] It was distributed in a capsule form, but was not approved for the treatment of chemotherapy patients until 1985.

From all the information I had gathered it sounded like it was going to be a long process. We didn't have that much time. I wondered if I could just skip all the red tape and buy marijuana on the street. That evening I hit the streets of Los Angeles looking for a "street vendor." I did not know anything about buying drugs, how much it would cost or whether or not the drug might be laced with something else. And once I was on the street, I never thought about it being dangerous. I was on a mission.

It turned out to be really easy to purchase drugs in L.A. I just walked out on the boulevard and asked the first person I met if he could help me find some marijuana for my sick child. The young man that I talked to told me to meet him at the same place tomor-row night for the pickup. He said for me not to worry, that the weed would be pure. I thanked him, and then we talked for a while. I told him about the process the hospital had to go through to obtain the drug and that I was worried Brian would have to suffer. He was sympathetic and told me that if he was in my position he would do the same thing.

On Monday morning Brian had a fever, dashing my hopes of an early discharge, but with no signs of infection, at least the NG tube was pulled. I hoped the order to start fluids would be forth-coming because Brian was still asking for water. Before nightfall I asked the staff to try to contact the surgeon again, but he did not return their calls. Brian slept while I slipped out onto the streets of Los Angeles with my $20 to fix the next foreseeable problem.

I met my "street vendor" on the same corner and picked up a large bag that literally looked like dried weeds. The man would not accept any money. He simply wished me well and disappeared into the night. I was so thankful for the help; I could not express how much gratitude I had for this dealer with such a big heart. Now my only problem was where do you store an illegal drug? You certainly couldn't take it into a private building, where there were children. I had not thought the process through. I decided to move my car onto a public street and keep the drug in my trunk.

Back at the hospital Brian looked over at me with tears in his eyes, I could just barely hear his faint whisper, "Water." I felt so bad, about not being able to fix this problem too. I was sure there had been some kind of mix-up that delayed the doctor's order. I tried to make it better by offering to buy Brian a new toy, but he just closed his eyes and he fell into another deep sleep.

On Tuesday morning, November 10, at 8:00 AM, still there was no order for fluids and the NG tube had been out now for over twelve hours. When the surgeon came in during the morning rounds he said that Brian's system was not ready to receive any flu-ids yet but that chewing ice would be all right. I mentioned to him that the interns were already talking about starting chemother-apy but he assured me that he would not authorize any treatment because it was way too early for that. Then he left for the day. No order was written for ice. Brian's mouth was so dry his lips were peeling. He could barely make a sound. It was so bad that even the nurses tried to page the surgeon but failed again.

When Brian's hematology doctor came in to order some tests on Brian's heart, I asked him about the ice chips. He said we needed to let the surgeon make that call and again declined to write the order. It was all so frustrating because we seemed to just be going around in a circle on this issue. Brian would have to go another full day without fluids. To add to my frustration, the staff told me that they were too busy to take Brian downstairs for an echo on his heart. I knew that without the test results we would not be able to go home anytime soon.

I took it upon myself to dampen Brian's lips and told him he was getting fluid from the IV and he only felt like he needed water, but he really didn't. I told staff that I could take him down for the echo. Once I got Brian into a wheelchair we went down to cardi-ology. The nurses got him into a room quickly but the technician refused to do the test while the IVAC (a portable intravenous [IV] pump that electronically regulates and monitors the flow of IV fluid) was on a battery backup. I left Brian and went back upstairs to get the electrical plug. Brian cried the whole time I was gone. Fearing that he could cause damage to his incision, one of the nurses heavily medicated him so that he would sleep.

I was so sorry that he had been drugged. Everywhere I turned I was losing control. I left the hospital to check on things back at RMH—I was still covering for the house manager. Pauline told me that one of the little boys with a brain tumor had been rushed back over to the hospital for a second surgery that morning and another little boy had died at the hospital just a few hours ago. She suggested that we clean the parent's room because they would not be returning to the House.

So many things were going wrong and now even the children were dying. I knew I wasn't the only one that was having a bad day. There wasn't a single family in that house that was not experiencing a crisis of some kind. Each death reminded all of us that our child could easily be the next victim. Pauline and I cleaned out the room and then I returned to the hospital.

I could hear the alarm coming from Brian's room as soon as I stepped off the elevator. The pump was indicating that there was air in the line. I looked around and could not see a nurse anywhere, so I ran up the hall to a neighboring nursing station and asked the first person I saw if she would check on the line. The nurse was very angry. "Who do you think you are?" she yelled. "You have upset all the other parents!" I looked around and did not see any parents, but she continued, "You are making me look like I am not doing my job and I won't have it." It was not the response that I had anticipated.

She stomped into Brian's room, clamped off one line, and plugged in another one. While she took care of the IV, I grabbed a pan of water and some towels to wash Brian down. The last intern had used too much ointment, and Brian, still under the influence of the sedatives, was fussing excessively about it. When the nurse turned around we collided, and I accidentally dropped the pan of water onto the bed. Brian cried. He had tubes and bandages everywhere. I couldn't blame him for being upset, but he was making my circumstances worse. I quickly told the nurse that I would change the bed and clean up the mess. She wasted no time giving me yet another lecture.

Once the bed was dry, Brian fell back asleep and I pulled the blue chair in our room over to Brian's bedside. I had not even thought to secure a second chair before nightfall. It was going to be a long night. At 10 PM a resident came into the room stating that he was going to start Brian back on chemotherapy. I told him "Absolutely not!" and as he stormed out of the room he announced that he had a "Chad Green situation" on his hands. Although everyone was talking about the Greens, I had not heard anyone direct such a charge toward any of the parents.

"Oh, please!" I responded in exasperation. I had already been told that there would be no treatment given in the hospital; thereby eliminating any chance of yet another infiltration.

Whatever the intern had touched while he was in Brian's room; upset the alarm again on the IVAC. The IVAC wasn't the only thing in the room that was feeling a little temperamental. When the same nurse came back into the room, she casually mentioned to me that they might have to call Child Protective Services. I rolled my eyes at her threat. Later I heard the nurse and the resident down the hall, commiserating about how uncooperative I had been. I asked Brian if he would pray with me. I had been convicted and knew what I had to do next. After I figured out how to reset the machine the room was quiet and Brian fell asleep. I left the room.

Over the last twenty-four hours I had worked to clean up all the loose ends and bring my life back under my control. When I brought my concerns to Jesus, in his light I realized what a mess I had created. Taking things into my own hands had caused me to purchase drugs illegally, angered the staff, and left my child still asking for ice chips.

I found the intern and apologized. I explained to him that the order for chemotherapy was in conflict with the surgeon's orders. I could tell by the look on his face that my good faith effort had not changed his feelings about me. I walked over to the nursing station but that nurse had already left the building. I figured her response would be similar, but it still didn't matter. I was reminded that the Bible tells us that once you have offended someone they are not easily won over. I had lashed out, a kneejerk reaction because of all that had happened in the past. Quickly putting my emotions in check, I reminded myself that Christ did not die on the cross for my excuses; he died for our sin. Whether I had acted out of something that happened in my past or not it was still sin; resolved by repentance.

Sulking in my own thoughts, I went back to the room. All of my actions had consequences. I retraced my steps prayerfully. In a few minutes one of the night nurses, came in to give me a hug. She told me not to worry, that they would straighten everything out in the morning.

I couldn't sleep and got up at 3 AM to walk the halls. Had I really threatened to remove Brian from the hospital against medical advice (AMA)? I had. For Brian's sake, I needed to stand firm, and stay focused.

I circled around and returned back to the room, a man was guarding the door. Without giving my reaction a prayerful thought I responded sarcastically with, "Perfect!" The words slipped out so easily. The man at the door said nothing, but everything I had said that evening had been documented in the nursing notes.

The next morning, daytime staff dismissed our guard. It was a new day bringing an opportunity to start again. I jotted down a list of questions I kept forgetting to ask the doctor. I hoped a list would help me on track:

- When can Brian have ice? When can he start liquids?
- When can we pull all of the IV tubes?
- What is the earliest we can go back to RMH?

During rounds, there was no need to ask any questions; everything was cleared up and preparations were being made for us to go back to RMH. I decided to get Brian up and walking. Staff was so busy and I knew the routine. Brian moaned when I pulled on his pajama bottoms, put on slippers and switched the IVAC to battery. He was already saying, "I can't, I can't." Walking was going to be a lot more difficult than just getting him out of bed and sitting him in a wheelchair. I told him we would just take a short walk to the end of the hallway and come back. His feet shuffled in slow motion. I felt the pain of every step. But when we got to the elevator he told me he wanted to go to school.

Brian lit up as soon as he walked into the hospital classroom. He joined the other children sitting down at the large round table near the window. He wrote this poem about his stay in the hospital:

<u>The Hospital and Me</u>
When I was in the hospital, it wasn't very fun.
And I was getting shots, one by one by one.

You better bring your teddy bear, 'cause I don't think
you would like it here.
It just wasn't fun.
    By: Brian Perigan

Note from me: I'm in the hospital, I'm getting out of here
tomorrow. I've stayed here for about a week now because I
had to have surgery.

When Brian returned to his room, his surgeon followed. We were being discharged that afternoon, November 11, to RMH for rest and recovery. Chemotherapy would begin the next day, and radiation would follow on November 30.

I thanked him for all he had done for Brian and then signed the discharge paperwork at the nurse's station. I borrowed a wheelchair to take Brian to RMH.

When we got back to the House, he wanted to write. I went down to the kitchen to fix him something to eat.

The mood in the House was very heavy that day because we had lost two members of our RMH family. Pauline was growing impatient, not knowing if Tony would even live long enough to have his next surgery. Waiting for something to happen was one of the most difficult parts of being a parent because you had to leave all of the decision making and actions in the hands of others.

That night, as our children slept, the parents of the House stayed up talking about losing the battle. Despite the fact that we believed our children were at the best hospital, getting the best possible care, having surgeries performed by top surgeons, our kids were dying. Those of us who had been fighting this battle for years tried to encourage those who were just beginning the journey.

Back in my room, I thought a lot about cancer research. I had learned that Wilms' Tumor makes up only seven percent of all the childhood cancers, and that it is caused by genetic changes; affecting one percent of all members in a family. We had discovered that the disease had probably come from my husband's side of the family even though I had thought for years that it must have been my fault. His family had a genetic connection to Wilms' that could be traced throughout several generations.

I wondered why there was so much talk about research when we saw few results at the clinic. All the chemotherapy that Brian had been on was discovered in the '50s and many of those drugs are still being used today.

- **Actinomycin D/Dactinomycin (DACT)** is a polyped-tide antitumor antibiotic first isolated in soil bacteria in 1950. It was first used to treat Wilms' tumor in the '70s.[28]

- **Adriamycin/Doxorubicin** is an anticancer/ antibiotic agent, derived by chemical semi-synthesis from bacterial species. It was discovered by an Italian company Farmitalia Research in 1950.[29] Cytoxan/Cyclophosphamide (CTX) is a synthetic alkylating agent, chemically related to the nitrogen mustards with anti-neoplastic and immunosuppressive activities. Discovered in 1954, it inhibits DNA replication and initiates cell death.[30]

- **Methotrexate/Amethoterim (MTX)** is an anticancer folate inhibitor, discovered in 1947. It was used by Sidney Farber to slow the progress of cancer in 1949. Also used for psoriasis, rheumatoid arthritis, and Crohn's disease.[31]

- **Vincristine/Oncovin (VIN)** is an alkaloid, discovered by Dr. Armstrong in 1963. It is derived from the Madagascar periwinkle and targets all rapidly dividing cell types while having little or no effect on the bone marrow. It inhibits the growth of tumors.[32]

I wondered if it had been the outdated and limited choices of treatment that had caused the Greens to look for something more current in the late 1970s. Today cancer still struggles to be the number one killer in the nation, running a close second to heart disease. According to the American Cancer Society death rates have gone down twenty-three percent in the past twenty-one years. However, many feel that finding an absolute cure is unlikely because there are so many different types of cancers.

- Technology and knowledge have improved the way we treat cancer today. Surgery techniques are less invasive using thin fiber-optic scopes, precise robotic arms, and radiofrequency ablations to remove tumors. Radiation therapy uses x-ray beams, stereotactic radio surgery and proton beams to target tumors more precisely with less damage to healthy tissue.

- Stem cell transplantation is another option if the right donor can be found. There are hormone therapies and biologic therapies that also work to inhibit the growth of cancer cells.

- Chemotherapy agents have been divided up into five classes:

  1. Mitotic Inhibitors disrupt a phase of cell division that uses antibodies and inhibitors.
  2. Alkylating Agents are active against blood-related cancers by damaging DNA.
  3. Antimetabolites interfere with DNA and RNA production.

4. Topolsomerase Inhibitors interfere with enzymes that replicate accurate DNA.
5. Anthracyclines are anti-tumor antibiotics interfere with DNA replication.[33]

Certainly progress has been made, but most agree that more needs to be done. I reached over and picked up Brian's latest poems and then I fell asleep with a smile on my face. My child knows I really do love him.

<u>Mommy</u>
My mommy is nice. She sleeps long.
I love her and she loves me
Because God says to love one another.

By the time I woke up, both kids were already awake. Crystal had been staying at the House since Kevin left on Sunday. Pauline had kept an eye on her in my absence. It felt good for all of us to be together again as a family.

No one wanted to go back to clinic that morning, but we had to be at the lab by 8 AM I agreed with the doctor that we should hit the cancer with all we had since it was now attacking other organs. After the physical, Brian was given the first low dosage of chemotherapy. He wore his hat during the infusion.

After just four days of treatment, we were allowed to go back to our home in Placerville. Treatment would be continued at UCD. The Hematology Clinic in L.A. wrote this note to the UCD:

Brian has started VAC therapy today in order to avoid problems with his GI tract (constipation, ulcers, nausea, and vomiting, etc.) so soon after his surgery; his doses for this course have been altered. We will send meds with him. He is scheduled to begin radiation therapy on November 30.

20

THE BEST CHRISTMAS EVER!

When we got home from Los Angeles, in the midst of a large pile of mail was a certified letter dated November 4, 1981, from our insurance carrier. The letter read:

Your claims have been received after the termination of your coverage. Under ordinary circumstances, benefits are available only for services received during the period of active coverage. We, therefore, cannot provide benefits for this (all) claim(s).

I was dumbfounded. When had our coverage been terminated? I called the insurance company and demanded to speak with someone who could help me. This time, I did not get the runaround. When the agent came to the phone, he had documentation in his hand verifying that coverage for Brian had been terminated in 1977. The agent told me he had been dropped thirty days after his first surgery because his medical bills had exceeded the $35,000 limit in a thirty-day period.

What the agent could not tell me to my satisfaction was why it had taken almost five years for us to find this out. I told him I had been asking about a termination of coverage for over three years and the service agents had always told me that we had coverage. He said only three names appeared on the computer screen and all three of us still had full coverage; Kevin, Crystal, and I.

As I opened up all of the remaining bills, I felt the sting of each charge. Now we were fully responsible. Bills were already pouring in from the last surgery; a room charge of $5,100, a surgery charge of $30,000, consults for $7,000. And I knew this was just a small portion that was owed on just one surgery. There would be additional charges for medication, supplies, anesthesia, the surgeon, x-rays, labs, unknown individual providers, ICU. The list was endless.

I made calls and faxed copies of the termination letter to all of our vendors, and then I placed a call to CCS. Our income had not changed and CCS was already taking the bulk of our money. My CCS worker told me not to worry, but I knew the thousands of dollars that we had already paid out could not begin to make a dent in all the debt we had incurred over the last five years. My plans to sell the house so we could pay off all our debt would never work now. Even if they took everything thing we owned it wasn't going to be enough.

Cancer became even more deadly that day. I already believed it killed everything in its path; but now it was going after things I had not even thought of. It would take our son, our house, our lives, my heart and soul. That deep pit that I had fought so hard to stay out of just kept getting bigger . . . but then I remembered, God's love was greater.

I took a deep breath; we had come so far. We were saved by his blood, buried with him through baptism, and filled with his Holy Spirit. I couldn't let this be about money. This was just another spiritual battle and I already knew that my God is bigger than all my problems. I had learned the lessons: I gave him control, I trusted, felt confident in battle, and experienced his joy and love. In prayer and supplication, I recognized that I could not handle this problem on my own. I stood firm and quietly repeated these words with confidence:

Therefore, I will continue to hold on. I will praise him for all that he has given me, for all he has brought me through and because I know that wherever he leads me I will follow him!

That night, behind closed doors, Kevin and I talked and prayed about our financial problems. He was calm and told me that we would just have to wait to see how it all worked out. We thought we had kept the details of our financial problems private. But the kids could see we had some financial limitations. Brian wrote this story, to show he understood.

Mommy & Daddy

My mommy and daddy are nice. They are still nice if they can't buy me a toy. I know why they can't buy me a toy because sometimes they don't have a lot of money.

I just hoped that we could hold off on our financial demise until Brian no longer needed any more medical care. If I worried about it, I gave it power, so I just let it go. Christmas was just around the corner and I had so much I wanted to do to make this Christmas special.

As we entered into the holiday season, I worked hard on changing my outlook. I had always been so fatalistic on birthdays, holidays, and special events, believing it would be Brian's last celebration. Then the next year I would do it all again. When Brian got a tutor I had mourned the loss of him being able to return to school and then he went back. I was sure our trip last summer had been the last thing we would ever do as a family but it wasn't. I needed to enjoy each day to the fullest. I trusted that God would tell me when it was time to stop.

On November 19, Brian received his infusion at UCD and the doctor sent us home with Thorazine 20mg. It was the drug that made him feel dizzy and impaired his thinking. The doctor told me that it was dispensed as just a precautionary measure for nausea and vomiting.

The next day, I noticed a rash on Brian's face and instead of taking him to the hospital, I drove four miles to our local pediatrician. I was worried that it might be shingles. It was embarrassing to tell the office that I would need to pay cash for the visit because we were having problems with our medical coverage (that was an understatement). When I left the office, I felt so stupid. I had paid $40 just to be told that Brian had a very dry patch of skin, probably a result of the drugs he was on.

Little was said during the consult with the doctor until I mentioned that Brian was being treated in Los Angeles. The pediatrician was outraged that we were traveling back and forth for a treatment that was provided locally. I was reluctant to hand over the phone number for Brian's doctor in Los Angeles, but the pediatrician insisted. When he came back to our room he looked very angry. Apparently Brian's doctor had told him to stay out of it. I agreed with the pediatrician, it might be easier on us if all of our services were provided by UCD, but I still believed Children's Hospital provided the best possible care and I wasn't willing to cut ties with them now.

We had less than six days left at home when Brian's new teacher, Flossie, came by the house and dropped off cards made by his classmates. She also brought a packet of homework that he could take with him to the hospital. Flossie's visit sent Brian over the edge; he was so happy to see her he could hardly speak.

Her visit was a reminder that people in our hometown supported us. Placerville would be where we stayed even after Brian left us. On Sunday I would make a special effort to attend church to thank members for supporting the blood drive. And on Thanksgiving Day we had dinner at Kevin's uncle's house.

As we packed up to return to Los Angeles, I had many concerns. Just one year ago, while Brian was undergoing radiation treatments, we missed having Christmas at home. And Brian was so sick; he really couldn't participate in any of the family activities. Already Brian had become so thin and there didn't seem to be any THC in our future as we were still waiting for approval. I had dumped our stash of marijuana long ago because I could not take the additional stress that came with carrying an illegal substance.

We checked into RMH the day after Thanksgiving. At the radiation clinic, Brian received several new ink tattoos on his abdomen and back, preparing him for treatment on Monday. The radiologist was also growing impatient waiting for the THC to be approved, but nothing more could be done. Radiation began on November 30, and the kids happily returned to the schoolroom at the hospital. I had made arrangements with Crystal's school concerning her long absences, but I didn't bother with all the red tape at Brian's school district. School was important to Brian but whether or not he met anyone's criteria was no longer a concern to me. Nevertheless, Patti, the school teacher at Children's Hospital, insisted that both children continue to work toward graduation. She even negotiated a plan to keep Brian enrolled.

Brian's treatment would continue through the first of the year. Treatment was five days a week, breaking only on the weekends.

Tony returned to RMH. He had recovered from surgery and was at the facility for more chemotherapy. Brian was so happy to see him that he no longer minded going to the hospital if it meant that he could play with Tony in the afternoons.

I thought it was odd that the similarity in treatments and surgeries seem to produce similar mannerism in the boys. They were both soft-spoken, enjoyed quiet play. Their gait was similar, small uneven steps, and they were guarded when they were approached by strange children. They both seemed to keep one arm held up close against their chest and held their heads high as they struggled to breathe. They were both very thin, picked at their food, tired easily, and shed tears when they couldn't keep up with other children. Although they never held hands, they patted each other on the back for encouragement. As they played you could feel the deep affection they had for one another. This friendship was a match from heaven. How great is our God that he would allow my son to have a best friend at the end of his life. Brian explained the closeness of the friendship when he said to me one day, "Mom, he is just like me."

As for me, I missed my new neighbors. In the past year our neighborhood had closely bonded. My next door neighbor remembered to write to me periodically about the everyday things that happened in the neighborhood. She wrote (in part):

Dear Penny:
　　I tried to call you before you left but your phone was busy. We got our Christmas tree and lights are up. Matt is sitting in my lap which makes it hard to write. He is talking more and more . . . .

I remembered how at the beginning of this journey, details of other people's lives once upset me. The normalcy of it drove home all that our family had lost, but now it was different. It was just the type of hometown letter that reminded me how much I missed being at home. I missed cutting down the Christmas tree, decorating the house, making cookies. Then I thought of the many holidays that we had missed when others just took their celebrations for granted. I had to turn it around before I worked myself into a deep depression. What had we gained? We gained insight into the purpose of our lives and learned the value of each day.

Before I put the letter away, I read the last page. It was from the American Red Cross thanking my neighbor for putting together the blood drive in Brian's name. I was reminded of the many blessings we had had that year. I couldn't be sad that we didn't get to have Christmas at home. We could celebrate Christmas anytime. We were not limited to a specific day.

The second week of December, Brian and I were sad to hear that Tony and his mom would be leaving on the weekend to go home. I was trying to stop myself from starting to feel a little jealous about them being able to go home for Christmas when Pauline told me the team was sending her home until they decided what they were going to do with Tony. His liver cancer was spreading rapidly. I had hoped the boys might be able to spend the holidays together, but that wasn't going to work out either. I would miss

Pauline terribly; she had become such a good friend to me over the last few months.

Because we'd been regulars at the House for so long, and because the holidays weren't really shaping up for us the way I had planned, Brian's doctor gave us three donated tickets to a new musical starring Sandy Duncan. Just knowing we were going to see a live production of Peter Pan lifted our spirits, but I feared that Brian's situation was so volatile I wasn't sure we would get to attend on Saturday.

It was late Friday afternoon when Brian told me he thought he would be able to go to the show. I scrambled because we had nothing to wear. I called my mother for help and was grateful when she provided clothes and called her purchases Christmas presents.

The kids didn't fuss when I told them we had to dress up and they only squirmed a little as we stood in line to enter the Pantages Theater. They sat very still as we waited for the show to begin. As soon as Peter Pan came out, flying around the stage, all eyes were on the show. Brian and Crystal sang "I Won't Grow Up" and "I'm Flying" for days. Sensitive as I was about being so near to the end of Brian's journey, I couldn't help thinking that the words from both songs were nothing short of being prophetic.

On Monday, Brian began to feel the full effect of the treatment. He was so sick. He went through violent waves of nausea, stopped eating, and shed many tears. By the middle of the week, the hospital had restricted all of Brian's activity for fear that bouts of dehydration would put a strain on his already toxic heart. The hospital warned us not to leave RMH because Brian was that fragile. Thoughts of escaping to my parents for a home-cooked meal on Christmas were stifled.

The busy Christmas week at RMH was a pleasant surprise since we were literally housebound. Volunteers came to the home and decorated all the public areas and even put up a tree. At night groups came in to sing, dropping off toys and cookies. The carousel that had been placed in the House last year mysteriously returned to the atrium. You could hear children laughing and playing throughout the House.

That week a Christian friend brought in bags of food for us. It was such a thoughtful gift, especially when our spirits were so low. I knew how special each purchased item was because the family that gave the most had so little to give. I appreciated the great sacrifice they made.

That evening the RMH had a wonderful Christmas party. It was an extravaganza compared to the year before, when the House was new and they were still drumming up support. RMH was one-year-old now and had touched the hearts of many. The community responded very generously that year. Santa and his helper, Kermit the frog, came and passed out presents to all the children. Ronald McDonald dropped by with hamburgers and danced with all the children. And then just as the party was ending, several of Brian's nurses dropped by after work and brought him gifts. Everyone had a wonderful time.

The next week, Brian's treatment started back up, and it was brutal. They increased the dosages to the highest level even though Brian was already so sick. I reminded myself that we had already enjoyed the holiday. We had been to see a play that we never would have been able to afford. Brian had been able to attend the RMH Christmas party and even got to dance with Ronald McDonald. We didn't need anything else. But I still called Kevin that night.

Kevin had already made flight reservations to spend the holiday with us. He had planned on flying to Ontario Airport, located 35 miles from Los Angeles where the kids and I would pick him up and drive to our friend's house for Christmas Eve. I wasn't sure how that would work because Brian was not allowed to leave RMH.

On Tuesday Brian was weak, but the radiologist had good news. The medical marijuana had finally arrived. The dark round purple capsule worked wonders. In just two days, Brian's stomach settled down and he was feeling hungry again. He took the pill three times a day for four days and never complained about feeling "dizzy." It was another small gift, another blessing.

Wednesday afternoon, Brian got the best Christmas gift; Tony dropped by RMH for a couple of hours, after a long day of testing. Both of the boys were worn out from their day at the hospital and could do little more than lie around on the floor and take turns pushing around a toy truck, but it was enough.

On Thursday, both of my kids were scheduled for another round of psychological testing, to see how they were adjusting. I thought we should cancel, but when Crystal said she wanted to do the test again, Brian followed her lead. The results were unchanged. Both children were developing within a normal range. I wondered how could these kids go through so much and still be normal. It was the gift I was most grateful for that year.

I was ecstatic when the radiologist thought to cut the radiation dosage in half that afternoon on Christmas Eve. I called Kevin to tell him we would be able to pick him up at the airport after all. We all drove to Rowland Heights, eager to start our family holiday celebration. The kids went to bed early that evening while the adults stacked the presents under the tree. I realized that Brian had so many presents and asked where they had all come from. Bob and Bonnie had spread Brian's story throughout our former community in Los Angeles, many people responded with donations to help make Brian's Christmas special. I was so touched by the thoughtfulness of total strangers. We went to bed and like children waited with great anticipation for what the morning had to bring.

Christmas morning was exceptional, there were so many presents. Brian excitedly unwrapped all of his own presents that year. There were space toys and books, but there was one toy that looked very expensive. That morning a friend of Bob's that worked at a toy company dropped off a new toy that had not even been released on the market yet. The name on the large black box read *Armitron*. Brian was very interested to see how it worked. He sat patiently listening to all of the instructions. He was having quite a time because he wanted to play with everything at once; and the day wasn't even over, there was more to come.

Early Friday afternoon we drove just twenty minutes to my parents' house. They were anxiously awaiting the arrival of their grandchildren. My parents had purchased a few electronic toys and bought the kids new bikes. I told my mom that the new clothes had been enough, but she replied "Your dad wanted to do this." The kids played with talking dogs, remote cars and cats that purred. Brian looked just as excited when he saw the homemade quilt that my mom's best friend had made as when he took the new red racing car out of the box that my dad had bought. He was such a good kid! But there was more.

Saturday night, all sixteen members of the Perigan family had dinner at Kevin's dad's house in San Marino. This time, the whole family shared a meal and took part in a gift exchange. I thought Kevin's step-mother was warming up to the family when she handed out several gifts, but then she mentioned she had bought her family expensive gifts and had bought all of us items at a garage sale. When Brian got tired, we went back to my parents.

Brian wrote this about Christmas when we returned to RMH.

Christmas
Christmas is a happy time. I love running around.
I love Christmas. I love singing songs.
I love Christmas. I love messing around.
I love Christmas!

He still loved Christmas when radiation treatments ended on December 31. But Christmas wasn't over yet. There were still presents under our tree at home and gift exchanges with all the neighborhood kids.

I dropped Kevin off at the airport Sunday after church and drove back to RMH. We were all filled with so much joy there was no room left for sadness. All of our old friends, family, and community had been so kind to our family. Brian looked truly happy. That night, just before he fell asleep, surrounded by a few of his new toys, Brian whispered in my ear, "This was the best Christmas ever." Those were the words I had hoped to hear as I was planning to have Christmas at home. On that day all my wishes had come true. But as I held Brian in my arms, I could feel him slowly slipping away and began to wonder if he would really make it till spring.

21

JANUARY 1982

On January 3, we attended Melodyland so I could thank the congregation for the gifts and support they had given us over the last few years and say goodbye. We would be heading back home soon. The words out of my mouth were thank you so much, but my heart was saying, you won't need to pray for us anymore; it's over.

Back at the hospital I waited an entire week to hear words that said we could go home. On Friday afternoon, January 8, after a long day at the clinic, we were told we could return to Placerville.

At the House I had already washed the sheets, remade the beds, vacuumed the rugs, polished the furniture, scrubbed down the bathroom, and checked out. I had left all the fruit and canned foods on the kitchen table for the remaining guests. I wiped out the kitchen cupboard and cleaned off our shelf in the refrigerator. It was sad knowing there would be no reason to return.

The doctors believed the cancer was still growing in Brian's lungs and colon and there was nothing else they could do for us. UCD would be taking care of Brian's needs from now on.

After a long drive home, I felt frustrated when I got the call from UCD notifying me of their plan to start chemotherapy again in just three days. What? I thought everyone was on the same page that we were all giving up. Once again I felt I was being forced back into that endless cycle of surgery, radiation, and chemotherapy.

I was surprised at the time of his physical to find out Brian had grown another inch. He was fifty-one inches tall and forty-eight pounds; he had lost half a pound. The doctor in Sacramento took the time to review Brian's current status with me. He said he knew the cancer was still growing in the lungs, but it was too early to tell if the radiation had any effect on the colon. He felt that it was not time to give up just yet.

Brian began an eight-day course of treatment in Sacramento on January 11th. On the weekend, Kevin took the family for a short drive to beautiful Lake Tahoe. It was cold, but the water looked iridescent next to its white snowy border. It was so peaceful there.

Deep in thought, I couldn't help but wonder what we were doing? Here we were five years into Brian's fight and still dangling somewhere between life and death. I had been locked into this struggle of uncertainty from the very beginning and was so tired. I wanted nothing more than to hold on to hope, but I didn't want to open my heart up . . . again.

Even the Lord had tried to speak words of encouragement to me that morning:

> Be very strong . . . But you are to hold fast to the Lord your
> God, as you have until now . . . because the Lord your God
> fights for you, just as he promised (Joshua 23:6, 8, 10 NIV).

It was up to me to make a "free will" choice to serve him. I knew that in him all things worked together for good.

The darkness lifted as I looked at such magnificent beauty all around us. My God, who created all of this, could take care of Brian's need even now. Didn't the Bible tell us that God even notices when a sparrow falls out of a tree? He loved Brian so much he had died for him so that Brian could have eternal life. I had nothing to worry about.

Brian and Crystal were already throwing snowballs when I stepped out of the car and I threw a couple back at them. We built a snowman and sledded down the mountain and then it was time to go home. Nothing made Brian happier than being at home in Northern California. He thrived in the fresh air, loved the snow, and played with the neighborhood kids. By nature, he had always been agreeable, but at the hospital he was complacent. I was encouraged to see his playful side return. He still had a life to live. I had written him off too soon.

On the last day of chemotherapy Brian told me again that he didn't want to have any more treatment. I let the doctor talk to him about it. The explanation was much like we had heard before; they wanted to continue the chemotherapy to get rid of the cancer that remained. We all knew Brian's quality of life would be impaired whether he continued to be treated or just quit.

Brian asked me if I thought it would work *this* time. I still did not know. Brian wanted to know if this last treatment had worked, so the doctor ordered a CT scan on January 25, and the next day we were asked to return to Children's Hospital. The results were not good. Apparently whatever was going on now could not be handled in Sacramento.

<u>22</u>

FEBRUARY

On Monday, February 1, I was sitting in a small yellow room, part of the outpatient clinic. We had been at the hospital all day long, waiting for test results. As in the past, I knew that when you wait for long periods of time, the results were probably going to be very bad. I did not know what was happening to Brian. He seemed to be doing better. He was able to eat and drink now without a problem. Was the colon cancer back and another surgery needed?

The doctor came into the room with a grave heaviness. His rigid posturing scared me; even though I had seen it many times before. I braced myself so that I could endure the next blow. He said they had found numerous tumors in Brian's lungs and they were all growing at an alarming rate. We should return home and wait for the "team" to make a decision. It was the same news Brian's friend Tony had been given.

The kids and I stayed in Los Angeles for the rest of the week because my uncle had died, and my mother offered to watch the children while I took my father to the funeral. My dad was failing and very thin, but he was determined to attend the funeral of his younger brother, despite the tumultuous relationship they had in the past. Just months ago, the two had come together and had begun the healing process; the timing could not have been better.

As the funeral date approached, my dad worried I was not strong enough to help him in and out of the car, so to ease his concerns I called Kevin and asked him to fly down for the weekend.

On the way to the funeral we drove through parts of East Los Angeles that my dad had not seen for many years. It reminded him of the good times he had growing up. At the funeral he was able to see his surviving siblings and several other friends and family members for one last time. It was a very emotional day for him.

Back at my uncle's house, my dad spent some time with my aunt talking about old times. As he stood in front of her, nearing death's door himself, she told him she did not blame him for what had happened between the two brothers. It was important for him to hear those words. The boys had been inseparable growing up. When he came back to join the group and the men decided to go outside to have a cigar and a drink, dad was ready to go home. He didn't want to be around for the drinking. It had been drinking that caused all the problems thirty-two years ago.

After church on Sunday, Kevin and I walked across the street to take the kids to Disneyland. Brian had no fears that day. He didn't need to wear a baseball cap because he had a full head of hair. He didn't need a wheelchair, but he was so cold we had to buy him an extra sweatshirt while we were all wearing short sleeves. The park was virtually empty; it was as if we had the whole place to ourselves.

We never saw Mickey or any of the usual characters; just Mary Poppins and her Penguin. The kids rode one ride each; Crystal chose Space Mountain and Brian drove the cars. Then we all piled on the train. After lunch we left the "happiest place on earth" and headed back home. It was Brian's last visit to the park. Both kids slept soundly during the entire eight-hour drive back home to Placerville.

School via home tutoring started on Monday morning. Brian had grown accustomed to the infrequent visits of his tutor. I was hoping we could get back to a regular routine again once we were finished with Children's Hospital.

When Nancy arrived Brian was happy to see her. He liked having sessions where he was allowed to move at his own pace. He was always in such a hurry to get through to the next lesson. I guess he knew he didn't have much time.

Over the next few weeks, we had to cut the tutor's visits down to twice a week. Brian was having pain and it was hard for him to concentrate. In the past he had always been able to act like he was fine no matter how he felt. But now he just cried out in frustration. Every task took so much of his energy that it was painful to watch him. Often he just sat and struggled to catch a breath. During one session he cried the whole time Nancy was there. She thought she should leave, but Brian wanted her to stay. I know he hung on to her visits because she was all that he had to look forward to now. His struggle was hard on all of us.

One day after a session, Brian wrote this is his journal:

<u>Home Teaching:</u> I have home teaching every year, when my sister goes to school. I have a tumor and it is a bad kind. I could die. I got it in my stomach and my side and chest, but that doesn't mean I can't do anything. I know God is with me all the time. And the most important thing is . . . that I'm me.

Brian always took the high road even in adversity. I needed to learn from him. On Tuesday morning, February 16, we were back at UCD for the second round of chemo. The doctors at Children's hospital felt that we should try another eight-day course. I worried because Brian was in constant pain and was having difficulty breathing. I consented only because I hoped the treatment would help, but it only made things worse. With the chemotherapy came the low blood count which always resulted in intensifying the pain. Brian's pain worsened and his breath became so shallow at night that I checked his pulse regularly to see if he was still alive.

The next morning when we got to the clinic, Brian's skin was so grey from the lack of oxygen that staff made sure he was the first patient the doctor saw that morning. He looked so thin, no hair, eyes deeply sunken in. The nursing staff expedited the infusion process so I could take Brian home. Without having to wait through a six- to eight-hour day, Brian was able to watch a little television and spend some time with his dad before he went to bed that evening. I raved to staff about what an improvement I had seen. Staff sped him through morning infusions throughout the rest of the week.

The next week, I started getting sick. I wasn't eating properly and I had been up for several nights pounding Brian's chest. It seemed like everywhere I looked things were not going well. It had rained all weekend and Brian was so disappointed that he couldn't go outside. I was feeling low because I wanted Brian to have another summer, but the tumors were growing so fast and the doctors were talking about doing another surgery. Brian didn't have a chance at seeing another summer and it was unlikely that he even had another month left. I read my Bible and sulked.

May your mercy come quickly to meet us, for we are in desperate need (Psalm 79:8 NIV).

On day eight, the last day of treatment, Brian woke up cheerful, but I had the flu. Kevin had to miss work and take Brian to treatment that day. I disinfected the entire inside of my house while they were gone worried that Brian might catch something. I spent most of the time in the bedroom and only came out when I was wearing a mask. Kevin had to take care of everything including the meals. It was the first time I had been sick with a cold or the flu for over five years.

On Thursday, Brian's classroom teacher in Placerville wanted to drop by the house and bring cards and letters that her students had made, but I had to ask her to come the following week because I was so sick. I told her how disappointed Brian would be that she could not come, so she said she would write him a note.

By Saturday, I was much better, and the rain had finally stopped, so I was able to stand outside while Brian ran up to get the mail. He was so excited that the letter in the mailbox was for him. He opened it and read:

2/25/1982

Dear Brian:

How are you?

Here is some work for you. Do a page of math and one English paper a day. Please write one story and two days later another story. Your spelling words for the week are: tomorrow, read, bad, pink, apple, because, shoot, upon, frighten, true.

We miss you. Good luck with your next operation.

Flossy

No one had told Brian that there would be another surgery.

23

MARCH

Brian's classroom teacher, Flossy, came to visit on March 3, bringing with her a large bag filled with cards crafted by his classmates. Brian was excited to see her, but privately he struggled to appear normal. He had to talk to her very slowly so he would not appear to be out of breath. While he could control his behavior, he could not hide his emotions. He had a very big smile on his face.

As soon as she left, he collapsed in pain. I pounded on his chest until Kevin got home. I had told the doctor that the Thorazine was not enough and yet they just refilled the same prescription as last month. Brian needed something much stronger now.

In March we continued in our cycle of ups and downs and trips back and forth. More tests at UCD showed that massive amounts of scar tissue restricted the lungs from filling up with air.

We left for Los Angeles on March 13 so I could spend the weekend with my parents. In the car I remembered that it was Lent. I was so wrapped up in my own circumstances I had forgotten to recognize who I belonged to and that Christ's death on the cross was for me.

Christians who observe Lent usually do so by abstaining from some kind of activity in preparation for Holy Week, which is the week leading up to Jesus' crucifixion. In the past I had given up superficial things, whatever it was, I felt I could not live without at that moment, whether it was chocolate or television. This year I would give up my time. It was what I coveted most. Brian required care around the clock. At night I read my Bible and prayed for the people in my life, but Jesus always required more. The time I spent in worship and praising him for the next forty days would be sacrificial, but crucial, in my spiritual growth.

They who seek the Lord will praise him (Psalm 22:26 NIV).

I was shocked when the test results in Los Angeles showed a marked improvement with the chemotherapy. Apparently it had been the scar tissue that had interfered with the reading of the former x-rays. Before any decisions could be made about Brian's current condition, the "team" thought we should wait and see how Brian did. But I knew what they really thought: that he would not live long enough for another surgery.

That night at RMH, the manager told me that Tony was in very bad shape and that he was receiving care from hospice. All they could do for him now was to keep him comfortable. I didn't tell Brian.

Before heading home my mom gave me her old car. My dad had bought her a new Buick. It was one of the things on his bucket list. He told me all of his funeral arrangements had been made and paid for. He and my mom had been in WWII and had plots in a nearby Veterans Cemetery. The car was a great gift, but the circumstances made me sad. Everywhere I turned, Brian, Tony, and my dad were all dying of cancer.

When the tutor called, I told her Brian was waiting for her but that the visits needed to be cut down to just once a week. She told me not to worry, she was still working with Brian's homeroom teacher, Flossy, and also with Patti at the hospital, and she was sure Brian could still graduate with his class.

When UCD started the chemotherapy on March 22, I told the doctors that even the Tylenol #2 was not going to be able to handle his nadir. I begged them for a stronger medication, but the doctors ignored my requests. They said they were not concerned about something that might happen in two weeks. Each day Brian struggled to move, struggled to breathe. I had to cancel school all together. Kevin and I were taking turns pounding Brian's back throughout the night.

On Friday, March 26, God granted us a reprieve. Brian had an entire day without pain. After chemo he went outside and played with the kids in the neighborhood. We were witnessing a miracle; he was running and riding his bike. I thought this couldn't be my child, but it was. God healed Brian's wounded spirit and turned everything around.

There was no denying Brian's improvement when we returned to clinic on March 30. The doctors at UCD were very excited and thought that even Brian's heart sounded stronger. Feeling hopeful I quickly removed the word "terminal" from my vocabulary. Then we got the bad news, and all our joy slipped away . . . .

24

APRIL

<u>Easter by Brian Perigan</u>
Easter is coming, Easter is soon.
Easter is near, Easter will be before noon.
Easter I love, Easter is a delight.
Easter is wonderful, Easter is bright.

It was Easter Vacation and Crystal was out of school. We were home at last enjoying a holiday. Brian had experienced nine glorious days without pain.

I just had one more week of Lent, and with the change of events in Brian's life, praise oozed from my grateful heart.

Brian was also showing signs of spiritual growth. He still read his children's Bible and sang spiritual songs, but suddenly he too began to have a relationship with his Lord and Savior. He was thankful for each new day. Even on the worst of days, he was happy just to be home. He never let an impending surgery damage a day. Each day stood on its own.

During the week, we were coloring eggs. When we finished, we hid them and let the neighborhood kids find them. When everyone got tired we put them in baskets and decorated the house with them. It was so much fun.

On Easter Sunday I was so relieved we had made it through the entire Holy Week without a single call from the hospital. After church, having gone eighteen days without pain, Brian prayed before our meal that Sunday:

Dear God:

Thank you for this food. Let us have a good time tomorrow and the next day and forever! Amen.

On April 12, back at UCD we waited to hear whether or not they had decided to go through with the next surgery. Brian and I were disappointed when we didn't receive any special treatment that day, but he was so much better that there was no reason to move him to the front of the line.

Sometime after three o'clock, the doctor could only tell me that they had "new concerns." He sent us home, no decision had been made. I wanted to know if the "team" thought Brian's life warranted another surgery or not. Later I heard that the doctors were at odds about whether they should take steps to improve his quality of life or just let him die.

On Wednesday, April 14, Children's Hospital still had not called. I understood that no one ever wants to give bad news, but we needed to hear something soon so we could move on.

Meanwhile, Brian continued to improve. I took him with me to run a few errands that morning. My CCS financial agreement had to be renewed and Brian needed more pain medication. As I pulled the car into our garage, I started to wake Brian up when I heard our phone ringing. I quietly opened the car door, and ran into the kitchen.

"Hello?" Pauline was on the other end of the phone, crying. I stepped back into the kitchen and shut the door. Pauline's son Tony, Brian's best friend, had died. All I could do was cry with her. She told me there would be a service on the weekend. I thought about the last time we saw Tony. He had looked very much like Brian did now. He still had life, but his light was dimming. I watched Brian get out of the car. He felt cranky and tired. He asked me for something to eat. I needed some time to think about how I would tell him.

After lunch, I said, "Brian, I need to talk to you about something."

He said, "Just tell me."

"It's about Tony." He sat up and stared at me. "Do you know what Tony did today? He ran off to heaven with a bunch of angels."

Brian looked at me and smiled, and then he took a deep sigh. "He died," he said, in a matter of fact tone. "I heard you crying."

He didn't want to talk about it and never mentioned it to his sister or his dad. I never took the time to explain where I went that Saturday. Grief work is something that is often done during a self-imposed period of isolation. We all mourned in our own ways. Tony was just the first imminent death on my list.

I drove 200 miles to Tulare to attend the saddest funeral I had ever been to. I sobbed uncontrollably all the way back home. I remember so little about the details of that day. Several years later, when Pauline's mother wrote to me to tell me Pauline had died in a car accident, she said my attendance at the funeral had meant a lot to the family. She told me I had been a good friend to Pauline. It was another loss and by then there had been so many. Brian, my dad, and my two brothers had all died of cancer by then.

I don't know what caused Brian's pain to come back so fiercely: a low blood count, Tony's death, or the growth of the tumors, but the pain reached a new level. Brian's chest hurt and his breathing was labored. I had been pounding his chest, but he pleaded, "Harder, faster, I still hurt."

I kept Brian so drugged that I feared he would succumb to an overdose of pain killers. His tolerance level after five years was high, so he needed massive amounts of the drugs to stop the pain. We went through 150 Tylenol with Codeine in what felt like days. The hospital encouraged me to give the medication more frequently. I gave him the drugs but worried that I was giving him too much. I wondered how I could ever cope with a death that I had caused.

One morning I panicked when Brian started gulping in air. Still haunted by Tony's death, I called Children's Hospital for help. "Brian is grey, he is not getting enough oxygen and I cannot manage the pain with the drugs I have!" It was late Friday evening before I heard back from them. The only option we had seemed futile.

Brian looked like a different child. His skin was ash grey, his body so thin and his big brown eyes were sunken. He was too drugged to write anymore or to think clearly. All Brian wanted now was for the pain to stop. The surgeon agreed to do the surgery but warned me once again that Brian might not make it. I thought it was ironic that in my effort to help, again I faced the possibility of killing him. There were no good choices, every resolution ended in death.

Driving back to Children's Hospital I felt like it was the right thing to do. I was comforted by the fact that the Hospital had been with us in the beginning and would take us through to the end. Brian's doctor had scoffed when I told him I had peace about Brian dying. He thought I was becoming more aggressive and tense. He was right. I was becoming a much stronger advocate for my child. But in my defense, I had not slept for two weeks because Brian was in such bad shape.

When I arrived at the hospital I began to feel uncomfortable almost immediately. It must have looked like I was trying to keep Brian alive at any cost. I knew it was really only about stopping the pain, but they didn't.

I talked to Brian about the surgery. I told him it might not work and that Jesus might come and take him home. He said he already knew that. We checked into the Ronald McDonald House on Sunday, April 25. He managed to write this poem, to let me know he was okay:

<u>Jesus</u>
Angels guard you, all around your bed.
God is watching over you, as you lay down your head.
Jesus was scared but he died for our sins.
For boys and for girls, for women and for men.

We need him forever and ever. We need him all day long.
We need him every year. Cause he is big and strong.

As I read the poems, I wondered how Brian could even begin to understand what Jesus felt as he faced the cross. Brian refers to Jesus dying for our sins even though he was scared. Brian may still have been working out some of his own fears about death or pain as he faced his last surgery ("take this cup from me," Jesus had prayed). In the last verses he seemed to have grasped where his strength lay. I should have known all along that only God could give Brian that deeper understanding of who he was.

Brian's surgery was scheduled on April 27, his eighth birthday. On the April 26, we went through the admitting process and got settled into a room that afternoon. Brian's nurse that evening was someone who had become very special to us over the last few years. She was appalled that the doctors had scheduled surgery on Brian's birthday. Whatever the date was, it didn't matter to me. Brian's pain was intense, and we did not want to delay in getting him the help he needed.

Brian was resting peacefully in the hospital receiving an IV drip morphine solution and all he wanted to do was sleep, but the staff made an exception for our situation. The surgeon postponed the surgery for twenty-four hours, and we were given a pass to go back to RMH.

It was a nice gesture, but Brian didn't feel well enough to enjoy much of anything. Surprisingly, though, the morphine held until Brian was able to return to the hospital. We stopped at McDonald's and ordered a Happy Meal. I had a long talk with my son about his life, his hopes, and his dreams. We talked like grownups that day. I finally relaxed a little and began to realize that the extra day had been a gift after all. I began to have peace about the surgery. Brian would walk boldly toward the light as he faced death, never flinching or turning back.

After he finished eating, I asked him what he wanted for his birthday. Brian liked a Discovery magazine called *Ranger Rick*. Every issue included pictures of exotic animals and colorful birds. I feared he might ask for a lion or a pet monkey as a birthday gift, but Brian wanted his own pet bird. "Like a parakeet?" I asked. "No, Mom, a cockatiel." He wanted to teach it how to talk and sing. We laughed about the kinds of things we would teach the bird to say.

When we returned to RMH, a birthday cake and a few friends were waiting for him. I was overwhelmed. What if all this had never happened? There were so many sweet memories that day and I savored each one.

Brian and I rode the elevator at RMH to the second floor. Just eighteen months ago, the house had been brand new and my kids ran up and down the stairs. It seemed like so long ago. We still had so much hope then. I tucked Brian into bed and waited for the medication to take effect. I watched him sleep for a few minutes. It took every muscle in his body to catch a breath and then he would exhale and struggle again. It had been a good day. God had blessed us.

I went downstairs to grab some coffee to help me stay awake during the night. All the families in the House were new, all strangers to me. The House manager told me we lost another little boy from our original group of the first sixteen families. Now only Brian was left, but even while we spoke his time was running out too.

25

MAY

Brian's thin little body barely pulled through his *tenth and final* surgery. The left thoracotomy for tumor accomplished little. The surgeon had gone in to remove the tumors but they were too advanced and could not be extricated safely.

Brian was in intensive care for eight days. Kevin had flown in the morning before, leaving Crystal with my parents, so that he could be with Brian. When the surgeon came out to talk to us, he spoke words that no one ever wants to hear. "There was nothing we could do," he said. He had removed as much of the scar tissue around the chest cavity as possible and he hoped it would make Brian a little more comfortable.

The Bible verses I had read that morning reminded me that I had already learned to walk through the darkness. The days in ICU had been intense, but the intensity had only drawn us closer to God. I knew God had given us many blessed days with Brian, and that eternity was what lay ahead. We could rejoice that Brian would soon be out of pain.

> Dear friends, do not be surprised at the painful trial you are suffering, as though something strange were happening to you. But rejoice that you participate in the sufferings of Christ, so that you may be overjoyed when his glory is revealed (1 Peter 4:12–13 NIV).

Brian was kept on high levels of morphine throughout his entire time in ICU. He was so drugged that I could see no visible signs of life. All hope for recovery was gone. I had no more tears left; we had run a long hard race, and now I just sat and waited for all pain to stop. But just like all the other times, Brian wasn't ready to go just yet.

On May 5 when Brian left ICU and was rolled into a private room on the third floor, the nursing staff had a big surprise for him. Still celebrating his eighth birthday, they had decorated his room with cards and banners from his classmates in Placerville.

It lifted our spirits to see all the brightly colored cards on the wall, and Brian almost smiled. Several days passed before he felt alert enough for me to begin to read every card to him. It was the card that never mentioned the hospital that he liked the best. It said:

> *To Brian:*
>
> *Once upon a time a boy named Brian had a birthday. It was exciting. It was very neat. He got a bike, motorcycle, a tuba, and a million dollars. It was terrific. Lee*

When Brian was discharged from the hospital, his surgeon and physician came in to say goodbye, but I couldn't speak. I had trusted God to bring us to this point. We had reached a level of certainty that all hope for saving Brian's life had been diminished. I was moving slowly toward total acceptance, but my emotions were so raw. Brian had lived through ICU but I could not let hope soar again. He only had weeks or maybe even just days left.

Last week, when I had called Children's Hospital in desperation, I was still fighting for Brian. The "team" knew it was over and yet they had rallied and had gone over and above what was expected with this last surgery. I could not ask them for anything else, they had given Brian their all.

It had been five years ago, almost to the day, that we had first entered into the hospital and now it was ending. I remembered some of the best times, the video in Laminar, Brian in the classroom at the age of three, opening day at RMH, the day drugs were flown in from Germany for Brian, and a time when staff gave us so much hope sharing stories about new cancer research. Brian and I had been included in every major decision. We had learned so much about the medical world, and I would miss that part of my life.

I had spent time with the Lord that morning, "We are very close to the day you have been preparing us for: Brian's homecoming." I had tried to visualize Brian in heaven, running down the streets of gold without pain. It was the only place he could go now and be completely whole again. The cancer could take his last breath, but it would never touch his soul. I had hoped that God would reveal to me the number of days we had left, but while I waited to hear his voice, we would continue to celebrate each day that was given.

I hugged all the nurses goodbye, but when I saw Patti, the school teacher, we exchanged phone numbers and addresses. I would miss her in this setting, but I would see her again. She had become a good friend.

As a teacher, she had taught Brian to read and write at three years old. She had allowed him to be creative and encouraged him along the way. She had also worked tirelessly with each child's school district to ensure that they met the annual requirements for graduation. Six months later she would write a letter that encouraged me to go on. Telling me how Brian's smile had captivated her heart and that it hurt her deeply to have Brian placed in God hands. Years later she has remained a loyal friend.

She had been involved in so much of what had made Brian's experience in the hospital a pleasant one that I suspected that she had something to do with the extravagant decorations that now covered every inch of his room. Before we left she handed me a story Brian had written the day before.

The Hospital

Have you ever been in a hospital besides when you were born? I have since I was three. I'm having shots, surgery, everything. I hate it but it's the only way I can get better. Cause if I was better I wouldn't have to go to the hospital. But I still hate it.

Brian still had hope that he would get better. Why else would I have brought him back to Los Angeles? I guess when we first arrived I still had that hope too. Then I thought about how much I would miss Brian's laugh, silly songs, stories, and the poems that I found regularly on my chair.

I packed up the room while the "birthday nurse" went to get the wheelchair. She handed me the instructions for the medication and said that Brian should take Tylenol #2 every four hours for pain. Then she told us about a follow-up appointment with UCD on May 10. It would be up to UCD to facilitate our first appointment with Hospice. I wondered if this was what it had felt like for Pauline. I felt pushed out and I wasn't sure I was ready to leave just yet. I signed the discharge paperwork and took the bag of medicine in one hand and my Bible in the other and we walked out into the bright sunlight.

There was something about going home that always revived my spirit and made me feel like we were free. Spring had come just like He promised. The nurse carefully rolled Brian up to the car, and then she asked me what I thought we would do now. I told her we were going to go home and try to enjoy the summer. She hugged me goodbye and said, "Go have a great summer!" We both smiled, but neither one of us believed Brian would live that long.

We got into the car and drove away. But we couldn't start toward home before making one last stop. Brian had not forgotten about his birthday request. He had reminded me about it several times while he was in the hospital. I'd found an ad in the paper for a six-weeks-old hand-fed cockatiel and all we had to do was go pick him up.

Born on March 1, it was just the bird Brian wanted. When Brian and his new pet were introduced, it was love at first sight. He was grey with a white chest and bright yellow and orange markings on his face. The bird was so little that he fit in a small shoebox already filled with bird seed and water. Brian held the box carefully in his lap for the entire 500-mile ride back home from Yorba Linda.

The bird's name was Hector, but on the way home we talked about changing his name. Brian was outraged. "We can't change his name because then he won't know who he is!" That made perfect sense to me; I was sorry I had brought it up. Adopting Hector was just the first step we took to embrace life—eternal life. Hector continued to serve as a symbol of that hope for our family for seventeen years after Brian died.

The hope I held now was not temporal, like the hope of physical healing, or hope that stopped the pain. My hope was now only for the eternal. I could see Brian spending eternity with Christ. Marching up to the mountaintop, he only had one lap left, his victory lap. I prayed that God would keep me strong so I could embrace all the wonderful blessings along the way.

Back at home, Hector was just what Brian needed to help him forget his pain. In fact, Hector and our neighbor's daughter, Melissa, were Brian's reason for getting out of bed each morning when he came home from the hospital.

Brian could not wait to share the bird with Melissa. She was a couple of years younger than Brian, still in kindergarten, but I think he liked that he was older and could show her the ropes. Melissa had become a frequent playmate. She was fascinated by the bird and seemed very impressed that the bird would soon be talking and doing tricks. Brian looked at Hector with high expectations; all I saw when I looked into the cage was something that looked like a little grey rat.

Almost everything we did started to focus on making Hector happy. We first bought a new cage and supplies. Then Brian wanted ladders and mirrors, just like he had seen in the pictures of his magazine.

The bird and his cage went everywhere Brian went. I carefully moved him from bedroom to bathroom. And in the afternoon he went from family room to the kitchen. I didn't mind Brian's intense involvement with the bird because Hector had become the only pain medication Brian needed.

I was surprised that Brian knew so much about birds. I knew he could identify most of the birds in our area, but he was the one who thought about using an eye dropper for water and covered the cage at night. I bought him several books on cockatiels and he studied them daily. It wasn't long before we were purchasing a much larger cage, bathtubs, and bells for the bird.

Kevin bought Brian a tool set and on several rare occasions you could find father and son in the garage building birdhouses for Hector. Mostly on good days, Brian spent the bulk of his time trying to teach the bird to talk or to whistle. On bad days, when Brian couldn't get out of bed, the bird was perfectly content sitting on Brian's head and chewing on his hair all day long.

May 10 seemed to creep up on us so quickly because I felt like I needed more time with Brian. Death was at our doorstep. Brian had a follow-up lab test in Placerville. The hospital had wanted to review the results to make sure that Brian had no internal bleeding after the surgery. The results were not good; his blood count was low. There had been a discussion amongst the staff, and we were called. The decision was made not to give Brian a blood transfusion even though he needed it. I should not have been surprised by the response.

On Wednesday, we went to UCD so the doctor could complete the final physical and then hand Brian over to Hospice. The social worker made phone calls to Children's Hospital and our area Hospice Agency. The agency would start coming to the house on Friday. My relationship with UCD had ended. It was sad, but I was getting used to saying goodbye.

Brian came home and could not wait to play with Melissa. They ran outside to explore the outdoors. That day they came across a stray cat that was eating a bird and deduced that it was the mother of several baby birds on our front porch. They wanted to rescue the babies but they were too far gone. When they all died despite our efforts to save them, the kids wanted to have a funeral. I went through all the motions; putting the birds in a box, burying them in the ground and saying a prayer. I spoke words that thanked God for taking the birds to his home in heaven, but the timing of the mock funeral had a devastating effect on me.

The children were satisfied that we had given the birds a decent burial. Indifferent to the emotions that such a ritual can sometimes bring, they simply laid a few freshly picked wild flowers on the gravesite. I could hear their laughter as they ran off to play. The cries of my heart came from a deeper place. The funeral was just a rehearsal for what I would have to face months later. I didn't want the birds to die, and I didn't really want Brian to leave me; all of it was too much to deal with. Jesus cried tears of blood before he faced Calvary. My broken heart cried tears of blood at the thought of burying my son. It all seemed so unfair. I still saw so much life in my child, but the lab work, the doctor's physical examinations, and the surgeons report confirmed that death was imminent.

You can say "God holds your future," but until you act on it and believe it you will never find his perfect peace. It all starts when you receive him as Lord and Savior, begin to trust that he has a perfect plan for your life and then walk with him daily until you get to your final destination—with him in heaven. Brian's days on earth were diminishing. I knew Brian's cancer had become widespread. It was time to completely embrace the fact that he would soon be with Jesus.

The Hospice worker came out to the house to do an assessment on May 14. She explained the philosophy: Death is a universal fact of life not something to be feared. She talked to me about why Brian met their criteria:

- The patient has a confirmed diagnosis of an illness that will probably result in death (within the next six months).
- The patient has a need for management of pain symptoms or psychosocial problems caused by the illness.
- The patient's primary physician concurs with the admission.

- The patient, family, and primary physician understand hospice philosophy.
- A primary caregiver must be available if the patient is unable to care for himself.

I was thankful for Hospice because I had not been successful managing the pain on my own. In the past I had not been comfortable giving Brian high dosages of a drug that could kill him. Angie, a retired R.N., was assigned to Brian. She only came weekly in the beginning, to check on Brian's decline and monitor all of his medication. She was very sweet, loved animals, and Brian enjoyed her company. I sensed immediately that she was someone that I could trust.

Later that day, I flipped the TV station to a Christian channel and heard words of encouragement:

The situation of the world is getting worse, but our Provider remains unchanged. His treasures have not been eaten away. Looking around there are many traps to get depressed in, but when we look to him there is not a one.

Many things were changing in our life but God had not changed. He still held all that we needed in his hands. I knew if I took my eyes off of him now, I would be lost.

The Bible uses the loss of a child to describe some of the most devastating situations. In Amos and Zechariah, God tells his people they will mourn "as one mourns for an only son." It was important to me to know that God knew my mourning was not trivial; it was a sadness that ripped out my heart. As Christians we cannot even begin to understand the sacrifice God made when he sent his son to die for us. He gently reminds us in scripture that such a loss is like no other. But when we look to God we can see his compassion for us in Jesus; the gift he gave because he loved us that much.

Three days later, just as I was finally wrapping my head around Brian's fate, UCD called. They had found something that was broken and they thought they could fix it.

I walked up our long driveway to get the mail. I felt pushed and pulled in opposite directions. Were we letting go so Brian could die in dignity? Or were we going back to the hospital and continuing to fight for his life? Maybe we were doing both. We would not fear death, not in this house, but we would continue to live life to the fullest.

I got excited when I saw the letter from Christian Television Network (TBN). I wondered if it had anything to do with the letter I had written to the Billheimers. It read:

The Lord is near to the brokenhearted, and saves those who are crushed in spirit (Psalm 34:18 NIV).

He that comes to me, I will certainly not cast out (John 6:37 NIV).

Behold I am the Lord, the God of all Flesh; is there anything too hard for me? (Jeremiah 32:27 NIV).

What I do you do not realize now; but you shall understand hereafter (John 13:7 NIV).

We present you and all those upon your heart to our Father in the name of Jesus and we thank Him for hearing this cry. His answer shall come!

With Jesus' love, Paul and Jan
TBN Trinity Broadcasting Network, Inc.

I remembered when Jan came to our church years ago, before she had become famous. Over 300 people accepted Jesus as their Savior that night, having heard her testimony. The words encouraged me.

On May 18 at UCD, Brian's doctor was excited about a new experimental drug that treated Wilms' tumor and he thought we should try it, but first he had to resolve the problem he saw with Brian's blood count. Brian's count was still dropping, but there would be no blood transfusion. We had to wait and see if Brian's body could resolve the issue on its own. I brought Brian back to UCD on Friday, but the blood count was still low and the level of pain was increasing. The hospital referred us back to Hospice and told us they were sorry.

I didn't understand why inflicting this level of pain on us was necessary. In Proverbs 13:12, scripture tells us that hope deferred makes the heart sick. It all seemed so cruel . . . "but you will understand hereafter."

UCD called on Tuesday to see if Brian was still alive. They ordered a local blood test, and this time it was good news. The blood count had come up by itself and was within normal range. Chemotherapy would start on Wednesday morning. "Is there anything too hard for me?"

AZQ (aziridinylbenzoquinones/2.5 bis carboethoxyamino) was an experimental drug that had been used to treat metastatic Wilms' Tumor. It is part of a large class of compounds that exhibited significant anti-tumor activity by disrupting mitosis. The agreement I signed with the hospital said that "children with Wilms' tumor that had a reoccurrence only lived for one to two years from the date of the original diagnosis."

I was shocked; no one had ever told me that before. Brian should have died before he reached the age of five. It all made sense now; the doctors thought he was living on borrowed time. He had already outlived everyone's expectations. He was a miracle. If my child had died while in kindergarten, I would have never known he wanted to become a doctor. There would have been no stories or poems. I could have never known he had a relationship with Jesus or even that he could train a bird. I had been blessed in ways that I had not seen before. Though the years had brought great sadness and much suffering, the Lord really had been with us.

In Psalm 34:17–18 David reminds us that when we cry out to God he hears us. "The Lord is near to the broken hearted and saves those who are crushed in spirit." He had been with us each day, loving us and encouraging us through his Word. And during the darkest part of the journey, when I felt that I could not go any further, I reminded myself again, how he had carried us through the valley.

The doctors wanted to explain the paperwork to me but I just signed it. Driven by the increasing pain, Brian had already agreed to try something new so I had no hesitations about being part of a clinical trial. The drug had all the usual side effects: hair loss, nausea, weight loss, lethargy, poor neuromuscular coordination, and bone marrow depression.

When we returned home, I had to make several phone calls. I needed to update Hospice on Brian's current status and follow up on an urgent financial matter. I had set all the bills aside, because for the next few days or weeks or however long Brian had left on earth I just wanted to focus on helping him manage his pain. And it seemed to work until I got a certified letter from the collection agency.

I had to laugh at the $16 request. Really? Don't you want $30,000 or even $300,000? When I called, the woman was so nice that I sent out a check on that same day.

I had one more important payout to make that week. I needed to take care of Brian's final arrangements. I had never had to plan a funeral before and I wanted Brian's to be well thought out and not just thrown together at the last minute.

On Saturday, May 29, while Kevin was home with the kids, I made plans to pick up Kevin's cousin Julie on the way to the mortuary to help me make arrangements. Everyone thought the idea was repugnant because Brian was not dead yet, but I forged ahead anyway. I had gotten a similar response when we started hospice. In my family, I had noticed that hospice was often called a week or two before the person died. It didn't make any sense to me. Why not plan ahead and use every possible resource available to make the death process easier on the patient and the family.

That morning we drove around and looked at all the big beautiful cemeteries in Sacramento. Then I decided on a smaller one that was closer to home. The mortuary in town had many funeral packages to choose from, but I chose something simple and inexpensive. Choosing the coffin was a little too intense for Julie, who decided to take a walk outside. I was glad she had not seen the coffins made for infants and had not been there when I had to pick out the light blue lining. I signed all the paperwork and wrote out an obituary.

When I got home I had just had one more thing to do. I had forgotten that our church was in the middle of a building program. We would have to have the service at the mortuary. I made one last call to make the arrangements. With that burden lifted, I went home to enjoy being with my son.

On the last day of the month, Kevin had the day off from work because of the holiday, and the kids were playing outside. I sat inside staring out the window, everything was in place. It was almost over.

As I watched the kids outside, I wondered why I was mourning; no one had died yet. I dragged out my suit of armor again and told myself to march forward. The breastplate of faith and love would protect my heart in battle. The helmet, the hope of salvation, protected my mind and reminded me to whom I belong.

> Since we belong to the day, let us be self-controlled, putting on faith and love as a breastplate, and the hope of salvation as a helmet (1 Thessalonians 5:8 NIV).

There would always be a daily battle of the mind, and at each junction I would have to choose who I would serve and then stand firm in my faith. I could already see that there were going to be many more battles that I would have to confront as I walked down this road with Brian. I felt confident that God could handle them all. When we are pressed there is only one option: to reach for him.

26

JUNE

B rian was back to having only a few bad days, but we were taking everything one step at a time. We were eager to start the next round of chemo on Wednesday morning because Brian was definitely showing signs of improvement.

By Friday afternoon Brian was back to his old self and was playing outside with the neighborhood kids. His illness no longer interfered with what he wanted to accomplish in life. The doctors were puzzled by the quick turnaround in his ability to breathe and function.

Who can love like this? We had more time with Brian than we could ever have dreamed possible. Only with God are all things possible. My spirit was so lifted up, but I didn't have the words to express my appreciation, not until years later when, during a lecture by Ravi Zacharias, I heard about a woman named Annie J. Flint (1866–1932). Flint was blind and suffered for over forty years from crippling arthritis. Her joints had become rigid, and she was confined to a wheelchair. In great pains she wrote a few lines on paper. In her song, "He Giveth More Grace," she clearly expresses what it is like to be on the receiving end of God's great love for us.

He Giveth More Grace

He giveth more grace when the burdens grow greater,
He sendeth more strength when the labors increase;
To added afflictions He addeth His mercy,
To multiplied trials, His multiplied peace.

When we have exhausted our store of endurance,
When our strength has failed ere the day is half done,
When we reach the end of our hoarded resources
Our Father's full giving is only begun.

Fear not that thy need shall exceed His provision,
Our God ever yearns His resources to share;
Lean hard on the arm everlasting, availing;
The Father both thee and thy load will upbear.

His love has no limits, His grace has no measure,
His power no boundary known unto men;
For out of His infinite riches in Jesus
He giveth, and giveth, and giveth again.[34]

Each day Brian woke up, jumped out of bed, and ran to Hector's cage. He put Hector on his shoulder and came into the kitchen for breakfast. He spent a lot of time training the bird. He even taught the dog how to fetch the bird when Hector flew into another room. Over time we learned to clip Hector's wings back so Brian could take the bird outside or to the neighbor's house. He really loved to showcase his pet.

On June 8, Hospice decided Brian might benefit from two weeks of art therapy. On the first visit, the therapist gave Brian a small notebook. The plan was for the two of them to fill the notebook with pictures representing Brian's feelings about dying. Overseeing the exercise, I felt very protective, once I realized that therapist did not share our belief system. I didn't want her to negatively impact Brian's healthy outlook, but Brian disagreed with me. He wanted to hear what she had to say. I respected his wishes and backed off. His body was that of a child, but his spirit was very mature.

On the second visit, she explained reincarnation and had him draw pictures of the afterlife. She was not satisfied when Brian drew birds flying to heaven. Listening to the discussion, I sat fuming in the next room. When she encouraged Brian to explore death, he drew the sun shining on brightly colored flowers. I don't think it was what she had in mind. She started feeding him ideas about how he should perceive life and death. She suggested he draw things like a child in a hospital bed crying. But Brian was articulate enough to express how he felt.

I talked to Brian several times about stopping the sessions. He rolled his eyes and said, "No, it's okay." He explained he did not want to quit until he had filled up all the pages in his book. So I allowed the therapist to keep coming.

In the beginning I did think maybe the sessions would tap into some feelings Brian hadn't been able to share with me or his dad. But by the end of the two weeks, when the book was full, it looked to me as if Brian envisioned heaven as a wonderful place to go to. He had just two pictures in his book of hospitalized children, but they all had big smiles on their faces and lots of new toys on their beds. The rest of the book had pictures of family, birds in the air, and angels—Brian had remained true to himself. I was relieved that his belief system had not been tampered with.

I think Brian wrote this to let me know he still knew who God was:

He Made the Earth

God made the earth and people built houses.
And birds all sang to the little mouses.
People play in the morning, they sleep at night
    and when they sleep,
they have good dreams they keep.

On June 11, Brian's aunt and her four boys spent one night with us before they headed north to Oregon. The boys played Pac Man on the Atari. Brian knew how to play the game and was able to keep up with them.

Brian wrote this story, after they left.

A Story About Pac Man

Pac Man was at work making power pellets when Ms. Pac was making dinner. It was Saturday. The next day Pac Man and Ms. Pac decided to get married. So they did and a week later they had baby Pac which was always hungry. The Pac family was fine until the ghost monster came along. The ghost monsters were hungry for Pac Man. Pac Man was tired from running around. Pac baby planned a picnic, but instead of going somewhere, he had it right at home. When Ms. Pac and Pac Man saw the Baby Pac decided to have a picnic, they got all ready and went to have a picnic. Baby Pac climbed up a tree and told on ghost monster. The whole family dug right in and they had ghost monster and power pellets for lunch and then went home. They lived pacfully ever after.

The day before his next treatment, Brian's report card arrived with a note that stated that he had graduated into the third grade with the rest of his class. It read:

Brian has good language skills, is a very good speller, and has no difficulty with written expression. He is an excellent reader and an attentive listener with good comprehension in both areas. Brian has good mathematical reasoning abilities and has no difficulty with new concepts. Brian has an enthusiasm about all science and a good grasp of nature's laws. And his artwork is outstanding.

I was so happy that he was still able to excel in school. He needed to have something he was really good at, especially now. It meant so much to him.

After the next dose of AZQ, Children's Hospital requested that we return to Los Angeles for more testing. I thought that was a terrible idea, I never wanted to go back to Children's Hospital and the dates interfered with Father's Day. Brian ignored my excuses and told the doctor he would agree to go. We left the next day. Brian wrote this story for his dad on Father's Day. He took great care in adding quotation marks and rereading it until he felt it was perfect.

Story

Danny the Dog was walking around and met Mr. Duck. Danny said, "Can I live with you?" "No." said Mr. Duck "Sorry." Soon Danny met Mr. Squirrel. Danny said, "Can I live with you?" "Sorry," said Mr. Squirrel. Then Danny met Mr. Skunk. "Can I live with you? said Danny. "I wish you could," said Mr. Skunk.

Then Danny met some friends. They played hide and seek and after Danny's friend found him. Danny left and met a lady dog. They fell in love and got married. They had babies and built a house and lived happily ever after. The End.

Then he wrote this as an afterthought for me so I wouldn't feel left out.

Mommy

When mommy gets up the doctor calls, then she fixes me and Crystal breakfast. Then me and Crystal play and turn the TV on until it is lunch time and when it is lunch time mommy fixes lunch and sometimes me and Crystal fix lunch. I play with Crystal and then it was dinner time we ate dinner. My daddy did too. Then we did some stuff and then we went to bed.

We saw smiles on many faces when we entered the hospital in Los Angeles. No one could believe that Brian was still alive. Throughout our stay, many of the old gang dropped by to see him.

The test results showed no drastic improvement in Brian's condition and yet his pain was mild. Brian was given another dosage of the drug on June 23 after I signed the authorization form. It read:

I understand that my child will be in a treatment program in accordance with a plan of clinical research approved by the institutional review committee of this hospital. I understand that I have the right to remove my child from this treatment at any time. Any physician involved in my child's care will answer any question I have regarding treatment. Subsequent treatment of your child at the Children's Hospital is in no way contingent upon participation in this program of treatment.

I was pleased that the process had become so formalized; it meant they saw some potential with this drug. The thirty-minute infusion went by quickly and had minimal side effects; the only downside of the entire trial was the commitment we had to make to have weekly blood draws.

Kevin's birthday was coming up and Brian was worried we would not make it home in time to celebrate. He went into the classroom and sat at one of the tables, feeling right at home, and wrote a letter to his dad.

Dear Dad: From Brian Perigan
How are you? How are the animals? See you in a week, I hope. I hope you get a raise at work. Do you like my letter so far? Well any way here is a little poster of you.
From Brian

We put the letter in an envelope and sent it out with the hospital mail. By the time we realized that we hadn't included the two most important words it was too late. We were both in such a hurry to get it in the mail that we had forgotten to say "Happy Birthday."

On Sunday we went to church at Melodyland and continued to seek God's will for Brian's life. I checked in on my parents one last time, as I did not anticipate any more trips to Los Angeles. On the way home we talked about plans for Kevin's thirty-second birthday.

We arrived at home before Kevin got home from work, but I was surprised to find my father-in-law and Helen in our house. I was surprised that anyone would just show up given Brian's prognosis. Trying to be helpful, my neighbor had given them the front door key.

Kevin's stepmother took it upon herself to reorganize my whole house. It was a little overwhelming because she had actually taken the sectional sofa apart and put pieces of it in different rooms. I wasn't sure why my father-in-law had not intervened because he knew how meticulous I was about my house. There was nothing I could say about it that would have been pleasant so I went outside to unpack the car.

She quickly followed me out the door and ordered me to come back in and fix them dinner. By then I was feeling a little agitated and suggested she might want to eat out. I told her the kids and I had been on the road for eight hours and we were going upstairs to take a nap.

As I started up the stairs I could see Helen's handiwork had not been limited to the first floor. She had also added her personal touches to the upstairs too. The most destructive thing she had done to the house had occurred in Brian's room.

When Brian walked into his room, he burst into tears. Crystal and I were right behind him. I was stunned that anyone would go into Brian's room and take down all his handcrafted model airplanes that were hanging from the ceiling. The planes had been tossed into the trash can. I wondered why she wanted to destroy something that Brian loved so much. When I marched back downstairs I demanded to know why she had gone into Brian's room. She defended her actions by telling me that those planes should not be hanging from the ceiling!

I quickly returned upstairs before I said anything else to her out of anger. Brian was sitting on the floor, sobbing hysterically. He was frantically digging into the trash can trying to put the pieces back together. I tried to help him savage any recognizable parts from the wreckage but it was no use. All of the planes had been so fragile. Nothing remained intact now except for the wheels and propellers.

Brian started to breath heavily; the outburst had taken a toll on his body. He was so vulnerable, it all seemed so senseless.

When Kevin finally got home, I told him about the planes and insisted he get his stepmother out of my house. He took his dad and stepmother out to eat and by the time that they returned I had arranged for the two of them to stay at Kevin's uncle's house. I was so distraught over the fact that anyone would come into my house and destroy things that belong to my children I could barely speak. As we helped them gather their personal items the conversation remained pleasant until they got ready to leave.

When I walked into the garage to tell them goodbye, that woman was putting Brian's bike into their car. I asked, "What are you doing?" She was stoned faced and her words were insensitive, "My grandson wants a bike and Brian doesn't need his anymore." I ran inside the house to tell Kevin to stop her, but by the time he got out the door, they had already left.

The planes which had been handmade were not replaceable and we couldn't ever find another bike like the one my dad had bought Brian. Brian suffered a major setback that day. I beat his chest for the rest of week, trying to make the pain go away. That night we had to move his bed into our room so we could keep an eye on him. He was so upset we feared his heart would stop. There was nothing to celebrate on that day.

27

JULY

It was already July and summer was slipping away. We had done nothing to make it a "great" summer. We had been so restricted by weekly blood draws, trips to the hospital, and visits from Hospice that we hadn't stop to enjoy any part of it.

I asked the kids what they wanted to do, and on July 3 we set out for Marine Africa World, the closest amusement park. We managed to see a couple of the shows but Brian couldn't tolerate the heat or being in the crowds.

Kevin's dad had given us his old Ford Truck when he got remarried. We bought a used camper for $300 to make the truck useful. We had hoped that by providing a comfortable space for Brian it would be easier for him to travel. We had gutted the camper and added new bedding, toilet, and curtains. My dad was an enthusiast for all my renovation projects and sent a battery operated television for the kids. On July 5, when Kevin's aunt invited us to her farm in Yreka, we decided it would be a great opportunity for our first camping trip. The kids fed the farm animals and learned how to drive a tractor. It was a good visit.

Brian started to feel a little better and was back to writing more stories and poems:

<u>Boys in the Park</u>
One time there was a boy who was playing in the sand.
Another boy came up and said do you want to shake my hand.
They played and played until it got dark.
And by the way one was named Larry and the other Mark.

<u>Pet Rock</u>
Have you ever had a pet rock?
He is heavier than a clock.
Every day he would jump in the hay,
And then come back with my sock.

The camping trip had been so successful we thought we would try another short trip. On July 17, we left for Carmel. It took five hours to reach the northern shoreline. There was something so healing about the sea. Brian just stood by the water, slowly breathing in and out with the rhythm of the waves.

Having the camper eased Brian's stress and gave him a place to retreat when activities became overwhelming. In it was everything he needed: his family, a bed to sleep in, and an ice chest full of food he liked to eat.

The beach was empty that weekend because of the low clouds, but the cool air made it perfect for us. Both kids walked around the beach dressed in sweatshirts. They played in the sand and let the waves chase them up the shoreline.

Much of the time Brian stood alone. As he gazed at the incoming waves, I wondered what he was thinking about but didn't disturb him; he needed those healing moments. Instead, I watched as the sun peaked through the clouds causing the waves to sparkle.

At night, we barbequed hamburgers on our small $10 Hibachi, while the kids looked for sand crabs. The next morning, I was able to snap a few pictures of the kids running near the ocean. The dense fog made the pictures look magical. No one wanted to leave; it had been such a relaxing trip, but Kevin had to be back at work on Monday morning.

At home Brian's pain returned and I wished we had never left the beach. As soon as we walked in the door Brian crawled up on the sofa and didn't move. His chest hurt and his heart was beating so hard. I called Hospice to let them know I was increasing the pain medication, but they just referred me to UCD. The doctors told me to give him whatever he needed and set up an appointment on the following Wednesday.

I immediately recognized that pattern; no one was in a hurry to see a terminally ill child. I had to reset my thinking; we were back on that road again. Once the doctors had discovered that the tumors were not decreasing in size, they knew there was no hope of survival.

When we showed up at the hospital, UCD staff examined Brian and sent him to Los Angeles. Brian's blood count was too high and they thought the problem stemmed from AZQ. We flew to Los Angeles the next morning. Because Brian was part of the research on AZQ it was important to determine what was causing the blood count to rise. Children's Hospital kept him for the whole week so they could run tests. It looked like our summer was over.

Hooked up to IVs, Brian was back on Demerol and morphine. It was both comforting and disturbing for me to watch him rest so well each night. He never wanted to be drugged, but I never wanted him to be in so much pain. It was very clear now that the door had swung the other way again and now once again I was looking at my despondent dying child.

They started him back on the AZQ and kept him under close supervision. On the fourth day of treatment, Brian needed only Demerol once every twelve hours. It was a major improvement since he had been receiving injections for pain every two hours since he had been in the hospital. But even with his pain managed, Brian complained, "It's no good, because it only makes me stay in bed and sleep all day." I told him it was a tradeoff, but I thought it would be good for him to let his body rest once in a while. Once we returned home he could regulate his own drugs. Then he told me he did not want to spend any more time in the hospital. Looking back, I was sorry I couldn't uphold his wishes, but it couldn't be helped.

Brian visited the classroom a few times, but it was summer and Patti was on vacation. We didn't recognize any of the new volunteers. The hospital continued to grow and change and we had lost our connection there.

On day six, Brian was discharged from the hospital and we flew home. As I sorted through the mail, I found a letter from our pastor in Southern California. It had been written on July 20.

Dear Friends in the Lord:

Greetings to you in the name of our Lord Jesus! Just a line or so to let you know you are remembered in our prayers. Be encouraged and lifted up in the strength of his might. To be sure, God's eyes are upon Brian and His hand is under him.

Hug him for me, Robert Kemp, Pastor

Brian had been busy writing again so I had a few more things to read. I sat back and read a couple of his stories.

The Bear Cub

Once there was a bear named Cubby, and he didn't have any friends. He went to his mom and said, "Where can I find some friends?" His mom said, "Why don't you go to the park there are lots of kids there?" So he went to the park. But all the kids had friends and were playing things. They wanted nobody else to play. One day Cubby and his mom went to have a picnic and so did Mrs. Bear and her cub. They met and Cubby didn't know it but he made a new friend. The End.

I wondered, *Brian, are you lonely? Do you still feel excluded?*

My Dadday and Mommy

When my daddy gets up he goes to work. But on the week-ends he stays home. Really on Sundays he goes to church with my mommy. Sometimes just my mommy goes. When they come back, we have some fun. We do some stuff.

It is getting dark so we have dinner and then go to bed.
The End.

Brian, after all that you have been through, I am so glad your life is fun!
Despite his circumstances, his words could still lift my spirit. All of Brian's writing told me so much about who he was, about his character and his integrity. He talked about how friends were so important to him, showed me his silly side and that he still had a sense of humor. The stories told me that he'd had a good day even when his body ached with pain. His journal, poems, and drawings continued as a sweet reminder of who he was.

In the back of his notebook, I came across something he had written over a year ago. I had never seen or heard about it before. He promised Jesus he would go to church. My heart sank and I felt guilty. He hadn't been able to attend regularly since we moved to Placerville. I had noticed that whenever he was asked if he felt like going, he always said he wanted to attend. I needed to be more mindful of meeting all of his needs. So many times I thought that dragging him to a service would be too hard on him.

The next morning, I called my mother to check in with her. An hour later we were packed and on our way to Southern California. It wasn't a hospital trip; we had decided to go on a cross country road trip in her new car.

I think I set out across the country because I believed if we ran far enough away, I could put off the inevitable. Many times on this journey I had wanted to run away, and here, at the end of it, I finally had this chance to just leave. It was my mother's idea. She had a new car and wanted to drive out to see her family in Alabama. My father had encouraged her because soon her cancer would be so advanced that she would not be able to travel. I hoped the trip would recapture some of the fun the kids and I had last year. It was foolish.

I left the state AMA (against medical advice). I hadn't even told Kevin we were going until I got to my mother's house. There was no plan and we didn't know when we would return.

Once we were on the road, the new car was easy to drive and was very comfortable. Brian had settled in the backseat and always seemed to rest so well in a moving vehicle. I told myself everything would be okay. Besides, my mother could take care of Brian's medical needs, and the kids loved the idea that we were staying with my aunt in Alabama.

The kids fell back into vacation mode, singing "Spankin' Spoon" again, but after several days of hearing the same song, I told them they needed to come up with a new song. It wasn't long before they came up with:

What Could It Be?
Over the hill there should be an animal.
Over the hill what could it be?
Over the hill there should be an animal
Over the hill there is a . . . .

We were in Dallas on Crystal's eleventh birthday. Like Brian's birthday that year, I could only promise to get her whatever she wanted when we returned home. She told me she wanted a Cocker Spaniel. I told her we would pick out a puppy as soon as we got home.

After a sixteen-hour drive, we arrived in Alabama on Sunday evening. On that day Brian's journal entry was a simple narrative about playing with his sister, but mostly he slept.

Crystal and Me
Crystal and me are playing boat. I have two stuffed eagles.
One is a baby eagle. Crystal has a fox and a hound.

At first the trip had seemed to be going well . . .

28

AUGUST

When we got to Aunt Gussie's everyone was tired and Brian was struggling to breathe. By the end of the week his skin had lost its pink tone because he wasn't getting enough oxygen. Last year in June the temperatures and the humidity had been very mild, but this year in August, the temperatures soared. My aunt's old farm house was cooled by a one-room air conditioner perched in a window. The cooler had almost no effect on the temperatures that had reached 95 degrees.

At first Brian was shy about letting people know how much pain he was in, but as the week wore on, he spoke openly about being in too much pain. I doubled up on the amount of pain medication but it was not enough. His cancer ridden lungs could not move air laden with so much moisture. At first I started to panic, thinking we would not make it back in time for him to die at home. Then I realized I couldn't afford the luxury of losing control of the situation. I had to do something to manage the pain before we started back.

On the weekend my aunt had a potluck at her house and called it Crystal's birthday party. The house was filled with relatives I didn't even know I had. It wasn't long before I was getting hammered with judgment for leaving home with such a sick child. But they were right and I felt terrible about it.

When I left for Alabama, I had acted so recklessly that I wondered if it would cost Brian his life. I thought I was doing something that Brian would really enjoy. I knew God saw my heart, that when I said I was sorry, he forgave me.

My mother and Crystal enjoyed lunch while I stayed in the back bedroom with Brian. Brian told me he had wanted to come to Alabama, but when that didn't seem to make me feel any better, he thought I was upset because I was missing Crystal's party.

After everyone had eaten, my aunt came in to talk to me and pray for Brian. "You need to live life," she told me. She went on to say that we should never sit around and just wait for death to come, that it was good I was able to still do all the things Brian felt like doing; that I was building memories and not living in fear. Her husband had recently passed away and she regretted that they had put off so many things they had wanted to do.

My aunt had taken it upon herself to come in to talk to me and to change the attitude in her house because, after all, we were celebrating a birthday. She invited me and Brian to come out and have some cake and ice cream, and we did.

I called Children's Hospital early Monday morning on August 9. I felt horrible about telling them what I had done. The on-call nurse in Los Angeles was punitive and gave me a lecture. She said I had disobeyed orders by leaving the state.

It was true. We were fugitives. We had run away, and now 2,500 miles from home I needed help. She told me she would leave a message with Brian's doctor. I chastised her and told her I needed to talk to the doctor right away. I was thankful when he called me right back. He explained that the strict drug laws in Alabama made it difficult for him to help me. I needed to find a pediatrician in that state who would be willing to prescribe narcotics, and he thought that would be virtually impossible. But as soon as I hung up, my family helped me locate a doctor and arranged for Brian to be his last appointment of the day.

It was 5:00 PM when the receptionist walked into the empty waiting room to tell me to follow her back into an examining room. The doctor was hesitant about prescribing a class 3 narcotic and wanted to speak to Brian's doctor in Los Angeles. Forgetting about the two-hour time difference, I thought we were doomed because an after-hours call was sure to roll over to an answering machine or an on-call staff member who knew nothing about Brian's case.

I handed the receptionist the number. Brian's doctor answered the call; it was just 3 PM in California. After a brief consult, we had a prescription for Demerol and Tylenol #3.

In the morning, I drove straight through to Dallas, just as I had done the week before. We spent the night with my Aunt Amy. The humidity was not as intense in Texas and her whole house air conditioning system had greatly improved Brian's condition.

The next morning my Aunt Amy surprised everyone with an unexpected announcement. She had packed her bags during the night and had decided to travel with us to California. My mother was thrilled with the idea that she would be able to spend some time with her sister. Just having her join us for the trip home was enough of a distraction to make us forget the seriousness of Brian's situation.

We were back at my mom's house in California in less than twenty-eight hours. It had been my aunt's idea to drive straight through to California, but I too was eager to get Brian back home where he could die in peace. The 5,000-mile trip had taken less than two weeks but had felt so much longer.

At my mom's house, my dad looked frail. The worry and stress of our trip had taken a toll on him too. He brought out gifts for everyone hoping to make everything better. He had bought me a new electric typewriter and my mom got a microwave oven.

We rested at the house for a few days before I called Children's Hospital. Brian was doing so much better that I wanted him to have a reprieve before I dragged him off to the emergency room.

On Friday, August 13, I made arrangements for Brian to be seen at the Outpatient Clinic. He was supposed to just get a physical, but the doctor asked us to stick around. My aunt took us all to the Ice Follies on Saturday night because she wanted to do something special for the kids. They loved it.

On Monday morning, the hospital called and told us to go straight to emergency. Brian was hospitalized overnight. The echocardiogram showed that Brian's heart was weak. The doctor explained that as Brian's tumors grew, they were putting more and more pressure on his heart and now his heart was giving out. There was nothing more they could do for him except to manage his pain while he was hospitalized. He was released on Tuesday. While the news was devastating, Brian was actually doing well and I chose not to be reactive. We would still live each day to the fullest.

Our best friends in Los Angeles followed us home to Placerville. They would take their week long summer vacation at our house. Brian was feeling so good, having been on Demerol and morphine for twenty-four hours and was excited to get back home. He missed his dad and the bird. When I saw Kevin finally back with his son, I realized I had to do something to make up for the impulsive trip I had taken. I secretly planned a boy's night out.

Brian couldn't wait to show off his bird to Traci. I was glad to see the bird had not forgotten Brian during that two-week timeframe.

By summer, Hector was beautiful, all his colors were brilliant. His dark black eyes followed you when you came into the room and then he would whistle at you as you walked by. Hector could say "Hello" and "Bye bye," and "What are you doing?" he knew all the words to *Yankee Doodle Dandy*. He had learned a few simple tricks: to ring a bell and put his head down.

For the rest of the week the kids kept busy. They played in the pool, searched for arrowheads at Sly Park, and we took them to visit a place called Fairy Tale Town in Sacramento. The night before our friends left, we took the camper out to Wright's Lake and spent the night out in the woods. The kids floated on logs in the lake and we barbequed on the grill for dinner.

Brian wrote in his journal:

<u>When Bob and Bonnie Came Up</u>
When I look for arrowheads at Sly Park it's fun. One time
I went with my friend. We took the camper and that time

is now. I wonder if my family and my friend and I will find any arrowheads?

I found four chips. My friend found some and so did my family. My mom found the perfect arrowhead. One time I went looking for arrowheads but that was on my vacation.

Brian continued to write more and more as his days got shorter. He must have known his poems and stories were little treasures we could hold on to.

Children's Hospital called on August 27 and wanted us to bring Brian in for another round of treatment. Brian's pain was increasing and he wanted to go back to the hospital. The doctors hospitalized him for three days to give him several infusions of AZQ, then asked us to stay for two more injections at Outpatient.

At the hospital I had to listen to another explanation about AZQ and sign new paperwork. An advocate came into the room and even explained patient rights to us. She told me we had the right to withdraw from treatment at any time without consequence. That was something new; it was something I thought every newcomer should hear.

We spent one night at our best friends' house and the last night at my parents'. We left Los Angeles with our prescription of Tylenol #3 and Demerol. On the way home, Brian wrote:

<u>Jesus Loves You</u>
Flowers can grow.
Trees are big and strong.
God and the angels love you.
Roads are so long.

Many of our roads had been long and painful, but once again Brian rallied and his pain medication was reduced back down to every twelve hours. August ended the summer months but Brian still had more gifts to share with us. As we entered into September I just kept pushing the envelope; looking for activities that would enrich Brian's life. We would run this race as long and as hard as we could.

29

SEPTEMBER

Sesame Street on Ice came to town on September 11th, and Brian was looking forward to going to see the show, just him and his dad. Sometimes just the anticipation of a new activity upset his ability to manage the pain, so I had been in contact with our hospice nurse all week. Angie supported our choice to continue with the AZQ, not because it was treating the cancer, but because it was helping Brian to manage his pain. She believed in maintaining the highest quality of life to the end.

Angie's biggest frustration was that we were not keeping Brian drugged twenty-four hours a day so he could remain pain free. She talked to both me and Brian about how important it was to be one step ahead of the pain so we could ward off the violent attacks. We always listened and respectfully nodded in agreement with her concerns, but Brian still fought being drugged; he had things he wanted to do. He knew better than any of us what the consequences were, so I continued to leave it up to him.

On September 10, I pressured Brian into letting me administer Demerol around the clock so he would be pain free on Saturday for the ice show. The drive to Sacramento would take an hour and then there would be long lines where he would have to stand and wait. But the whole time I was working to make sure the next day went well, I worried that no matter what I did it probably wasn't going to work out.

After a day of drugs and bed rest, Brian was up early and ready to spend the day with his dad. Brian gave me a funny look as he and Kevin stepped into the garage to get into the car. He couldn't believe Crystal and I would miss such a great show. For just a moment I wanted to toss out all the plans so that Crystal and I could go too, but I owed Kevin the chance to spend some one-on-one time with his son. Kevin needed to see the magnificent young man Brian had grown up to be over the last few months. Through his mother's eyes, Brian still looked good, a little thin maybe. But I thought no one would ever guess he was standing at death's door.

Crystal and I laid on the bed all afternoon and watched science fiction movies until Kevin and Brian got back home. It was a special day for us too. We never had a chance to just be at home and hang out.

Brian was all smiles when he returned home, but he was tired. What a relief that he had made it through the entire day. He was exhausted from keeping up the charade of feeling fine. It was what he did now when he was in public, smiling when everyone else did, holding his arms down by his side rather than up at his chest, acting as though there was nothing wrong; it was important that "they" believed he did not have cancer, that he was just a normal kid. But now that he was home, he curled up on the couch so I could beat on his back to stop the pain.

The next week, UCD wanted to run more tests, but I postponed it. There had been so much testing. I reluctantly agreed to the blood draw on Wednesday, only to comply with AZQ requirements.

Brian had started back to school with his home tutor. He spent many days doing homework, drawing pictures, and writing stories. He practiced his cursive writing skills and loved to do math. I found drawings of animals on almost every page of the newspaper, in magazines, and on pieces of mail.

It was the middle of September, and we still had not found a cocker spaniel puppy for Crystal. For some reason, that breed of dog was difficult to find in Northern California. On Saturday, Crystal and I went out on a mission to find a puppy, any puppy. If she couldn't have a cocker spaniel, another dog would have to do. That day we went to the animal shelter as a last resort. It was disappointing that none of the dogs looked anything like a span-iel. As we walked past all the cages, we saw one small dog, the only dog close to a cocker spaniel size. We couldn't really tell what breed she was because she had just been rescued and was still dirty and her hair was matted. We decided no one else would want her and we could give her a good home. I was surprised when the facility said she was a Cockapoo mix. We carefully lifted her into the car, but when we closed the door we quickly realized that not only had she looked like she needed a bath, she smelled like it too. The ride home was really bad.

We named her Missy. But when we brought Missy home, no one was very excited to meet her. Kevin just shook his head. Brian looked out from the bedroom disapprovingly and said, "Oh Mom." Neither of them could believe we would bring home such a dirty little mutt. But Missy was cute once she was bathed and trimmed, and she loved Crystal. She was very smart and learned how to do several tricks right away. She could stand on her hind feet and twirl around when you asked her to do a "pretty dance." Whenever Crystal left the house, Missy sat faithfully at the win-dow, waiting for her to come home. Missy frustrated Brian be-cause she never wanted to play with him, but he understood that Missy was Crystal's dog.

Brian started to spend more time upstairs as his pain in-creased. On "bad" days, he wanted me to be near him. He did not like any noise. He could not stand having the television on and didn't want to do anything except write and draw pictures. As he wrote, I noticed how the words were written so neatly on lined paper. Each word had a purpose and was written boldly. He rarely made any mistakes or crossed anything out. His stories had pic-tures and most of his poems still had rhyming words.

In most of his stories, birds learned to fly or animals went to church, but in this simple short story, the mother dog told her puppy he had to go to school. He wrote this story for Crystal and then she drew the pictures to go with it. On that day they were playing school and she was the teacher. He was just starting third grade.

The Dog Who Didn't Want to Go to School

There was a dog. He didn't want to go to school. He didn't have any friends.

His mom said, "You need to go to school. It's good for you." He said, "Do I need to go to school in two days?" "Yes," said mom.

Soon it was two days. He went to school. In a few days he made friends. He was happy. When he came home, he saw one of his friends. They got to play. Now it is dark, his friend had to go home. Now the dog went to bed. The End.

As Brian wrote, I prayed. Daily I sought God and found his loving arms waiting for me. Sometimes I wondered what would happen if I hadn't been a believer? I knew this experience, with all the uncertainty, all the emotional and financial pressures, would have destroyed me. Or what if, as a Christian, I had gotten angry and blamed God because I thought I deserved something better? If anger only breeds hate, then the results would have been horrifying for my child. I couldn't image what it would have been like for Brian if his father and I had not been grounded, if our home had been divided or if we were so focused on ourselves that we hadn't had time for the children's needs. All of those things would have only made this journey more difficult.

I thought about how I used to approach God, before I recommitted my life to him. I used to dump all my problems on him and then just walk away. I thought I was doing my part by confessing and asking for forgiveness. I hadn't realized that I actually had to come to terms with the sin and change my behavior. I didn't know God wanted me to use my experiences to help others. I used to casually pray about things that did not bring eternal rewards. Do you think God really cares what lamp you buy, when he made the sun? Does he care where you live, when you should be living for him? Do you pray for the homeless, when you could be feeding them? I began praying for souls to be saved and that God would use me for his glory.

It had been the fact that I had a relationship with God, spent time in his presence, and listened to his words of guidance that had gotten me through all those "deep valley" days. At the end of Brian's life, I needed only to turn to scripture for strength. When the apostle Paul prays for the church Ephesus to have a deeper faith in the book of Ephesians, he says:

And I pray that you, being rooted and established in love, may have power, together with all the saints, to grasp how wide, and how long, and high and deep is the love of Christ . . . (Ephesians 3:17–18 NIV).

The church in Ephesus needed to grow so they might glorify God. In verse 3:13, Paul tells them not to lose heart because of the trials, for it is the trials that elevate our faith. God has sent his Holy Spirit to us to empower our lives. Because of Jesus, we are already rooted in God's love. He had already given me all I needed. Nothing could happen now that was outside of God's grasp.

On September 19, God spoke to me so clearly about Brian's death that I knew the time was near. I asked the Lord, "Will you take Brian or heal him? Brian is asking me what you are going to do." I read in His Word:

Will not the land tremble for this, and all who live in it mourn? (Amos 8:8 NIV).

Are you really taking Brian now?

I will turn your religious feasts into mourning and all your singing into weeping (Amos 8:10 NIV).

Lord, is this really from you, I have to know that I am hearing from you, let me hear your words one more time.

"But you, son of man, listen to what I say to you. Do not rebel like that rebellious house; open your mouth and eat what I give you." Then I looked, and I saw a hand stretched out to me. In it was a scroll, which he unrolled before me. On both sides of it were written words of lament and mourning and woe (Ezekiel 2:8-10 NIV).

Even though the words were tough to hear, I knew without a doubt we were at the end of the road. I would have to find a way to tell Brian.

That evening, I was praying that I would say the right words. I wondered about the sadness Brian would feel, leaving his family, facing the fear of the unknown . . . and God said to me, ". . . and (he) went home praising God" (Luke 5:2 NIV).

The words were so comforting because it didn't matter what I said to Brian. He would be ready to go when it was time. Then I asked, "Lord, what about us, if you take Brian will you get the glory?" I read Isaiah 15:1,3,7:

Surely in a night—devastated and ruined. . . . Everyone is wailing, dissolved in tears . . . . the abundance which they have acquired and stored up, they carry off over the brook of Arabim (NASB).

Lesson 10: <u>E</u>ternal Rewards

I believed we would mourn Brian's loss, but the abundance (that which was over and above) which we had acquired and stored up (the weight of his glory) during our journey would remain. We had gathered some of the essence of God's nature and had been changed by a deeper walk with him, a greater faith, and a belief in a love that never failed. This weight of his glory would remain with us and help us to carry on.

C. S. Lewis in an essay entitled *The Weight of Glory* states that in heaven: "We will be with Christ, be like him, and have glory." Our activities on earth are not frivolous but a call to do everything for his glory.

There is a physical aspect in the description of glory; the weight (*kabod* in Hebrew means: weight/burden; glorious). It is the part of God that remains in us—we see that part as a reflection of Him.

I talked to Brian about what his journey would look like now, at this final stage. Brian responded by looking up at me and saying, "It's okay, Mommy, I know Jesus is with me." The only words I could say back before I fell apart were, "I know that too."

I brought the bird upstairs into our room and set him up next to Brian's bed. Sometimes we had to cover Hector's cage because he was so noisy, but Brian wanted Hector there next to him. I would have to bring all of his meals upstairs now on a tray. As his pain increased, so did the amounts of Demerol he was receiving.

On Monday, September 20, UCD arranged for us to come into the clinic for an x-ray. The doctors were concerned about internal bleeding again. They thought that he might need to be hospitalized. I envisioned the cancer growing everywhere in his body because the level of pain he was experiencing was unbearable.

On days when Brian felt like he could manage the pain, he wanted nothing to do with another hospitalization. But on the very bad days we were both conflicted. We knew the IV drip of Demerol and morphine killed the pain better than anything we were using at home. I still wanted to let him die at home but I could not see how it was going to happen.

UCD wanted to send us back to Children's Hospital, and again I pushed back the date. Time at home was important and I was so conflicted about going on back to Los Angeles. On Thursday

Crystal's band performed and on Friday I went to church to hear Barry McGuire sing. I was doing anything I could think of to avoid another trip. After having a few days to think about what we should do next, I went ahead and made arrangements to fly to Burbank on Sunday.

The flight from Sacramento to Burbank took less than forty-five minutes, and our best friends picked us up at the airport and dropped us off at my parents so I could borrow their car. We stayed in Los Angeles for nine days. Brian started back on daily doses of AZQ on Monday. Brian's doctor gave us a prescription for Methadone. On Wednesday after the morning infusion, Brian was feeling better. On October 5, we flew home.

30

OCTOBER

B rian had a few good days back at home. He couldn't ride the new bike we bought to replace the one Helen had taken. Sometimes he just sat on the seat of the bike or held it upright. He still took Hector out on the front porch for a few minutes each morning. Inside, during the last two weeks of his life, he drew pictures of Hector and wrote poems. This poem is the most important one to me, because in all that pain, God was still good.

<u>God Is Good</u>
God is good, he is not bad.
Jesus is good, and we are glad.
Angels we know are above our heads,
While God is watching over us, as we lay down our head.
Everybody knows God will come down soon
And later we will be right over the moon.

Brian's tutor called to see if we were still going to try to have school that week. I told her Brian still wanted her to come. It was her last visit. I always bathed him now before his weekly tutoring session. The warm water seemed to loosen his stiff joints and the steam helped him to breathe a little easier. He had to be helped down the stairs, but even though he never said anything I could tell he would have preferred to come down on his own.

As he sat at the kitchen table to wait for Nancy to arrive, he started to cry. "Where is she?" he asked. "I am not going to make it." I knew it would be at least another ten minutes or so before she got there. I tried to get him to lie down on the sofa, but he was afraid. It was difficult to breathe when he reclined. He was afraid he would die before she got there. I could see his heart pounding. I had doubled up on his painkillers, but it wasn't enough to kill the pain. Brian refused another dose knowing that he would not be able to function if he took any more. I was trying to figure out what else I could do when I saw Nancy pulling into the driveway.

When Nancy came in, Brian was alert and still feeling creative, but his body was weak and frail. The lesson plan for that last day was simple math, after which she had Brian create a picture using pastels. Brian finished his page of math problems in minutes and was ready to draw. He drew a picture of two flamingos standing on a hillside near a pond. The colors were so vivid. The green grass, the deep blue water of the pond, and the bright pink flamingos posing in a way that only flamingos can. He added a yellow sun at the top of the page and five birds flying through the clouds of the light blue sky. It was a beautiful picture. I marveled at his ability to create something so perfect even now. He was on the verge of collapse. It was so hard to see him this way.

I re-read the words from a friend, who had written to us exactly one year ago, on October 5. The words helped me through the very tough times. She said the Lord told her to send this to us:

<u>Picture Him</u>
Picture him running
Leaping into the arms of God
Cuddled
Greeted by a loving Father
Who loves him even more than you
Picture him loved
Resting upon my bosom
Happy, joyous
Basking in my love

Picture him whole
No tears
No sorrow
Made perfectly whole
Being what he could not be on earth
Picture him found

I had to let him go now. I couldn't even pretend anymore that he was doing well enough to stay. God would make him whole again in heaven.

On October 8, UCD called to remind us of our weekly blood draw. The results were not as bad as I had imagined. Brian's count was slowly decreasing; his red blood count was 9. He had 230 platelets and his white count was 2.3. But in the next few days as the blood count dropped I feared the nadir would really kill him this time. Meanwhile the pain continued.

I started looking through all of the articles I had collected about cancer patients and their pain. I found an article comparing terminally ill cancer patients in the United States to those in Great Britain. Here in the United States cancer patients suffered severe pain at the end of their lives because of the high tolerance levels they developed for painkillers. In the final stages, when pain is relentless, the pain-relieving drugs are no longer adequate. British patients were given heroin to ease their suffering.

Research there showed heroin to be 2.7 times as potent as morphine, and patients who took it were pain-free and alert. They were able to socialize, keep busy, and enjoy the last days of their lives. But the American Medical Association, the U.S. Government's National Cancer Institute, and the American Cancer Society all opposed prescribing heroin; they claimed morphine was just as effective. It made me angry to read that in other countries they did all they could to help, but here, we simply wrote it off as not effective. How could they know that? Did they even care? This unbearable pain was preventable.

I had also kept an article from the *Los Angeles Times* dated May 16, 1982, which stated that "in the last stages . . . morphine, Demerol, and Dilaudid will be inadequate to do the job. In more than thirty nations heroin is legally available to doctors for treating patients . . . injected it is clearly superior for pain relief."

I wondered how I was going to get the heroin. I bet I could get it in San Francisco, but I couldn't leave Brian.

On October 11, Brian was still having trouble breathing. He needed help, but the only thing I could do was to pound his chest. It was picture day at Crystal's school and I tried to juggle everyone's needs around until I was able to get her on the school bus.

Brian hurt so badly that I just kept increasing the dosages, but it didn't help. I was sure that in the late hours of the night I had given him too much Demerol again, but he woke in the morning needing more.

On Tuesday, the morning was pretty normal, but by the time Crystal left for school, Brian's breathing was shallow. Even with the help of Hospice I did not know how to let him die. When he told me he needed help, I called UCD and the doctor made arrangements to meet us in the emergency room. I knew by now the blood count had to be at its lowest level. The doctor suggested a blood transfusion might help.

I called Kevin at work and told him to meet us there. When we arrived at the hospital, Brian was gray, there was no parking and so I left the car on the side of the building and carried him in. The medical team admitted him right away and gave him something for the pain. The doctors tried to draw blood to see what his count was but they could not find any good veins. They just kept trying until they got enough to run the tests. Both Brian and I were exhausted when they came back and said his count was within a normal range. It meant the trip had been a waste of time. He didn't need a transfusion after all.

I asked the doctor to order penicillin because in the past it had worked to clear up any infections that were hindering his breathing. The doctor said infections weren't the problem. Lack of oxygen in the blood and organ failure was making it difficult to control the pain.

He showed me the latest x-rays. Both of Brian's lungs were filled with tumors. I asked for penicillin again anyway, and the doctor wrote me a prescription. There was nothing else anyone could do for Brian except admit him into the hospital to manage his pain. I knew that was not what Brian wanted and so the doctor did not push it. We both knew that if Brian was admitted to the hospital, he would die there. When Kevin arrived, the doctor said the obvious out loud: that Brian could die any time now. Kevin listened to what the doctor said, but I couldn't bear to hear any more. I could barely handle the minute-to-minute plays that were flashing before me, nothing more.

Before we left, I finally had enough presence of mind to ask about the colon cancer. I wondered if the cancer was attacking all of his other organs. But the doctor looked stunned. He said the colon cancer had been completely healed, that it never came back. I had been waiting for over a year to hear those words. The colon cancer had disappeared. God had healed him of that, just like he said he would!

I remembered when God spoke to me: "Brian will not die from the colon cancer." He had touched Brian at a time when we could not take any more. My soul rejoiced! "Lord, I did hear your voice!"

I am the good shepherd. I know my sheep and my sheep know me (John 10:14 NIV).

In the years ahead there would be so much more to learn, but that moment confirmed for me again that I really had all I needed. He had *circumcise*d my heart so that I might hear his voice. I committed myself to the Lord, nothing was impossible for him. In resolute trust I was confident in battle. He lifted my spirit above my circumstances and gave me unspeakable joy. His mantle of love carried me until I was able to come to a complete surrender. I became his instrument of praise thankful for all that he had given me, all he had brought me through and for wherever he would lead me. Now as I rested in sweet communion with him I reaped the eternal rewards that were waiting for me. I used his words to praise him.

> You alone art the Lord. You made the heavens, even the highest heavens, and all their starry host, the earth and all that is on it, the seas and all that is in them. You give life to everything, and the multitudes of heaven worship you (Nehemiah 9:6 NIV).

This is the God I worship. He is the God I put my trust in. I will praise him because I know that my journey will serve his purpose and bring him glory.

Just hearing that Brian had been healed, from the very doctor who knew Brian so well, was good news. He knew that Brian had been healed because he had followed Brian's progression, reviewed the x-rays and could show me the results in the body scans. But it was the confirmation that I had clearly heard God's voice in a moment of profound weakness that restored my soul. God had waited to fill me with joy. He had guarded my heart for this very moment. The affirmation would carry me through. Death would not sting.

When we got back to my car, I had forgotten about leaving the car parked on the side of the building, and I had a ticket on the windshield. I just sighed and started to put it inside the car. I deserved it, there are always consequences when there is disobedience, but the hospital social worker intervened. She took the ticket and said she would take care of it for me. I hugged her goodbye and got into the car. Kevin placed Brian gently onto the back seat before finding his own car. Brian was resting peacefully now. We drove home with Kevin following.

Kevin's Journal: The doctors say Brian is in his last days. He can die anytime now. It was a long drive home from the hospital. Brian is breathing much better now after the injections of pain medication. Picked up penicillin for Brian.

Kevin knew his time with Brian was short. He had three prayer requests that day;

1. He wanted to be with Brian when he died.
2. He wanted Brian to die in peace.
3. He wanted God to let Brian die at home, just like Brian wanted.

Back at home, I wanted to keep Brian heavily sedated, but he shook his head no, so I started the penicillin. Wednesday was a terrible day; Brian had an allergic reaction to the antibiotic. His body was breaking down and instead of clearing his airways, it caused severe itching. I called UCD. I had pushed too hard for the medication and it had been the wrong decision.

I followed the doctors' instructions, forcing Brian into a warm tub dowsed with cornstarch. The bath helped, and he was ready for a nap as soon as I got his pajamas on him. UCD had also suggested that I push fluids and increase the pain medication.

After a few hours of sleep, Brian wanted to go downstairs and watch some television. He saw an ad for the Make A Wish Foundation. He turned to me and said he had a wish. He wanted the foundation to arrange for him to spend the day with a policeman. I didn't respond. He waited, looking impatient because I wasn't saying anything. Then he said, "You better hurry up!" But I didn't know how to make something like that happen now. Brian could read me well. He said, "It's too late, Mom, isn't it?" I still didn't know what to say. Through my tears I could see the light in his eyes grow dim as the truth was starting to sink in.

Kevin's journal: Rode into work alone today instead of car-pooling, in case. The boss is still sick, work is hectic, proba-bly better for me to keep busy. Penny called; says Brian had allergic reaction to penicillin. Pulled muscle in my back at work. Go home emotionally drained. Put Brian to bed. Feel like the battle is almost over. Not hungry, just very tired.

On Thursday, Brian felt a little better. Brian's doctor at Chil-dren's Hospital called to see if the pain medication was adequate, reminding me that I could increase the dosage if needed. He told me about a new drug that was coming out that might help. His words were hopeful; but we had already moved from a temporal mindset to an eternal one.

On Friday, Brian was a lot worse. He was coughing and couldn't catch his breath. He threw up bile. He lost control of his bladder and wet his clothes. The bath upset him. He didn't eat. He didn't smile. He couldn't stand any noise. He cried if anyone walked into the bedroom, or spoke. He cried when the social worker called to see how we were doing. Brian even asked me to cover Hector's cage to keep him quiet. It was the beginning. He was leaving us.

I kept asking him how he was doing. I wanted to know if he needed any pain medication. He didn't want anything.

That night, even after Kevin came home from work, I just stayed upstairs with Brian. He wanted someone with him at all times now. I couldn't blame him; it must be frightening to feel like you are suffocating. That night I wasn't just keeping him company, I felt like I needed to talk him through this part of the journey.

I took a deep breath, I was crying, so Brian started speaking first. He told me not to cry, that he was having a nice day. He had al-ways tried to comfort me, and he was even doing that now. He told me *he was not afraid to die*. He said he thought about heaven a lot. It was a very emotional time for me, and I cried some more. Brian was leaving us. He had already separated from Hector and now he was telling me he would be okay. I still wasn't ready to let him go.

On Saturday, because Brian had such a hard time on Friday, I pleaded with God once again to intercede on our behalf. God heard my prayer. That morning when Brian woke up he was hungry. He ate two strips of bacon, one piece of toast, and drank a half glass of punch and a half glass of water. It was the most he'd eaten in days, maybe weeks. After he had finished eating he told me *he would not be able to eat food anymore*. He said the words in such a way that made me believe they were true. It was his last meal. His words were the first of several prophetic utterances.

Winter was coming. We'd been planning to buy a woodstove because our heat pump was getting too expensive to run. But with Brian in the condition he was in, Kevin and I both hesitated to leave the house unnecessarily. It was a relief when Kevin mentioned going to the hardware store, just a few miles away, and both kids wanted to go with him. That was the answer; we would all go. Brian couldn't walk, but he hung tightly to his dad's neck while Kevin carried him around the store. We saw a few church friends there and said hello, but then quickly purchased the stove we had picked out months ago. We came straight home. It was the last thing we did as a family. Brian had been with us to purchase something that would warm our house and our hearts when he left us.

At home, Brian tried to watch TV, but that only lasted half an hour. All he really wanted was a warm bath. After I got him dressed for bed he asked me to check his nails on his fingers and his toes, he wanted to make sure they were clean. Then he asked me to clean his ears, he did not want his ears to be dirty. Once he felt clean, I sensed a wave of peace in our house.

I didn't understand the importance of him being physically clean. He didn't want a quick tub bath and then to bed. He insisted that he be thoroughly cleaned, from his head to his toes. Was he doing that to wash away sin? Jesus had already done that for him with his blood. Or was the bath to wash away any remaining part of earth in preparation to meet Jesus?

I knew Brian had been circumcised, both in the flesh and in the spirit. A physical circumcision took place when he was just three days old. His foreskin was cut away.

> In the Old Testament circumcision was a sign of the covenant with Abraham. When the nation of Israel wandered for 40 years in the wilderness the rite of circumcision ceased for a generation that refused to enter the Promised Land. Once the journey ended the blessing returned. Circumcise again the sons of Israel (Joshua 5:2 NIV). Circumcision involved a universal blessing. God extended the blessing in a way that would show the nations God has touched us.[35]

Brian was just four-and-a half years old when he first went up to the altar at church to accept Jesus as his Savior, but at the age of six he fully committed his life and began living for Jesus. It is this circumcision of the heart that cuts deep and goes to our very essence, our attitudes and relationship with God. Brian had prayed that prayer with Pastor Kemp just days before his eighth surgery.

> In him you were also circumcised, in the putting off of the sinful nature, not with a circumcision done by hands of men but with the circumcision done by Christ, having been buried with him in baptism and raised with him through your faith in the power of God, who raised him from the dead (Colossians 2:11–12 NIV).

For an adult the cutting away of our former life is painful, but for Brian it was easy. He had always had a relationship with Jesus and believed Jesus was always with him. Jesus gave him so much confidence that he never questioned why he had to go through the fire. He accepted his lot in life and never wanted to be anyone other than himself.

Finally, I decided that this washing ritual wasn't so much about Brian as it was about us. This was the path we needed to walk so the separation would not be painful. I was preparing him for his transition.

I wondered what was going to happen next. Would Brian just stop breathing? He put his fingers up to his lips and said, "Shhhh! No more talking."

31

FINAL DAYS

On October 17, when the Sunday paper arrived, I glanced over at the cover of the television guide and walked away. I felt like everywhere I looked God was sending me a very clear message; we were entering the final hours. The cover read "Dying Days."

On Monday morning, with Kevin at work and Crystal at school, I stayed close to Brian, watching him take every breath. It was a difficult day, because when he woke up he wanted ice and yet he didn't want me to leave and go downstairs to get it. He moaned and cried out whenever I left the room. His crying spells used up so much of his energy that he had nothing left to pull air back into his lungs. Each time it happened I sat and waited to see if he would recover.

I kept a log by his bed, documenting every dosage of medication. Brian showed no resistance to drugs that day because he was in so much pain. I tried to stay on top of it, but at this late stage of the game with no other viable options, it was impossible. He had codeine at 7:00 AM, and methadone at 10:00 AM I had found that alternating the drugs seemed to help.

It was almost noon when I asked, "Brian, would a warm bath feel good?" He answered, "No, but you need to wash my feet."

After that, he poured water into a basin and began to wash the disciples' feet, drying them with a towel that was wrapped around him. Simon Peter replied, "not just my feet but my hands and my head as well." Jesus answered, "A person who has had a bath needs only to wash his feet; his whole body is clean" (John 13:5, 9–10 NIV).

Brian had already bathed; he was clean physically and spiritually as well. I believed that his prayer for forgiveness had given him complete absolution from sin; but he had not yet been baptized in water.

> Jesus sets the scene . . . to show his disciples the full extent of his love. For the love that is evident in the laying down of life at the crucifixion is also demonstrated in the laying down of life in humble service in the foot washing. John's introduction to the event ensures that we understand God's glory (humility, intimacy, a share in an inheritance) is revealed in Jesus in this sign. Many note that the word wash (*louo*) is from a word family commonly associated with baptism and thus take this washing as baptism.[36]

As I washed Brian's feet, I felt like God had given me yet another opportunity to show my son how much I loved him. At the time I thought that something powerful was happening but I wasn't sure what the significance was. I only knew that Brian felt his feet were dirty and he needed to have the last remnant of earthly soil gone before he could reach his heavenly destination. When I finished drying his feet, I felt like I was walking on holy ground. Brian had laid down and was already sound asleep. I prayed, "He is ready now, Lord."

I kept an eye on Brian while I straightened up the room and cleaned the bathroom. At 3:00 PM, he was starting to wake up, so I whispered that I was going out to get the mail. He moaned and rested his head back down into the pillow; I knew he did not want me to go. I turned to him and playfully said "Don't be silly—I will be right back."

I stepped out into the rain and ran quickly to the mail box and then back up the stairs. I was gone too long—when I got back, Brian was sitting up, trying to catch his breath. He gave me a look that told me I had caused the episode. He didn't have to say a word because I quickly promised not to leave him again. He asked for more methadone.

For the next few hours Brian kept repeating, "Mom, I don't feel good." I knew something new must be happening inside his body. I was sorry I didn't have heroin—I had nothing else to give him to ease the pain. I offered more methadone, but he didn't want it. He was exhausted from being upset and trying to speak, so he just lay back down. I asked him if I could turn the television on for a minute. He nodded his head. The television set was turned to a Christian station and a minister was talking about the *day of delivery*. I turned it off. Today was our day of delivery, I already knew that. I was sure that by the end of the day Brian would be delivered from all this pain. I wanted to feel triumphant, but instead I turned away to secretly wipe away the tears.

The pharmacy called about a wheelchair Brian had requested the last time we were at UCD. When Kevin called to check in on us, I asked him to pick up the wheelchair on the way home. There were so many calls that day. Each time the phone rang, it upset Brian. I planned to unplug the phone as soon as Kevin and Crystal were safely home.

Several days earlier, while I was flipping channels, I had stopped to listen to a new song that was being played on a Christian television program. The song was being sung in preparation for communion. I remembered that day because it was the first time Brian asked me why people took communion. I told him that Jesus had asked us to take communion often so we would not forget what he had done for us. With the breaking of the bread we acknowledge our sins, the sins Christ died for, and with the wine, his blood, we are cleansed. Brian and I had taken communion while Jeannie Johnson sang a song titled, *In This Very Room*. I could hear the words. Jesus was in our room chasing away all the sadness and filling us with his love, his joy and an undying hope in him that could not be denied.

The words were comforting and helped me to remain calm and have peace. God in his great wisdom had provided a way for me to endure the next few hours by filling my head with the powerful words of that song.

"Lord," I prayed, "I know you'll be taking Brian soon. I know it's time because his suffering is great, and his faith in you is strong. But before you take him, will you let me see him smile just one last time?" I was being selfish, but I knew I didn't have much time left. I was asking for a sign that would assure me that Brian was doing okay.

Brian opened his eyes. *He had half a smile as he looked up at me.* Then he reached up and squeezed my nose and laughed. It was the kind of thing he used to do, on a good day. For that moment I was suspended in time. I held on to it with my whole heart and gathered every precious memory. Then it was gone, over in just a few seconds. He had already closed his eyes again and drifted off.

The rest of the day, if I even tried to talk to him, he repeated that unusual behavior he had used for the first time several days ago; he put his fingers to his mouth and said, *"Shhhh."*

He grew more and more sensitive to noise. He moaned when Crystal came home and he heard the door shut. Then he was restless when water ran from the faucet or the dog got excited. When Crystal began to practice her flute, he cried. I offered to go in and ask her to stop, but he shook his head no. Shortly afterward, Crystal stopped practicing and stayed in her room quietly doing homework. She must have known something was wrong.

Kevin came home early with pipes for the new wood stove. The leaves were turning and it was starting to get cold at night. I asked him to go back out to pick up the wheelchair and the new medicine the doctor had ordered for itching and anxiety. I wanted to have more medication for the night if Brian started to get worse. Kevin took one look at Brian and did not want to go back out, but I insisted. I wanted to be prepared for this mortal night.

Brian woke up when Kevin came back home. When I told Brian we had gotten the wheelchair, he was very upset. He told me, "No, take it out of the house." He was angry; he said he wanted to go downstairs and warned me that if he saw it down there, it would make him feel sick. Kevin hid the chair.

I was surprised by Brian's response. I didn't think anything that happened now could invoke so much anger. He had wanted the chair, but now days later it was too late. There was nothing this earth had to give him that he needed now. I wondered if he had gotten angry because he had fought so hard to be independent. Nothing was going to stop him from walking straight into the arms of Jesus. Brian would never sit if he could stand. He never wanted to be seen as anything less than completely whole. Soon all that would come true for him. He would be brand new, better than he had ever been before.

Kevin spent some time holding Brian while I answered phone call after phone call. First UCD called, then our best friends, my parents, and two of Kevin's cousins. All these interruptions were taking a toll on Brian. I had been on the phone for over two hours. All the time I was spending with other people robbed me of those precious last moments with Brian. But then I looked over at Brian and saw that my distractions had been God's way of allowing Kevin some time to be alone with him. I finally unplugged the phone so I could fix dinner.

I made spaghetti, our favorite family meal, but I don't remember anyone eating it. We all just sat quietly listening to Brian gasp for air. I gave him one medication at 6:00 PM and forty-five minutes later I gave him another medication, separating the itching medication from the dosage of methadone.

Brian was propped up against me, finally able to rest. I longed to hold him close and tell him everything would be okay, but I didn't dare speak or move because it had taken him so long to get comfortable. Each breath he took was slower and shallower than the last. I continued pleading with God for the reassurance I needed: "Lord, won't you just let me hold my baby in my arms just one more time?"

In his grace, God allowed me another special moment. Brian suddenly sat up to reposition his body. *He laid his head across my heart and held on to me.* I could feel his heart beating close to mine. I hoped he knew how much we had loved him. I knew God had given me yet another gift.

That evening, just like millions of other families in America, we all sat in the living room together and watched an entire episode of *That's Incredible* on television. It was an incredible moment. Brian had not been able to spend more than just a few minutes downstairs because he had been in and out of consciousness, could not stand any noise including the sound of people moving or talking, and yet there he sat engaged in a program for an entire hour staring at the screen, even laughing a few times. For a moment, it felt like everything was fine. We were a normal family again, just watching TV on a Monday night, the way other families did.

When the show ended, Brian wanted to go to bed. Kevin carried him back upstairs. The four of us would never be together again. It was 10 PM and Brian walked from the bed into the bathroom and then climbed into bed by himself. I wondered how any of that was possible. He was so weak and he had not eaten since Saturday, and had very little liquids. It had been well over twelve hours since he had gone to the bathroom. Yet he didn't ask for help; he was a strong little guy.

After getting back into bed, he lay down on his back, his head slightly raised by the pillow, and he patted his chest. The tumors in his chest were so large now that he could not rest in any other position. I pinched at the skin on Brian's arm. Brian didn't flinch. I was checking to see if he was dehydrated, but his skin recovered immediately. The few sips of water and ice had sustained him. As he closed his eyes and struggled for breath, I sat near him holding very still.

I was determined to stay up all night. Jesus was coming to take my son and I didn't want to miss it. I prayed and read my Bible for most of the night.

Out of the depths I cry to you, O Lord. I wait for the Lord, my soul waits, and in his word I put my hope (Psalm 130:1, 5 NIV).

I prayed, "Yes, Lord, my soul does wait for Thee, for you will redeem Brian from all his iniquities today!" I patted Brian and gave him a few small pieces of ice. At 11:15 PM, he cried out to me, "Where are you, Mom?" "I am right here," I assured him. He must have known he was leaving soon. I prayed he would feel ready. I gave him more methadone and he began resting easier. I wondered if he would be gone by midnight. I cried out to God, "Answer me O, Lord. Thy loving kindness is everlasting . . ."

Brian's body continued to fight to get air into his lungs. I looked over at our bed and saw that Kevin had finally fallen asleep. At 11:36 PM, Brian called out to me again. "Mom, it's there." I don't know what he saw, but I knew it was almost time for him to go.

I stayed close, patting him to sleep. It was after 2 AM, Brian was still breathing, and Kevin had just woken up. I don't remember leaving Brian and climbing into my own bed, but that's where I was when Kevin woke me up at 5:15 AM He had taken my place on Brian's bed. Now Kevin asked me to watch Brian while he got up.

It was so dark outside when I walked over and knelt beside Brian's bed. When Kevin returned he looked down at Brian and said it was over. Then he told me Brian had asked for water at 5:00 AM I thought to myself, hadn't Jesus himself said "I thirst" while he hung on the cross?

Later, knowing that all was completed, and so that the Scripture would be fulfilled, Jesus said, "I am thirsty" (John 19:28 NIV).

Jesus' last request had completed his mission on earth and he then spoke his last words; "It is finished."

As Brian lay dying he had spoken many words we would not understand until after he was gone. But at this hour, while he was alert and sober, having gone six hours without any pain medication, the message was clear. His time had come.

I looked at Brian and he was still taking slow shallow breaths. He would not leave without letting his mother say goodbye. "Brian," I asked, "Are you afraid to die?" Still conscious, he shook his head no. I said, "I love you, Brian. I can't hold on to you anymore because you hurt." He took three more very calm slow breaths. And then he stopped breathing just before dawn; it was 5:30 AM. Nightfall had ended, and it was the beginning of a new day. Brian was with the Lord. My soul shouted, "My son, look, your joy comes in the morning!"

Awake, Brian, you are clothed in his beauty. Rise up, the chains are broken, you have been redeemed. God says to you, "Here I am, I bring good news: salvation." And you can now shout with the victory that your God does reign (Isaiah 52 NASB).

Brian, you can see now what you always knew to be true. The Lord walked before you and was your rear guard. Nothing in your life happened without him being there. Surely our grief he himself bore. Our sorrows he carried . . . and by his scourging, you are healed (Isaiah 53). And now, as the angels of the Lord take you to heaven, my soul rejoices.

Brian, "receive the crown of life which the Lord has promised to those who love him" (James 1:12 NIV).

32

—

SOAKED IN THE SPIRIT

Kevin asked what I thought we should do. I told him nothing. "It's okay," I said. It really was okay. Brian had gone to a place where diseases were not allowed. "Thank you, Lord," I said softly. We knelt down next to Brian's bed and prayed. I was sure I could still feel the presence of angels, God's spiritual warriors, forming a tight ring around the bed. They must have come to take Brian home. We needed to let him go now so they could leave.

I held Brian one last time and kissed him softly on the cheek. I could still hear the communion song in my head as I stepped away from the bed. *Lord Jesus, you are in this very room.* I opened my Bible and read, "Where is the Lord? (2 Kings 2:14 NASB).

"He is here with us," my spirit answered.

"Where is Brian?" I asked.

"The Spirit of the Lord has taken him up . . ." (2 Kings 2:16 NASB).

"And the Lord opened the servant's eyes, and he saw" (2 Kings 6:17 NASB).

We saw the glory, the reflective splendor—a moment that awed us into silence. Suddenly it was 10:00 AM Where had all those hours gone? I touched Brian's skin and it was cold. We must have been caught up in the oneness of God. We had experienced his glory, where time and space no longer existed. We had not slept, but we felt renewed by his peace. There were no tears, no sorrow. Brian had been made whole.

I called the mortuary, then went to Crystal's room to tell her Brian had gone to heaven. I told her she could go next door and stay with the neighbor while we made the final funeral arrangements.

Instead of feeling overwhelmingly sad or even relief because Brian was out of pain, I walked around the house feeling a sense of awe. I wondered, *Did I really see thousand angels surrounding Brian's bed?* They stood so close together that their wings touched. How could five hours pass in just a moment?

Brian had died without the tubes and machines that had plagued him his whole life, retaining his full head of hair despite all the medication. His body had simply slowed down and stopped. We had been able to prepare, say goodbye, in every way we needed to. God had granted Kevin and me the opportunity to spend time alone with Brian. He also fulfilled every last wish, the smile, the hug, and the normalcy I so coveted for our family. He fulfilled Kevin's request that Brian die peacefully at home with his dad at his side. I even heard Brian laugh that night, seven hours before he went to be with Jesus. Brian had given all the love he could give, shared his life through stories and pictures, and left us with a beautiful legacy. He had been strong, showing no sign of fear, staying true to his sweet disposition, making sure I knew he would be all right.

Just moments before he left this earth, he spoke the words that told us he was thirsty. The cup he drank here on earth had been bitter, but he would never thirst again.

And the Spirit and the bride say, "Come." And let the one who hears say, "Come." And let the one who is thirsty come; let the one who wishes take the water of life without cost" (Revelation 22:17 NASB).

Where our suffering had been abundant, just like Paul promised in Corinthians, so was our comfort. Brian left us in peace. And then without warning, God allowed both Kevin and me into his presence, his power, and his love. "Brian, I won't be sad. You are where you need to be."

I showered and dressed just before the morticians arrived to remove Brian's body. I was concerned that there might be a problem because we waited so long to call, but they never said a word. The two men were kind, but they did mention that a death at home warranted an autopsy by the coroner's office.

The words were an abrupt interruption of our peace; I was horrified that they wanted to do an autopsy. There had already been too many surgeries, too much disfigurement. "Lord, hasn't Brian been cut open enough times already?" I called UCD, and the doctor said "not to worry" because Brian had been under a doctor's care recently and had Hospice. They would make the necessary calls to the mortuary and send the appropriate paperwork. I re-entered that place of peace.

Phone calls to family and friends were short; I would ask a few friends to make the calls back with the date and time of the funeral service. I made calls to all of our providers, but the most difficult call was to Brian's primary doctor at Children's Hospital. I left a message and he called me back.

I was thankful that I'd made all of the funeral arrangements ahead of time, when there were no time restraints. Making them now would have been overwhelming and we still had many things to do.

That afternoon we went to the cemetery to purchase a plot. I hadn't even thought that our small local cemetery might be full. With only a few plots left we walked the grounds to pick out the best one. There was one over by the trash cans and a few others near a drainage ditch.

I prayed, "Lord, why is doing this part so hard? Does Brian's plot have to be what is left over?" Then I realized I was making it hard. I still wanted only the best for him, but the physical location was not important; where was my humility? I understood now and prayed, "Okay, Lord, we will do whatever you want; I humbly accept any space that is available." We headed back to the office to make the purchase.

Just then, the woman in the office ran out to us. She had found one empty site, at the top of the hill. It was the most beautiful site, shaded by a large tree. I had to smile, "Really, Lord? You are the God that takes care of all my needs. We were willing to bury Brian at the bottom of the hill, knowing his soul sat with you on high, but instead you gave him the very best spot. You elevated him beyond anything that we could have imagined." He would be buried at the highest point overlooking the foothills. I could only say, "Thank you."

We didn't have the money to pay for the funeral services ourselves and the woman agreed to wait for twenty-four hours, when the funds would be available. My father-in-law had graciously offered to pay for the plot, and my parents paid for the mortuary.

Next we had to order flowers. Unfortunately, the small flower shop in town had a busy week. I wanted a blanket of white carnations to cover the casket, but the woman told us the supply was too low. When I mentioned that it was for a child's casket, she said that she could make it work. The blue silky ribbon that draped down to the floor would read, "To our beloved son, Brian." We wrote her out a check.

The next day I followed up on several phone calls while Kevin took the wheelchair back to the pharmacist. When he told them we no longer needed it, the pharmacist refunded all of our money. He already knew we had lost Brian because the obituary had been published in the morning paper. The whole town knew Brian had died. The obituary read:

Brian A. Perigan
Brian A. Perigan a Diamond Springs youth and student of the Charles Brown School, died in his home on October 19 at the age of eight . . . Funeral services will be held October 22 at 10:00 AM officiated by the Rev. Jim Hill. Internment to follow. The family requests remembrances to Cancer

Children's Services c/o Ronald McDonald House 4560 Fountain, Los Angeles 90027.

Next to his obituary was the name of another small child. I thought about how much pain that young couple must be feeling. I thought about how hard it would be for them to make the same type of arrangements we were making right now. Then I realized how hard it should have been for us to make those same arrangements, but we had been so blessed.

The next day the school principal sent out this message, with our blessing, to all the parents at Brian's school which included the time and place that the funeral would be held. It read:

We have been deeply saddened by the death of Brian Perigan, a valiant little eight-year-old–boy in our school, who passed away Tuesday from cancer. Our thoughts are with his family at this time.

Our pastor at our local church called to ask how we wanted to conduct the services. I had not given any thought about songs or speakers. He said I should have something in mind when we got together to plan the funeral the next day, leaving me just one day to pull something together.

I knew that Brian's funeral had to be all about him. At my mother-in-law's funeral, the priest who performed her service had not even known her in spite of the fact that she'd attended the church for over twenty years. I wanted Brian's service to be all about him. Brian had been well known throughout the community, but there was so much about him people didn't know. I knew that the burden to share who he was would fall on my shoulders. I would have to say something if I wanted people to know there was so much more to him than they were able to see.

The hospice worker suggested I display some of Brian's artwork at the funeral. That afternoon, I just focused on picking out some of his best artwork and placing them in frames.

Later that day the mortuary called to let us know we could attend a private viewing of the body on Thursday, the day before the funeral. I thanked them and made arrangements to be there at 7 PM.

The following day, all of the funeral plans fell into place despite the fact that I had done nothing to prepare for the day. Early that morning Kevin's cousin, Mark, called to say he felt the Lord had given him a song to sing. He wanted to see if our best friend Bob would join him in a duet. Neither had ever had to sing solo before, but Brian loved them both and I knew it would be just what he wanted.

Then a man from our church called to ask if he could come and share his testimony at the funeral. His wife and child had died recently in a car accident and he felt God had given him a message of encouragement and comfort to share. I told John Cowper how pleased I would be for him to come and do that.

By the time we met with our minister and his wife that afternoon, we had a plan. We would have special music, a personal testimony, and then our minister would speak. I asked him to speak specifically about heaven and the peace the Lord had brought to us. I also asked him to leave a spot open where he could squeeze me in, in case I decided to say a few words. Mrs. Hill helped me pick out songs that Brian liked to sing, and we were done. It was that easy.

When we returned from the meeting, one of my neighbors came to the house and brought several bags of groceries. I asked her how she could possibly know that it was exactly what I needed. She could not speak, but her kind gesture was greatly appreciated. I had over fifteen house guests coming that evening.

It was starting to get late, and even though guests were arriving, we had to leave for the viewing. The small private viewing room was so quiet and peaceful. Brian looked so good. He was a beautiful boy both physically and spiritually. I no longer saw a little boy racked with pain, laboring for each small wisp of air. I saw a young man who embodied perfect peace. Kevin and I prayed, then leaned over Brian and kissed him goodbye. I lingered near the coffin. His face looked so angelic. "He's gone," I told myself. "I am looking at an empty shell." But my heart couldn't let go. "Brian, I hope you know how much I love you. You have been a mighty warrior; death was the last enemy you will ever have to conquer. You know now that Jesus does love you more than I do."

> He who overcomes will inherit all this, and I will be his God and he shall be my son (Revelation 21:7 NIV).

Many people had come for the funeral. I wanted them all to stay with us. I needed them to fill up my house so I couldn't feel the emptiness. The house only had three bedrooms but people slept in the living room, family room, and loft. Some people had even thought to bring sleeping bags and slept on the floor.

My parents took our bedroom. Kevin's dad had to travel alone to the funeral and out of consideration for our many guests made arrangements to stay with his brother-in-law at the farm. I felt bad that Helen would never understand that the funeral wasn't about how it made her feel; it supported the family and showed respect for one that was gone.

Kevin and I moved Brian's bed back into his room and slept there. All the rooms to my house were open to everyone, with one exception. I kept Brian's room locked. I wasn't ready to have anyone touching his toys or moving his things around. Just like Brian, who had been so traumatized when Goofy had stolen his hat and revealed a secret he had tried to hide his whole life, so had I been traumatized when Brian's room had been invaded and his most precious treasures destroyed. I couldn't trust anyone with his things, at least not yet, and maybe never.

Around midnight that night, I woke up suddenly and plugged in that new typewriter my dad had given me over the summer. I needed to prepare a few words for the funeral. I hadn't been sure if I could speak in public. I didn't know if I would be too overcome with grief. I thought the last thing this funeral needed was a weeping mother, but I felt compelled to say something even if it was brief.

33

THE FUNERAL

At 10:00 AM, the small chapel at the mortuary was filled with over 200 guests. There were friends, family, neighbors, medical staff, and classmates from Brian's school. I was surprised that our hospice worker as well as staff from UCD and Children's Hospital had come. Even Brian's teacher had managed to get the day off. Brian would have been so pleased.

Back at our house several members from our church were preparing for the potluck which followed the service. I stood at the door of the chapel, greeting guests, while Kevin circulated inside.

I was sorry that Brian would miss seeing all the people he loved. I wanted to tell him it was such a good day. It was a day of celebration, not of tears. Rain had been in the forecast, but on this day there would be no rain. It was autumn and the trees and flowers were bright with color.

I was surprised that members of our church had put together a small pamphlet for all of our attendees. They had placed a large oak tree on the front of the program. Because Brian loved birds so much I could image all the birds living in the tree even if you couldn't see them. Inside the pamphlet was a poem. It read:

<u>In Remembrance</u>
God hath not promised skies always blue.
Flower-strewn pathways all our lives through.
God hath not promised sun without rain,
Joy without sorrow, peace without pain.
But God hath promised strength for the day.

Rest for the labor, light for the way.
Grace for the trails, help from above.
Unfailing sympathy, undying love.

In Memory of Brian A. Perigan
A native of California, born April 27, 1974.

Passed away in Diamond Springs, on Tuesday,
    October 19, 1982.
Friday, October 22, 1982 at 10:00 AM
Officiating: Rev. James Hill

We bowed our heads and prayed *The Lord's Prayer:*

Our Father, which art in heaven; hallowed be Thy name.
Thy kingdom come, Thy will be done, on earth,
    as it is in heaven.
Give us this day our daily bread, and forgive us our debts,
    as we forgive our debtors.
And lead us not into temptation, but deliver us from evil.
For Thine is the kingdom, and the power, and the glory,
forever. Amen.
    (Matthew 6: 9–13 KJV).

Then all joined in and sang the three songs that had been so
carefully selected.

- *In His Time* by Diane Ball,
- *Surely the Presence of the Lord is in this Place* by Lanny Wolfe
- *Amazing Grace* by John Newton.

Then it was time for the special music, sung by Mark and Bob.
I didn't know what song they were going to sing but I already knew
it would be perfect. *And it was.*

<u>Jesus I Come</u>
Out of my bondage, sorrow, and night, Jesus I come,
   Jesus I come;
Into Thy freedom, gladness, and light, Jesus, I come to Thee.
Out of my sickness, into Thy health, Out of my want and
   into Thy wealth,
Out of my sin and into Thyself, Jesus, I come to Thee.
Out of the fear and dread of the tomb, Jesus, I come,
   Jesus, I come;
Into the joy and light of Thy throne, Jesus, I come to Thee.
Out of the depths of ruin untold, Into the peace of
   Thy sheltering fold,
Ever Thy glorious face to behold, Jesus, I come to Thee.[37]

It was my turn. I had written the following:

Brian's life was centered on living. Although he suffered from cancer for five of his just eight years here on earth, he did not regard his suffering as anything but normal. He loved the beauty of the clouds, found entertainment in just watching birds. He always had a sense of security, knowing that Jesus was always with him.

Having a sharper eye than many of us will ever have, he was fully aware of the fact that he was dying and was not afraid. He wrote poems about angels, heaven, and his creator. We rejoice that today Brian is with the Lord; without pain, without fear, without suffering. Praise be to God, He will beautify the afflicted ones with salvation.

Then Rev. James Hill and John Cowper talked about God's love and the place Brian had gone to. When it was over, Kevin went up and thanked everyone for coming. Only a few people joined us at the grave site. A few white clouds hovered in the sky, but the sun shone brightly as we laid Brian to rest.

We had gotten through the day, but when they prepared to lower my child's casket into the grave, I had to remind myself that his body was just an empty shell. If it had not been for the potluck and the obligation I had to my guests, I would not have had the strength to tear my heart from the gravesite.

As we turned to get into the car, we knew Brian was not in that grave, he was with Jesus. Our mourning had disappeared with the clouds. We knew without a doubt that he had been set apart, circumcised—God had touched him. We drove home to greet our guests. The fellowship and love of friends and family supported us throughout the rest of day.

It wasn't until people started to leave our home that I realized Pauline and her mother had come to the funeral. She said it was so hard to see Brian because it brought back all the sadness she had felt when she lost Tony. I hugged her and we cried together. Only a mother who has lost her child to cancer truly knows the road we have had to travel. I thanked them both for coming. It was the last time I saw Pauline.

We had received many bereavement cards and letters. Three were especially meaningful. One was from our six-year-old neighbor, Melissa, one from Brian's school teacher, and one from the Medical Team at UCD.

Penny, I'm sorry that Brian died. He was my very very, very best best friend. We had very, very much fun together. I liked him very very, very very much. And he liked me very, very much. I was crying very much.

Love, Melissa (our neighbor)

Dear Mrs. Perigan:

Thank you for your help this year. You and Brian have made us all grow. Brian was a priceless treasure and you have made our year a more meaningful one.

Flossy (Brian's schoolteacher)

Brian will not be forgotten. He will always be admired for his gentleness and bravery. His nursing team at UCD

We still had one last thing to do; we needed to purchase a marker for Brian's grave.

Kevin's cousin suggested that I might want to personalize the grave marker. I liked that idea but didn't know where to start. I wanted the marker to tell Brian's story. Crystal, Kevin, and I each added something to the design. It would take months before we could afford to have it placed on the gravesite.

When Christmas came, I realized that some of our friends still hadn't heard about Brian's death. I sent out a Christmas letter to let everyone know we were doing well.

Dear Family and Friends:

We are writing to you this year to wish you a wonderful holiday. As many of you know, the Lord has done something very special for us this year. He has taken Brian home. This separation has not been a difficult one because we know that the Lord is providing much more for him than we ever could. We have not been left empty-handed but have been filled with a:

JOY unspeakable,

PEACE that passes all understanding,

HOPE in Him that does not disappoint.

Make this Christmas more than giving a gift, or picking out a tree, or sending a card. Make it a true celebration of God's gift, JESUS. We hope that His love penetrates your heart so that you might share with us in a love that is everlasting.

In His Love,

Kevin, Penny and Crystal Perigan

If you confess with your mouth Jesus as Lord, and believe in your heart that God raised Him from the dead, you shall be saved; for with the heart man believes, resulting in righteousness, and with the mouth he confesses, resulting in salvation (Romans 10:9–10 NASB).

Almost six months had passed since we'd ordered our specially designed grave marker. On Brian's ninth birthday, we had the marker placed on the gravesite. The Bible verse that Crystal had picked out was written across the image of a large, open faced Bible. I had added a picture of a small boy running into the arms of Jesus. Kevin had added the birds flying overhead. The marker read:

<u>Brian Anthony Perigan</u>
Apr. 27, 1974
Oct. 19, 1982
Come unto me . . . and I will give you rest (Matthew 11:28)

When Brian died, this verse brought me great comfort as I envisioned Jesus beckoning young children to come to him. Over the years I have come to realized Crystal's scripture has a deeper message. Burdened by the weight of this world, all of us are called to come to Jesus. When he calls us to submit to him, there is a promise that he will lighten our load. The scene is not so light and whimsical as I first thought, because our need is dire. When Jesus opens his arms to welcome us there is a great relief. Under the authority of his Father, Jesus is the ultimate Provider.

Like Brian, our needs are great. Jesus is waiting. We need to run to the arms of our Savior, knowing that he alone makes us complete. It is his divine love that heals every void. He is all that you need.

When we first brought Brian home to die, we didn't believe he had much time left. But God had been gracious and allowed us six months more than the doctors had predicted. God gave us twenty-four hours to say goodbye and then he gave us five-and-a-half hours more, an extra hour for each year Brian had lived with the cancer. He healed a damaged arm, a burned hand and he rid Brian's body of colon cancer. God's hand guided Brian's sanctification, the communion, the baptism, and the request for water to signal that the time had come. And even in the throes of death, Brian died without pain or fear. He had died so beautifully. There in itself was the victory. Cancer hadn't won this battle.

Today, I can only stand in awe for all God has done for us. My soul sings out. He giveth and giveth and giveth again! How great is our God! And Jesus said:

I have given them the GLORY that you gave me, that they may be one as we are one (John 17:22 NIV).

*   *   *

We had many losses that year. We sold the house, took care of my parents, and then I went to work to help pay off the debt. In1990, eight years later, CCS closed our account and paid off the remainder of our debt.

At eight-and-a half years of age, Brian left this earth and entered a new dimension. He had never wanted to be seen as a sick child. He was so much more than his disease. He would always say, whether he was fragile or strong, "It's still me inside."

Even today when I think of Brian, I can still hear him whisper, "I am alright, Mommy, Jesus is with me."

I Can Picture Him

Picture him running, leaping into the arms of God, cuddled, greeted by a loving Father, who loves him even more than you.
Picture him loved, resting upon my bosom, happy joyous,
    basking in my love.
Picture him whole, no tears, no sorrow, made perfectly whole.
Being what he could not be on earth—Picture him found.

RESOURCES

Bacz, Jacek. "Commentary on the Problem of Pain." *Newman Rambler*, Spring 1999.

Bakker, Jim. *I Was Wrong.* Nashville, TN: Thomas Nelson Publishers, 1996.

BibleGateway.com. "Jesus Washes His Disciples' Feet." John 13 commentary, 2011. https://www.biblegateway.com/resources/commentaries/IVP-NT/John/Jesus-Washes-Disciples-Feet

Billheimer, Paul. *Don't Waste Your Sorrows.* Ft. Washington, PA: Christian Literature Crusade, 1977

Bingham, Rowland. "Annie's Story." Bible Memory Association, 1900.

Cure's Cancer Updates, Research & Education. "Making Sense of Cancer Therapies." *The Seventh Annual Cancer Guide*, 2012.

Department of Health and Human Services. *Young People with Cancer: A Handbook for Parents*, 1982.

Friedman, Robert A. "Circumcision of the Heart," Jews for Jesus, 2006. https://jewsforjesus.org/publications/issues/issues-v01-n06/circumcision-of-the-heart

Mechoulam, Dr. Raphael, and Gaoni, Ychiel. Synthesized THC, 1984.

Messner, Tammy Faye. Tammy: *Telling It My Way*. New York: Villard, 1996.

Milazzo S., and Horneber, M. "Laetrile Treatment for Cancer." *Cochrane Database of Systematic Reviews*, 2015.

National Cancer Institute/National Institute of Health (NCI/NIH). "What You Need to Know About Wilms' Tumor," Pub. No. 81-1570, Bethesda, MD, 1981.

Scheible, Sue. "Chad Green's Short Life." *The Herald News*, July 25, 2007.

Stetzer, Ed. "What Does It Mean to Have Abundant Life?" Christianity Today, 2015. http://www.christianitytoday.com/edstetzer/2015/march/what-does-it-mean-to-have-abundant-life.html.

Wigglesworth, Smith (1859–1947). Sermon: "Live Ready: A Spirit Soaked Life," 1921.

ENDNOTES

1. "Glory (religion)," *Wikipedia, The Free Encyclopedia,* 2017. https://en.wikipedia.org/w/index.php?title=Glory_(religion)&oldid=769564216
2. "Maranatha," *Wikipedia, The Free Encyclopedia,* 2017. https://en.wikipedia.org/w/index.php?title=Maranatha&oldid=784906256
3. "What You Need to Know About Wilms' Tumor," National Cancer Institute/National Institute of Health, No. 81-1570 (Bethesda, MD: 1981).
4. Elmer L. DeGowin and Richard L. DeGowin, *Bedside Diagnostic Examination* (New York: Macmillian Publishing Co., Inc. 1976), p. 500.
5. Jamieson, Fausset, and Brown, *Commentary on the Whole Bible* (Grand Rapids, MI: Zondervan, 1975).
6. "Vincristine," *Wikipedia, The Free Encyclopedia,* 2017. https://en.wikipedia.org/w/index.php?title=Vincristine&oldid=780861363
7. Understanding Blood Tests: A Guide for Patients with Cancer, 1995.
8. Department of Health and Human Services, *Young People with Cancer: A Handbook for Parents,* 1982.
9. Jacek Bacz, "Commentary on the Problem of Pain," *Newman Rambler*, Spring 1999.
10. Ed Stetzer, "What Does It Mean to Have Abundant Life?" *Christianity Today,* 2015. http://www.christianitytoday.com/edstetzer/2015/march/what-does-it-mean-to-have-abundant-life.html.
11. Paul Billheimer, *Don't Waste Your Sorrows* (Ft. Washington, PA: Christian Literature Crusade, 1977).
12. The American Journal of Pediatric Hematology/Oncology, Summer, 1979.
13. Smith Wigglesworth (1859–1947), "Live Ready: A Spirit Soaked Life," 1921.
14. Carol and Ron Harris, "Special Delivery," performed by Evie Tornquist on the album *Never the Same*, 1979.
15. Southern California Ronald McDonald House, 1980.
16. "The Greatest American Hero," *Wikipedia, The Free Encyclopedia,* 2017. https://en.wikipedia.org/w/index.php?title-The_Greatest_American_Hero&oldid-78573956
17. Mike Post and Stephen Geyer, "Believe It or Not" (New York: Elektra, 1981).
18. Tammy Faye Messner, *Tammy: Telling It My Way* (New York: Villard, 1996).
19. Jim Bakker, *I Was Wrong* (Nashville, TN: Thomas Nelson Publishers, 1996).
20. S. Milazzo and M. Horneber, "Laetrile Treatment for Cancer," *Cochrane Database of Systematic Reviews*, 2015.
21. *The Candlelighter's Foundation Quarterly Newsletter,* Summer 1981.
22. Scott Berman, "Pediatric Informed Consent Rights," 1981.
23. Sue Scheible, "Chad Green's Short Life," *The Herald News*, July 25, 2007.
24. Elmer L. DeGowin and Richard L. DeGowin, *Bedside Diagnostic Examination* (New York: Macmillian Publishing Co., Inc. 1976), p. 541.
25. Ibid.
26. Ibid.
27. "Tetrahydrocannabinol," *Wikipedia, The Free Encyclopedia,* 2017. https://en.wikipedia.org/wiki/Tetrahydrocannabinol
28. "Dactinomycin (Actinomycin)," *Wikipedia, The Free Encyclopedia*, 2017. https://en.wikipedia.org/w/index.php?title=Dactinomycin&oldid=772193260

29. Ibid.

30. "Cyclophosphamide (Cytoxan)," *Wikipedia, The Free Encyclopedia,* 2017. https://en.wiki-pedia.org/w/index.php?title=Cyclophosphamide&oldid=782892983

31. "Methotrexate," *Wikipedia, The Free Encyclopedia,* 2017. https://en.wikipedia.org/w/index.php?title=Methotrexate&oldid=783157481

32. "Vincristine," Wikipedia, The Free Encyclopedia, https://en.wikipedia.org/wiki/Vincristine

33. "Chemotherapy, *Wikipedia, The Free Encyclopedia,* 2017. https://en.wikipedia.org/wiki/Chemotherapy

34. Annie J. Flint (1866–1932), "He Giveth More Grace," (Lillenas Publishing Co, 1941).

35. Robert A. Friedman, "Circumcision of the Heart," Jews for Jesus, 2006. https://jews-forjesus.org/publications/issues/issues-v01-n06/circumcision-of-the-heart

36. "Jesus Washes His Disciples' Feet," BibleGateway.com, John 13 commentary. https://www.biblegateway.com/resources/commentaries/IVP-NT/John/Jesus-Washes-Disciples-Feet

37. William T. Sleeper and George C. Stebbins, "Jesus I Come," 1887.